On to the Rescue

On to the Rescue

A TALE OF THE INDIAN MUTINY

GORDON STABLES, M.D., C.M.

GYAN

Published by

Gyan Publishing House
5, Ansari Road
Daryaganj, New Delhi-110002
Phone: 011-47034999, 9811692060
E-mail: books@gyanbooks.com

Distribution Network
gyanbooks.com
India, USA, Canada, UK, Australia, France

ISBN : 978-81-212-9480-5 (PB)
First Published, 1894

2nd Impression 2023

Printed at: Gyan Press, Delhi.

On to the Rescue
Author: GORDON STABLES

ON TO THE RESCUE.

"Willie had raised himself, and was gazing wonderingly on the speaker." *p.* 43.

On to the Rescue.

A TALE OF THE INDIAN MUTINY.

BY

GORDON STABLES, M.D., C.M.

(Surgeon Royal Navy),

AUTHOR OF "FACING FEARFUL ODDS;"
"FOR ENGLAND, HOME, AND BEAUTY;" "HEARTS OF OAK;"
ETC. ETC.

"Stars and moon and sun may wax and wane, subside and rise,
Age on age as flake on flake of showering snows be shed:
Not till earth be sunless, not till death strike blind the skies,
May the deathless love that waits on deathless deeds be dead."
—SWINBURNE.

NEW EDITION.

Dedication.

TO

INDIA'S GREATEST PRINCE

AND

BRITAIN'S FRIEND,

HIS HIGHNESS THE NIZAM OF HYDERABAD,

This Book is Dedicated

WITH EVERY GOOD WISH

BY

THE AUTHOR.

CONTENTS.

Book I.

BEFORE THE OUTBREAK.

Book II.

THE MUTINY IN FULL SWING.

Book III.

GENTLE PEACE RETURNING

On to the Rescue.

CHAPTER I.

BALAKLAVA LODGE.

WAS that the moon red-rising over hills and woods?

"Surely no one could mistake the moon," one might say. Ah! true, reader mine; but had you been a perfect stranger in the glen, and had you been unable to tell which was east and which was west, you would have been for a few moments puzzled indeed; for turning your back to one fiery ball, you would have seen, glimmering in a blue-grey haze, and near to the horizon, precisely such another. Yes, that is the sun, and it gets larger and more crimson every moment, till it sinks from sight behind the far-off mountains.

And yonder is the moon, moving higher and higher every minute, getting a trifle smaller too, and less and less red, until her broad, round, yellow disc has shaken itself clear of the horizon's haze, and is shining softly, sweetly over hill and dale.

Then a star struggles out; then another, and it is night.

But not until three or four more stars dot the dark blue of the cloudless heavens, does the mavis cease to sing.

It is a wild, happy, ringing melody that of his, sounding out from the pine wood, and making echo ring from tree to tree.

Well, that bird has reason to be happy. It is springtime now, or soon will be. Already there are buds on the trees and on the hedgerows, wee green dots on the white-thorn, brown, sticky burgeons on the horse-chestnut, long, smooth buds on the sycamore. Already the goat willows are hung with silver, the leaves are out on the honeysuckle, and in the haughs not far from the river's brink half-open primroses are coyly hiding in the grass.

A happy, hopeful time for the mavis! His nest is built and lined, and well hidden in that low spruce tree. And only to-day his speckled-breasted mate laid one egg therein, black-ticked and turquoisine. Ah! no wonder he sings, until the sight of the stars and the night wind, low whispering through the pines, drive him for shelter to his cosy nest.

Higher and higher rises the moon!

It is smaller still now, smaller and brighter, and its mellow light silvers streamlet and lake, silvers the village church spire that points heavenwards like a finger high above that cloud-land of fir-trees, silvers the dew that lies low in the meadow, silvers the gauzy mist that hangs over the woods, softens and spiritualizes everything.

And now that the moon is so high above the glen, and night has really and truly come, scarcely is there a sound to be heard, save now and then the fox-like barking of a farmer's collie.

Hark! though, that is someone whistling, someone whistling a bright and merry melody as he comes trudging along by the edge of the wood, a dog by his side. The notes of the mavis even were not more blithe and happy than these.

But suddenly he stops.

"Bruce," he says, "come here."

Bruce, his honest sheepdog, is by his side in a moment, gazing up into his face with his ears well back on his neck, for he seems to know instinctively that he is about to listen to something that is not quite pleasant.

Willie Saunders lifts a forefinger to emphasize his words.

"Doggie," he says in Scotch, "ye maun gang hame. I'm gaun, the nicht, where it is best ye shouldna follow. Hame, Bruce, hame!"

Bruce gives just one pleading glance up into his master's face, but seeing no signs of relenting there, he turns and trots sadly homewards.

Willie Saunders buckles his plaid more tightly round him and trudges on. He walks in silence now for fully a mile; for Willie is kind-hearted, and would not like his gentle and loving collie to think his master could be happy without him.

But spring and youth-time are the seasons for song

and love as well, and soon Willie begins to whistle once again, and then to sing, for whistling did not appear quite to meet the requirements of his case.

A blackbird near to her grass-lined nest crouches low as Willie passes her tree. Not through fear, for no one who could sing like that would harm a bird, but to listen. "There is music in that human biped's voice," he tells his wife; "and if my own song that Nature taught me were not so sweet and melodious, I might borrow some notes from him."

The mavis listens also, and, half-asleep though he is, he tries to remember some notes which, swaying on the tall larch-tree to-morrow, he will try to mimic.

But in the fresh green briard* yonder is a nest of a different kind. Thereon a lark sits low on her four dark-brown eggs, and near to her is her bonnie bold mate. He listens, but it is not with pleasure, for he sings in the clouds all day, and even at night there are times when he will mount in the starlight to trill his song, as if angels called to him to join their hymns, or as if he were so full of joy and happiness that he could not wait till day. *He* will not borrow the note of a human biped. No; he is the bird that Shakespeare sings of—

"Hark! hark! the lark at heaven's gate sings,
And Phœbus 'gins to rise,
His steeds to water at those springs
On chalic'd flowers that lies;
And winking Mary-buds begin
To ope their golden eyes."

---

* Springing corn.

But what cares Willie Saunders? Birds may like the song he sings, or birds may not. It comes straight from his young and happy heart, and, indeed, I am not at all sure that he is aware that he is singing, so full is that busy brain of his with thoughts of the pleasure that is before him.

The country is very still to-night up in this rural district of the North, yet it is but early in the evening. There is but little need for Willie to hurry, therefore, and if it were not that his steps seem to insist upon keeping time to his thoughts, he would not walk so quickly, for the dance will not begin till nine.

"First guests," he said half aloud to himself, "are seldom the most welcome. I'll even slacken my pace."

As he did so he looked up into the bright starry, moonlit sky.

"What a heavenly night!" he murmured. "I never saw a clearer sky, nor one more darkly blue; and the stars look so big and bright and so near, it appears as if I could touch them with a salmon rod. And yonder is the moon, the sly old moon. If I walk slow she hardly moves; if I were to run ever so quickly she would keep pace by my side. How she nods and blinks and bobs at me. It really seems as if she knew my secret, and were wishing me joy."

"Only a cold, dead world"—he was continuing his reverie—"no atmosphere around it; no bright and beautiful clouds to herald the sunrise; no grass or trees to clothe its glens with green; no water in its lakes, its streams all dry. Ugh! it makes me shudder to think of it. And yet, may be, there was a time when the moon was young; when forests waved in her straths and glens; when her hills were clad with verdure; when her blue lakes slept peaceful in the sunshine; when streamlets and rills joined hand in hand, and went singing seawards over their pebbly beds; when cattle or kine, perhaps, roved over her meadows, and blithe-voiced birds sang joyously in her woodlands. A happy time for the moon, the days of her youth. If so, then fell coldness and blight and death. I wonder if it came suddenly, in the very midst of her joy? Young lives are blighted at times. Ugh!"

Had the night turned suddenly colder? he wondered, as he drew the looser folds of his plaid around his shoulders.

"I feel," he said now, "as if somebody were walking over my grave. Well, of course I have a grave—somewhere; for not long ago the minister told me that as soon as a child was born into the world Death hurried away and dug his grave. That was only spoken figuratively of course. But it wouldn't take a great deal to kill me—a deal of grief I mean. Now, if Annie Lindsay is unkind to me to-night, I shall wish to be dead, as dead as yonder moon."

He had slackened and slackened his pace till now, as he spoke the last words, he stood stock-still, with his eyes on the ground.

Well, I am not in a position to calculate the amount of evil that grief in its bitterest form—namely, that of unrequited love—might work upon a sturdy young frame like that of Willie's, but to look at him now as he stands in the moonlight, to study him physically, one would think Willie Saunders would take a deal of killing. Though not more than twenty-one, he is sturdy and strong. The tweed kilt suit he wears, and the plaid, surely never before were worn by a more handsome young Scot. His brow is high and white, and his face is manly. Yet, had you criticised his features narrowly, you could not have helped noticing that there was an air of innocent simplicity in that face and in those light blue eyes that, although engaging enough to witness, would lead men of the world to believe he was easily moulded clay. Perhaps he was; but youths like Willie develop into heroes at times, when they become what sailors call "sea-fast."

Before a sailor can become so he must weather a few storms, and it is the same with men in their voyage across the sea of life. Storms of grief and trouble alone can make them brave and sea-fast, and grief indeed may oftentimes become the parent of fame.

Willie heaves a kind of half-stifled sigh, and resumes his journey. But he is not singing now; neither is he whistling. He is simply thinking.

In his own half-shy and simple way he had long loved Annie Lindsay, but he had never told her so. He had often told his heart's story to the birds that sang in the woodlands; he had whispered it to the wild flowers, and breathed it in song to the winds; but as far as words went Annie knew nothing about it. Nor, strange to say, had Willie said a single word about it to Jack Morrison, although this young man was the best and dearest friend he had on earth, and a near neighbour as well as a friend.

Annie Lindsay lived miles and miles up the glen in which we first meet Willie to-night. A light-hearted winsome lassie was Annie. She was just turned eighteen this very day, and it was to celebrate this event that her parents, who were very fond of her, permitted Annie to give a party. Indeed Annie herself had proposed it weeks ago. She was an only child, so was refused nothing—at all events, her father never refused her anything.

Colonel Lindsay, her father, had won the Victoria Cross, gained his promotion, and lost a leg, all in one day at the battle of Alma. A one-armed soldier is passable, but a one-legged one is no longer capable of serving his Queen and country, so Lindsay had retired even before the war was over, and here he now lived, hearty and hale, and still in the prime of life. The good soldier had some private means, and this had enabled him to make his little place, which was called Balaklava Lodge, quite a beautiful spot. It had been a kind of a wildery anyhow, a turbulent little stream with a natural waterfall went roaring through the grounds; banks and braes covered with scented drooping birch trees, with here and there a tasselled larch; bold bluffs of rock clad with heather and furze or whins that in springtime was all a blaze of bloom, the scented home of the rose-linnet, and skite; and high above all, on a bold-terraced height, the old-fashioned house itself, with solemn pine trees waving dark above it. The whole was sheltered by green and heath-clad hills from the cold spring winds of north or east. It needed but little aid from art to change a spot like this into a very romantic and lovely place indeed; and the Colonel spent all his time in his gardens and grounds, and with John, his gardener, was ever planning some new improvement.

Annie Lindsay I do not mean to describe, farther than to say she was *petite,* dark-haired, and very beautiful, because this is not a love story, but rather a tale

> "Of moving accidents by flood and field,
> Of hair-breadth 'scapes i' the imminent deadly breach,"

and of many a wild adventure, reader, incidental to a soldier's life.

Annie's father and mother had taken great pains with her education and culture. She could play well and sing very sweetly, but above all she could talk and read well. It was just such a girl as this that was bound to captivate a hero like Willie Saunders, because she was out of the common; that is, Annie was really a girl who had been brought up in refined society in the far South, and therefore not like the maidens Willie Saunders was wont to meet at church, who, however fresh and bonnie they might be, were somewhat wanting in *bon ton.*

Willie Saunders had known Annie for only a year and a half; but, dear me! that seems a lifetime to one in the days of youth. His father was what is called a laird in Scotland—not a rich one, however. He simply owned the farm he cultivated, with its woodlands and sheep-hills, and its haughlands stretching along by the river-side, where, in many a smiling field, the corn is now sprouting green and tender, and where in autumn the song and the laugh will be heard all day long as the farm lads and lasses mow down and stook the yellow grain.

Before Colonel Lindsay bought that place at this glen head, Laird Morrison, who lived about two miles from Raven's Nest—Willie's father's home—was a very frequent visitor indeed both in summer and winter at the Nest, and if now his visits were not quite so numerous, it was only because both he and Laird Saunders went so often to spend the evening at the Colonel's house.

The trio had soon become very good friends indeed, and the darkest or stormiest winter's night that ever blew did not prevent the "twa lairds" from rolling their plaids about them and striding up the glen to Balaklava Lodge, to spend an hour or two with him, often listening to the wondrous stories the soldier had to retail concerning his life and wanderings. But Willie and his friend Jack always followed on, a few hours afterwards, to bring their parents back.

It was during these visits that Willie Saunders had lost his heart so irretrievably to winsome Annie Lindsay.

* * * * * *

But why is he alone to-night, on this night of all nights? Well, the fact is that Jack had gone from home, but promised to turn up at Balaklava about ten or eleven. So his friend Willie has gone on without him.

Is Willie very sorry to do so? I must candidly tell you he is not. Before the colonel came to the glen our hero had thought Jessie Morrison, Jack's young and only sister, the sweetest girl in all the countryside, and perhaps she was; but now ——

Anyhow, to-night Willie determines to know his fate. He had repeated to himself, over and over again as he was dressing, with more care than usual, the lines—

> "He either fears his fate too much,
> Or his deserts are small,
> Who dares not put it to the test,
> To win or lose it all."

But now at a turn of the road he comes at last in full view of the Lodge, the lights from the windows of which struggle out through the tall pine trees, and do battle with the bright rays of the now clear and silvery moon.

The hustling noise of the waterfall or linn falls upon his ear in a kind of drowsy monotone; but Willie pauses not to listen to anything. He must hurry on now.

One thing he knows, one thing he feels, and that is that he will return to-night either the happiest young man in all the glen, or a youth to whom life can have no more charms. Which will it be?

CHAPTER II.

A BIRTHDAY BALL AND WHAT CAME OF IT.

"WHAT, my lad," cried Morrison cheerfully when Willie entered the drawing-room, "are you all alone then?"

"Yes," said Willie, smiling, "Jack has gone to Drumarran, and won't get here till pretty late, so I thought I wouldn't wait."

The Colonel and the two lairds were having a three-handed game in a quiet corner, for Mrs. Lindsay could not join them to-night.

"Come and sit down then," said Laird Morrison, "and have a hand with us; we want just one."

Willie laughed now outright.

"No, thank you, sir. Would with pleasure, you know, but I really feel more like dancing."

"Quite right, my boy," said the Colonel, "go and enjoy yourself, if you don't dance at your age, you won't at ours. Off with you."

There was one special room in Balaklava Lodge that deserves just a passing word or two. This was quite an ideal sort of a room, and I hardly know what to call it.

Happy thought! I shall shirk the responsibility of naming it at all, but leave the reader to do so. It opened then off one end of the drawing-room by a curtained doorway, but it was as large as three good-sized drawing-rooms. Quite a hall did you say, reader? Yes, almost a hall, and it was lighted partly by a glass roof, it was lined as to its sides with shrubs of tropical foliage and beautiful flowers; to this extent therefore it was a gigantic conservatory, but there were seats here and there half-hidden by the greenery, and there were singing birds here, there, and everywhere—to this extent it was an aviary, though the floor was laid for roller skating. "A rink," you say. Well possibly, but to-night there was an orchestra of violins, clarionets, and a harp at the farther end, and they were even now tuning up. "A ballroom!" Thanks, I knew we would get at it presently.

Well, by a doorway near to the place where the music was stationed, you could enter a well-lighted and real conservatory, and thence you might emerge on to a beautifully-kept lawn. If you crossed this, behold, you were on a strong but rustic bridge above the linn, and this would lead you to sweet-scented birchen woods that rose over the braeland, and that to-night were bathed in a flood of silver moonlight. Annie, on this particular evening, looked like—like—well I do not really know altogether what to liken her to, for similes of all sorts that are worth anything have been used up over and over again. "Fairy" won't do for Annie, she hadn't fair, floating hair, short green skirts and a gilded tinsel wand. No, she wasn't a bit like a pantomime fairy. "Houri of paradise!" How would that suit? "Too far fetched."

"A vision of beauty?" Vision of fiddlesticks; no, let me cut the gordian knot and simply call her a fascinating and pretty girl neatly dressed in white, with a pink rose in her bosom and one in her dark, bonnie hair. There were roses also on her cheeks.

But she wore no diamonds except those that sparkled in her eyes, and no jewellery of any sort; only clasped around her neck was a double chain of pearls that her father had brought from India long, long ago.

After all what need has a girl like Annie Lindsay to be adorned with gold or jewels? Leave such gewgaws to maids who are in the sere and yellow leaf. My *petite* heroine was robed in the beauty of her own innocence and youth. She needed nothing else.

But later on that night there was a song sung by a bold young student from the University that seemed just to suit Annie, and Willie Saunders felt that he wanted to choke the fellow, because as he sang he cast languishing looks towards Miss Lindsay.

You know the song, reader, and if you don't, the sooner you learn both words and melody the better for you. One verse runs thus—

> "Her brow is like the snaw-drift,
> Her neck is like the swan;
> And her face it is the fairest
> That e'er the sun shone on."

The student who sang this lovely old song took not the slightest notice of Willie Saunders, when he came up a few minutes afterwards to claim Annie's hand for the next waltz. Beautiful dreamy music it was, and as the young couple went floating around the floor, there was no one in the room who did not take notice of their dancing. The two seemed made for each other, seemed indeed to be the very embodiment of the music that was being played.

Willie wanted to choke that University man now more than ever. What right had he to dance so well. What right had he to dance with Annie Lindsay anyhow. Why he was positively whispering in her ear, his face far closer to hers than it had any right to be. Was he making love, Willie wondered, and then he wondered which way this young fellow went home, for he had half a mind to lie in wait for him in a wood, and to challenge him to fight as he passed.

But the music ceased at last, yet the bold student still lingered by Annie's side; and she had had her tablets in her hand.

Willie Saunders would not see any more of this. He rushed through the conservatory and out to the lawn.

The hum of the waterfall fell on his ear and calmed him, and the night air cooled his heated brows. He took a few turns up and down on the grass, then returned. He found Annie sitting alone in a corner, looking somewhat sad; but she made room for him on the sofa, and welcomed him with a smile.

Willie forgot everything now save her presence. He even postponed the fight with the student *sine die*. He would let the fellow live a little longer. The fellow at this moment appeared to be enjoying himself very much indeed, dancing with a young lady of quite a different stamp from Annie.

"The next two dances are ours, Annie," said Willie Saunders.

Annie inclined her head, and smiled.

"Suppose now," he added, "we dance the first, and sit the second?"

"Oh, that would be very delightful!"

"Come, then."

Willie Saunders's dancing of waltzes attracted no special notice of a very flattering nature, at all events. It was not so airy or so graceful as that of the University man. It was not the poetry of motion, at least not quite. There was not much poetry in the motion, for instance, when Willie cannoned off one couple and completely floored another. Our hero thought it was the correct thing to retire after that, so he led his smiling partner to a seat.

"Waltzing isn't my strong point," he said, wiping his brow.

"I rather think," said Annie mischievously, "that it is a very strong point."

"Now, Annie, you're laughing at me. I wish I could dance as well as that student fellow; you might care for me more.

"But," he added, "after all, waltzing is not dancing; and I think in a Highland reel I can hold my own even with him. Are you warm?"

"It *is* warm."

"Do come and take a turn on the moonlit lawn, then."

Willie's heart seemed to be playing at pitch and toss as he spoke. Would she refuse?

But she did not.

He left her in the conservatory for a few moments, and flew round to the hall to fetch thence a soft little snow-white Shetland shawl.

With this floating around her shoulders Annie looked like a sylph. So Willie thought, and so he told her.

"Only," he added somewhat clumsily, "you are ever so much more beautiful than any sylph that ever was born; that is, if sylphs *are* born."

"I couldn't say; I never saw one except in a picture."

Annie was looking at the moon, and Willie Saunders was looking at Annie.

They moved slowly across the lawn, and soon found themselves on the rustic bridge that spanned the cañon. They stopped for a moment to gaze down at the misty linn, then strolled on once more, Annie's hand resting lightly on Willie's arm.

There was a seat not far away on the braeland, and just under the boughs of two spreading birch-trees, the sweet, healthful perfume of whose leaves scented the air.

Many times and oft they had sat here before, reading, or studying botanically the specimens of wild flowers they had collected in their rambles over the moorlands and hills.

But that was in summer, and very happy Willie Saunders had been then.

He was less so now, solely because he felt awkward and shy and stupid. He would have given a good deal just then for the affable and cheerful mannerism of the student whom he called "that fellow who danced."

"You're sure you are not cold?"

He made that remark once, he made it twice, and when he made it the third time within two minutes, not having spoken a word during the intervals, she looked up into his face and laughed.

She could not help it, rude though it might seem. Then he blushed, and felt more like a fool than ever; but speak he must now, and speak he did, though the commencement of his speech was not by any means elegant.

"Oh," he said, "I don't care whether you are cold or not! I mean," he added awkwardly, "that when I asked the question I don't think I knew what I was saying. Oh, bother, I wish I was that fellow who danced! Seems to me, Annie, that I can't do anything right. I can't dance, and I can't talk, and ——"

"What is the matter with you to-night, Willie?" said the girl, looking at him wonderingly.

He grew desperate now.

"I'm going to tell you a story; I ——"

"Tell me a story?" laughed Annie. "Why, you will want to sing a song next. But is the story a very long one? because I'll be missed, you know."

"No, it is not a very long one, but it is a very old one."

"Oh, if I've heard it before, better not tell it."

"You never heard it from *me* before, Annie."

The young man was now looking so solemn and miserable that Annie was getting frightened.

"Is there anything the matter, Willie?"

"Yes, very much the matter; I'm in love!"

"Oh, is that the story?"

"That is the story. Just listen one moment, won't you?"

"Yes, with all the pleasure in the world, because, mind you, if there is going to be a wedding, I am going to be there."

"Certainly, I mean you to be." Willie was getting braver now every minute. "The fact is, Annie, the wedding would be nowhere without you. You see ——"

"Go on, I am all attention."

"You see I am an only son, and my dear mother and father are both very fond of me. Well, our place is very pretty, and I—I—I——"

"You thought of getting married? Is that it?"

"That is it. I half told mother, and she seemed so happy about it. But I haven't spoken to the young lady yet; only I made up my mind I would do so to-night."

"Well, if I were you, Willie, I should, and I think I can guess who it is."

"Do guess then."

"You danced with her twice to-night."

"I did."

"Her brother has not come. Am I right?"

"She—she hasn't got a brother that ever I heard of."

"What, is not Jessie Morrison the young lady?"

"No, Annie Lindsay, it is *you!*"

* * * * *

* * * * *

Those two lines of asterisks represent the fall of the curtain on Scene II. Act I. of this story. I have told you already that ours was not a love tale in the true sense of the word, so I could not keep it up a moment longer.

But see, the curtain rises once more, and the scene is once more the woods and wilds, the hills and dales, still bathed in the soft light of the moon. But, oh, how sadly shorn of her beams and her beauty the moon appears to Willie Saunders now, as he goes plodding homewards all alone! The trees around him and the hedgerows, green-budding in the hopes of summer soon to come, look cold and dismal now. The wind still whispers through the pine trees, but there is no music in its murmur now. The brooklets went merrily singing over their pebbly beds when Willie passed this way only a few hours agone. They are singing even now, but it is in a sad and mournful key. The song is

"A lilt o' dool* and sorrow."

What answer had Annie Lindsay made to Willie that caused him such grief? Perhaps she hardly knew herself. It was a disjointed one anyhow. She felt sorry for Willie. She liked him. She had liked him from the first. But she had never thought it would come to this. Marriage she had never dreamt of yet. Besides, she was too young, and—and—well, she said no more, but burst into tears.

She dried her eyes at last, however. Duty was duty. Her mother would miss her, and also her friends.

Willie led her as far as the conservatory, and there they parted. He would not go in just yet, he had said,

---

* Grief.

but take a turn or two all by himself. But she had taken his hand in hers in a kindly, sisterly way at the door of the conservatory, and as she gazed up into his face her blue eyes swam in tears.

He never forgot that look.

"You're not angry, are you, Willie?" It was all she had said.

Half an hour after this Willie had gone back into the ball-room.

Jack Morrison was dancing with Annie. She looked very, very happy.

Willie sighed, and retraced his footsteps towards the conservatory. He sat himself down in a corner. Nearly half hidden he was by a bank of sweet-scented flowers.

Presently two young ladies sat down near him, evidently unaware of his presence.

Here is a brief epitome of the conversation Willie had been obliged to listen to:

"Yes, and they do look a nice couple! Jack is so tall and manly. He is just my beau-ideal of a young laird."

"More like a highland chief."

"Well, yes, like a highland chief, the sort you see in books and on the stage."

"And it really is all arranged, you say?"

"Oh, yes, I had it from Mrs. Chataway, and you know she knows everything. In three weeks' time they will be called in the church."

"Do you think Miss Lindsay will have any tocher*?"

---

* Fortune.

"Not much, I suppose; but I think it is a real love match; and I am quite sure, from what I know of Jack Morrison, that he would be the last man in the world to think of marrying for money."

"Well, I'm sure I hope they will be happy."

Willie groaned, and was discovered.

He had arisen slowly from his seat after this, taken one last look into the ball-room.

Jack stood beside Annie Lindsay.

He was talking low.

She was looking down and nervously crushing some rose leaves in her white fingers.

How bitter Willie had felt at that moment.

"She has crushed more than rose leaves to-night," he said half aloud. "She has crushed a life."

He had turned away at once.

He had gone round to the hall and thrown on his plaid.

Then bidding good-bye to none, had left the house, had almost fled from it indeed.

No wonder, then, that all beauty had gone from the landscape, and all music as well. The mournful cry of the brown owl, as it flew past him overhead, was more in accordance now with his feelings than song of mavis or glad melody of blackbird would have been.

When he reached home at last he went straight to his own room.

His faithful collie lay on the rug, and rose to bid him a loving welcome.

At first Willie Saunders rudely repelled his advances, and poor Bruce looked truly wretched.

"What *have* I done, master?" he seemed to plead. "Oh, master, what harm have I done?"

"No, no, doggie, it isn't you, it isn't you. I have still someone to love me, though it be but a dog."

Willie Saunders threw himself on the rug, and hiding his face in the faithful collie's mane, burst into tears.

CHAPTER III.

THE HIGHLAND SEER.

WHEN Willie Saunders awoke next morning, for a few brief moments he felt a heaviness at his heart that he was unable immediately to account for. Then he remembered all, and his great sorrow came welling over his heart and brain, and almost swamped his reason.

"I don't feel over well." That was the excuse he made to his mother that day, as he sat before an almost untasted luncheon. "Caught cold, I suppose," he added, observing her looks of concern. "Oh, I'll soon get over it, mother dear! I'll go and walk it off, or I'll work it off.

"Bruce and I," he added, "will go for a run, I think, away over the hills. I'm almost too old for bird-nesting, but I like to look at the eggs, and I like to see the birds, because they seem so happy. I'll take some bread and cheese with me in my bag. The fresh mountain air is sure to give me an appetite. Come, Bruce. By-bye, mother; it may be supper-time before I get back, but you'll know I'm not lost."

The feeling next to grief, now uppermost in Willie's heart, was one of bitterness—bitterness towards almost everyone and everything. The world had suddenly grown colder, he thought. Probably it had always been cold to him, though he had not observed it. No one in it, at all events, cared anything for him now.

For a time as he trudged onwards *en route* for the hills, he tried to hug this thought to his heart. He felt a pleasure in melancholy, a pleasure in being a lonely soul that no one loved. This was certainly a very morbid state of mind to be in, but there was no doubt some excuse to be made for the poor fellow.

When he gained the top of a neighbouring hill he threw himself listlessly down on his back, and Bruce, who had been trained to this trick, lay down to form his master's pillow.

The cool breeze was calmative in the extreme, so too was the stillness all around. You might have heard the lambs bleating on the braelands, and the loving call of their answering dams, the purring of the grouse, and now and then the scream of the whaup high in air; but all else was still and quiet.

Calmness begets health in a case of illness like Willie's, and his brain soon gave evidence of returning to a better frame. He grew less and less bitter. The world was surely not all so black as he had painted it. His mother loved him. Ah! indeed she did, and his simple-hearted father too, though he was never of a demonstrative nature. And then he had Bruce. Ah! there is a deal of comfort reader, to be obtained from the love of a faithful dog. His master is all the world to him. Others may hate you, may turn from you; but your dog has always a welcome for you, always a soft tongue to lick your hand, always a fountain of unfathomable love for you, and you alone, dwelling deep down in his dark brown eyes. Surely this is something to be thankful for in a cold and selfish world like ours.

But at this moment Willie's thoughts reverted more to his mother than to anyone else. For never until this morning had he kept a secret from her. And had he not even told her a lie. He feared he had. Well, one good resolve he could make, and did make, that as soon as he regained his home that night he would tell her all. Not that he wanted pity or consolation; this was an impossibility under the circumstances. No; all he wanted or expected was a little sympathy in his great sorrow, and forgiveness for having kept anything hidden from her.

After making this resolve he felt a little happier, and sighed a kind of sigh of relief.

Then his heart reverted to Annie Lindsay and to Jack Morrison, and the bitterness all returned to his heart. He did not blame Annie so very much. She had seemed to love him. She had confessed to liking him. What could she more?

But Jack Morrison, the friend of his boyhood, the almost brother.

"Bah!" he cried aloud, "what is such friendship worth?"

He would never see Annie more. On this he was

resolved, and he would avoid Jack in every way he could, and treat him with cold contempt if they met. He must not meet him, though, if such meeting could be obviated. He might say things to Jack that were better far unsaid. He might—oh, the thought for all the bitterness he bore him was too dreadful to contemplate!—he might strike Jack. And Jack was such a gentle, honest-eyed fellow, so good-natured and kind too. Fancy hitting Jack! Fancy Jack's blood upon his knuckles and hands! The very thought made him shudder. His good angel tried to get a word in edgeways just here.

"What harm has Jack really done you?" said the good angel. "It may not be Jack's fault. Are you sure even that the story is all true? Are you ——"

But Willie drove the good angel right straight away out of his heart, and opened its portals wide for the demon of bitterness to enter in and dwell.

I think, as his historian, that Willie Saunders made a very great mistake. To harbour anger or enmity even against our enemies does harm even to ourselves, because anger is a heart depressant. If we would live long and healthful lives in this world, and, let pessimists say what they like, it *is* a beautiful one, and there is far more of joy and gladness in it than there is of grief and sorrow, we must avoid every feeling of the mind that causes dejection.

Well, if it be foolish to continue angry even against our enemies, it is ever so much more silly to be angry against a brother or friend, and to be so without a cause, or without making positively certain that the cause does really exist, is a downright sin, and one that will assuredly be recorded against us if we do not repent and get forgiveness.

I will give Willie Saunders the credit of a kindly heart at all events. I have no more right to judge him harshly than he had to judge his friend Jack hurriedly. And I believe that if my hero had lain on that breezy hilltop only a short time longer, and had considered the whole situation, the demon of bitterness would once more have been banished far away, and the good Angel of Charity have taken its place. But poor Willie was tempest-tossed, in a manner of speaking. His grief was very real. He felt that his young life was not only clouded, but rent with a rending that time itself would fail to repair. He must get up and move on, rest only made him chafe the more.

So he walked on and on and on, caring little whither.

Bruce, the collie, must have wondered what his master meant by all this walking without any apparent result.

There was a result however that the dog could not appreciate, for there seemed to come to Willie's heart at length some surcease of sorrow. A kind of listless, dreamy feeling, born of the exercise, the sunshine, and the fresh pure air, took its place, and he seated himself on a grassy knoll not far from where a stream, escaping from a little lake, came tumbling down the glen. A very high-spirited and impetuous rivulet it had been at first, just as most human beings are in the days of youth. But now, when near to the bottom of this bonnie glen, it was far less mad in its career, and although sometimes roaring over its stony bed, it sometimes went quite to sleep in quiet flowery nooks, where rushlets bent down their tufted heads to kiss it. From these pools brown and speckled trout leapt up occasionally with joyous spring, entirely regardless of a keen-eyed otter, that was hungrily watching them from his den in the rocky bank.

The rocks all round were heather-clad; green now, but when autumn should come, they would be bright with the crimson and purple glory that neither pen nor pencil ever yet did justice to. There was beauty enough in the glen, however, albeit summer was yet a long way ahead to give, pleasure even to "dowie"* Willie Saunders, as he gazed around him. For a wealth of spring tints were scattered widely over bush and brake and brae. See how lovely those curling fern-fronds are, and the grass itself green-nodding in the gentle breeze. There are few flowers out yet, it is true, only the mauve-coloured day-nettle, and the day-nettle with wee white bells, and the starry golden dandelion, and the modest primrose. Pretty beetles with shining metallic backs go creeping hither and thither, each bent no doubt on some little but highly important business of his own, while ever and anon one of these creeps up and up a stem of grass, then, lifting its horny jacket, spreads gauzy wings and goes floating away out into the sunshine.

Here comes a great bee flying fiercely round and round and humming a song to himself. He was sent out by his queen, he tells Willie, to gather honey, but where in all the world is he likely to find any.

* Dowie—sad-hearted.

Here comes a bright yellow butterfly flying slowly straight ahead, and not coquetting round and round as it would in summer time. Born a little too soon perhaps* and can't find a mate, and wonders why it was put into the world at all, at all.

And here is another big bee just coming home to his bike or hive, in the very bank on which Willie and Bruce are sitting. But the foolish fellow is unable to find the entrance thereto. He thinks twenty times over that he has it, and twenty times over he is disappointed.

"Let me see," says the bee considering, "there was first a dock-leaf and then a day nettle, and then—then; oh, yes, then a bit of hemlock! Ho! ho! I've found the hole at last." And in he pops.

There was something soporific in the air, perhaps, and in the droning sound that the bee had made; or the bronze-backed beetles that climbed the heather or grass stems and flown away in quest of adventure, may have taken Willie's thoughts and spirit with them away and away and away till landed in dreamland. I do not know, but this I am certain of, that this hero of ours fell fast asleep.

He awoke at long last, but he lay still for a short time before opening his eyes, as one will at times, wondering where he was.

"And a' these braes were red wi' blood"—it was a voice almost close to his elbow—"blood dyed the grass

* These early butterflies, however, have not, as many suppose, recently burst from the chrysalis, but have been born in autumn and hybernated all the winter.

and eke the heather cowes;* blood and brains were on the very stanes, and the streamlet and linn ran red wi' the blood o' the slain, but aye the fearfu' fight raged on and on."

Willie had raised himself on his elbow and was gazing wonderingly at the speaker, whom he soon however succeeded in recognising as a curious but harmless old man who, armed with a huge pole or sapling, used to roam about in these wilds, and who was called Fey Fraser.

The word "fey" is meant to express a peculiar kind of madness that is supposed to take possession of some people who are soon to die an accidental or unnatural death. But if Fraser was "fey" he had been "fey" for twenty years and over, and was not dead yet.

"Daft" would have been a better adjective by which to describe Fraser's mental condition than "fey." But there he sat at any rate, whether daft or fey, looking neither to the right hand nor to the left, and talking, if I may so express myself, as if some one were talking through him, and he were but the medium of some spiritualistic demonstration.

Strangely enough Bruce, the collie dog, although an excellent guard, had never either barked or growled at him.

Fey Fraser was a very old man—some averred that he was over a hundred—but he was straight as a rush, though lean and bony. He was dressed in a tattered kilt of shepherd tartan, with a jacket to match. His

* Stems.

beard was long and white, and from underneath his broad blue, well-worn bonnet his grey hair escaped in tangles.

"The fearfu' fight," he continued, "raged on and on; the air aroun' resounded wi' the fearfu' cries, the mingled screams o' pain, the oaths, the thuds as sword met shield, as skulls were cloven and shoulders split. Lowlan's and Hielan's had met in deadly tulzie; but Lowlan's must win or die in the glen. For ahint them, though miles and miles awa', was the town, the city, they had come out to defend, and there, weepin' wifes and bairns were awaitin' for the husbands and faythers they ne'er again might see."

"Did the Lowlands win?"

It was Willie Saunders who spoke now.

And the seer—for seer indeed he seemed—replied, without taking his eyes from the hills, "The Lowlan's won that fearfu' fight. Back towards their mountains the clans were driven, yet quarter had they nane. But ever at a rock or at a river ford they made the other stand, and there the corpses lay next day in dozens for the eagles to devour, for the corbies to pick."

The seer turned slowly round now, and his eyes and Willie's met.

Willie shuddered somewhat, for those of the seer were of a strange granite-grey colour, and as low in the head as if the man had lain for months in the grave.

"You are young," he said; "you are strong, you are bonnie. It isn't for the like o' you to stay at home in peacefu' glens when your country's cause beckons you abroad to fight, when the blood o' slain soldier and civilian reeks hot to heaven on Asia's sunny plains. It isn't for the like o' you to rest in peace when the tulwars o' a savage foe are dripping red wi' the blood o' murdered wives and bairns. Rise, lad, rise, and help to avenge the woes o' Scotia's sons and daughters! Love is the plaything o' the carpet knight; the sword, the sword, is the weapon for men and for heroes. Rise, lad, rise, your country needs you!"

Fey Fraser, by means of his sapling or pole, had helped himself to his feet, and as he spoke the last words he towered 'twixt Willie and the evening sky, gaunt and awful, till even Bruce appeared frightened; but instead of seeking safety in flight, he lifted his chin in air and gave vent to a mournful howl or wail that the very rocks and hills re-echoed.

"Fraser," said Willie, "I would speak—I would ask you ——"

But the wandering seer behaved as if he neither saw nor heard. He turned slowly round and glided silently away down the glen, and Willie gazed after him until his strange figure was hidden behind a rock.

Could there be any truth, Willie began to think, in the words the seer had uttered?

If there was, then he was fated to be a soldier. Why should he not be? True, he could not enter the army as an officer and gentleman, as many of his forbears had done, winning both honour and distinction; but he could carry a gun and bayonet for the Queen, and a man might be a gentleman, even though serving in the ranks.

Was there really going to be war? Willie would not care to be an idle soldier. In times of peace he thought he would repine, but in action and in change of scene he could forget his sorrow, forget his love. Well, if he could not, he at least knew how to die. He might be better dead. In the grave there is forgetfulness, and it might be that when she heard that her lover had fallen, sword in hand, she might drop a tear to his memory.

All mere sentiment. All mere romance—I hear some one remark. The sentiment and romance of a love-stricken youth not long out of his teens.

Well, perhaps; yet it is as well to remember that many a hero who has fought and bled in his country's cause, can trace the commencement of his career to sentiment just like this. I myself would never speak lightly of any feeling of the mind that should move a young man to action and to deeds.

This old Fey Fraser, who, by the way, had himself been a soldier in the days of his youth and manhood, might possibly be but a dotard, but the country-side thought him a seer. There *are* more things in heaven and earth than are dreamt of in our philosophy. The possession by some old men of second sight has been believed in for ages in Scotland, especially in the Highlands. They thought that this man possessed it.

His looks, his motions, and his bearing were strange and almost fearful. Even as he gazed at his retreating figure, lines from that weird poem of Campbell's recurred to Willie's mind, and some of them were really *a propos*.

> "Lochiel, Lochiel! beware of the day,
> For dark and despairing my sight I may seal!
> But man cannot cover what God would reveal.
> 'T is the sunset of life gives me mystical lore,
> And coming events cast their shadows before."

Willie sat there, deeply buried in thought, till the shadows of evening began to gather round him. A long strip of orange-red light lay along the western horizon; but in the east the stars had already begun to twinkle, and presently the moon rose slowly over the mountains.

"It is my destiny! It is my fate! Bruce, my dear dog, I am going to be a soldier."

And Willie Saunders walks slowly homewards now; but he had made a resolve, and he would keep it.

CHAPTER IV.

A PEACEFUL SCENE—MOTHER AND SON.

THE soldier or sailor who has no home-life to think about when far away, no cottage, be it ever so humble, to which his thoughts can revert by night in camp or on deck on the lone sea, is to be pitied.

Do you remember, reader, the beautiful poem called "The Soldier's Dream"?

Let me transcribe a few lines. Miss them, or skip them, if you do not care for them; but do not forget that we have soon to journey afar to scenes of adventure and strife, and it is only by contrasting the *agremens* of Peace and War that we can decide on their relative merits or demerits.

But the soldier in the poem had laid him down to sleep, thinking, no doubt, about his far-away, peaceful home in England or in bonnie Scotland.

"Our bugles sang truce—for the night-cloud had lower'd,
And the sentinel stars set their watch in the sky;
And thousands had sunk on the ground overpower'd,
The weary to sleep, and the wounded to die.

"When reposing that night on my pallet of straw
By the wolf-scaring faggot that guarded the slain,
At the dead of the night a sweet vision I saw,
And thrice ere the morning I dreamt it again."

It was a dream of home that this soldier had dreamt, and he thought he was back once more among his friends, back among the green fields and rolling hills that in his boyhood he had so often wandered over. The mountain goats were bleating, and upwards from the cornfields floated the song the glad reapers sang. And here was his own little cottage, and his joyful wife and children to welcome him home. As they kissed him a thousand times o'er, no wonder they pleaded with him to stay.

"'Stay, stay with us; rest, thou art weary and worn!'
And fain was their war-broken soldier to stay;
But sorrow returned with the dawning of morn,
And the voice in his dreaming ear melted away."

Ah! there is pathos in that poem, and even my own experience of life abroad tells me there is also truth in every line.

* * * * *

Take a glance now at the peaceful home of our would-be soldier, Willie Saunders, and I believe you will think with me that the grief which led him to take leave of it must have been bitter indeed. I have but to close my eyes for a moment, and the whole scene rises up before my mental vision. A wide-spreading glen it is, almost a strath, in fact. Room enough here for field and farm, forest and stream, between the wooded banks of the rapid river and the rugged hills or mountains.

A village nestles among a mass of foliage at the very bottom of it, a straggling sort of a village, showing but little from a distance save the rooftops, one or two white gables, and the tall steepled church. If you pass through its principal street and keep on for half a mile, you will come to a road leading off to the left, that will take you straight to Willie's home—the Raven's Nest. The road winds upwards and bears the name of loaning, which is equivalent to saying that the farm stands on elevated ground. It does, for as soon as the loaning broadens out, you find yourself on quite a plateau, and keeping on to the right you come to the steading, a beautiful roomy square of tall stone buildings surrounding a well-paved courtyard, with its byres, its stables, coach-houses, its mill and grain loft, but nothing to offend the eye or sense of smell, such as the slimy pools and manure heaps that exist on English farms. There is here neither sight nor sound nor loathsome odour to annoy the eye or disgust the senses; nay, and if you even enter the byres, you would wish to linger there, so sweet is the breath of the sleek fat kine.

The dwelling-house itself stands not far from the steading; it does not keep proudly aloof therefrom, as some more modern-built houses do. It is Laird Saunders's house, the laird is a farmer, and he is not one whit ashamed of his calling.

The house altogether is so quaint and intricate, that without a diagram pen fails to describe it. Goodness only knows how old it was in some parts, nor how recent in others, for since its erection it must have been greatly added to and altered.

Just take one peep at the kitchen, because it is really and truly Scottish, and especially Northern Scottish. Laird Saunders, you will observe, did not believe in what is called the bothy system for his men-servants. The bothy is little more than an outhouse roughly furnished, in which men live and cook and sleep, in a far more rude and primitive way than do pioneers in the Australian bush.

The laird's men-servants had their meals in the kitchen then. The back-door is sheltered by a roomy porch quite closed in, so that in winter, however wildly the wind may roar and howl, it cannot sift the snow in beneath the door to invade the kitchen itself. This kitchen is very large. You could not roast an ox here at the fireplace, but you might a whole sheep. Yes, it is a low fire with an immense iron crane over it, on which half a dozen pots at a time can swing in comfort; a hearth on which logs of wood and peat can burn, a hearth that a dozen happy and contented faces can scarce encircle on a winter's forenight. The rafters above the kitchen are visible, not plastered over, and from these hams hang and bunches of onions dry; they are crossed too with shelves, where cheeses may "win." The furniture is simple and strong, one long tall dais, one large table against the wall where the men dine or have supper, stools, chairs, and a bookshelf.

In a corner by the fire is a high-backed chair of huge dimensions, and of an evening it is no unusual thing for the laird himself to sit here and tell stories to the lads and lasses round the fire, mingling therewith many a word of good advice, and now and then a quotation from

Holy Writ. Then every night the laird reads a chapter in the parlour and says a prayer, the servants filing quietly out afterwards and soon going to bed; for early hours are the rule at the Raven's Nest.

In front of the house is a very pleasant rose lawn, and this is separated from the garden proper by a high ivy-covered wall. One might, if one chose, call it the kitchen garden, but it is not wholly devoted to vegetables, nor to fruit either, for here are all things combined—truly an old, old-fashioned garden. The gravelled walks are bordered with broad grassy bands, inside these is the brown soft earth sacred to flowers of many a hue, such as scent the air around them, and need but little tending. Primroses, primulas, and auriculas of every colour, daisies, lupins, carnations, pinks—a goodly show indeed, with at regular distances along these borders alternate rose and gooseberry trees. Not standard roses, that would have spoiled the whole effect, and substituted primness for breadth; no, these rose trees grew from their own roots, and the glorious roses when dew-laden bent groundwards or even rested on the earth itself. A delightful spot this, Sandie used to think, in which to spend a summer's evening with a favourite author; and when tired of reading or lounging in the heather-thatched summer-house one has only to open a door in the wall, and lo! here are the green fields. Away down beneath spreads out the bonnie glen, with the smoke of the village cottages curling up through the trees, and beyond a broad shining elbow of the silvery river.

If inclined for solitude you must turn your back towards the village, and by a devious footpath ascend the brow of the hill. A few minutes' walk will take you to as lonesome a scene as you could wish to gaze upon. For a tall-treed pine wood waves on this hilltop, and when you enter this you seem to leave the world far behind and beneath you, so still and silent is all around; nought of life to be seen save occasionally a hare or a rabbit scuttling swiftly across the footpath; nought to be heard save the song of the blackbird or mavis, or the love-cooing of the cushat dove deep down in yonder thicket of spruce. But push on and in twenty minutes or less you will be clear of woodland and forest, then for miles on each side of you spreads out a heather-clad peaty tableland, a wild and wide hobgoblin moor.

*　　*　　*　　*　　*　　*

When Willie Saunders and his collie returned that night, he took the nearest cut through the garden and across the daisied lawn, over which the light was streaming from the parlour window.

His mother sat sewing in her easy-chair by the cosy fire; his father had gone to bed. But supper was spread for the wanderer.

"Late, boy, late," said the mother, smiling fondly on her son. "I am sure you must be hungry."

"Oh, yes," said Willie, "of course I am hungry, and so is Bruce, so we will both have supper together."

He was unusually silent while he ate, and as this was not his usual form, Mrs. Saunders now and then cast an uneasy glance at his face.

Having finished, he took a low stool by her lap, on

which he leant his arm as he gazed for a time into the fire.

"Where have you been all day?"

"Over the hills and far away, mother. And whom do you think I met?"

"Your friend the colonel, perhaps, and your sweetheart his daughter. Is that so?"

"Ha, ha, ha!" Willie laughed. "Now, what little birdie told my mother I ever dreamt of sweethearts?"

His mother did not answer directly. She passed her hand over his brow and hair caressingly.

"To see my boy is to love him," she murmured.

"Mother, I must tell you all now. I have been dreadfully wicked in not doing so before, but I could not till now. You have always been so good to me, and I knew I should have your sympathy; still, I could not tell you this morning. But I have been alone all day among the woods and wilds and solitudes, and see everything more clearly now."

He paused for a moment.

"Mother," he resumed, "I am heart-broken! Don't answer yet. You see it was all my own fault. I was a fool! I mistook her friendship—sisterly regard, I might call it—for love, and I asked her to—to—to promise to marry me. But ——"

"Willie dear, of whom are you talking?"

"Didn't I tell you? Of Annie, of course—Miss Lindsay."

"And she refused you?"

"With tears and sorrow, mother, that I know were genuine; but still ——"

His mother sighed.

"How time has flown," she said mournfully. "I cannot think of you, Willie, as anything but a child. A child you are still to me, and now you talk of being married!"

"Oh, mother, I did not mean just yet! But I just wanted to make sure that Annie would some day be mine."

"Some day Annie may, dear son."

"Ah! no, no, no," cried Willie woefully; "she is going to be married, I was told—or, rather, I overheard it—to Jack Morrison. That makes it all the more bitter. Because he never told me, the friend of his boyhood, me who would have died for him, his secret, never told me a word about it.

"Mother," he continued, "no one knows how much I liked Jack. Had he not kept his wooing secret, had he been square with me, had he come and said to me, 'Willie, I love Annie Lindsay, and I am going to ask her to be my wife,' then, oh, believe me, mother, I never, never, would have breathed a word of affection to the girl, and Jack should never, never, have known that I loved her too. I should have been a true friend to both for ever and for aye.

"Do not try to comfort me, mother. My heart is broken. I have lost my love, I have lost my friend, and Jack's duplicity stabs me to the quick!"

What could Willie's mother say to comfort him? Nothing. She spoke, it is true. She told him he was young, that he would outlive all his care and sorrow, that he was not even old enough to know his own heart, and that Jack's conduct was no doubt capable of being satisfactorily explained.

Willie only groaned.

"I'll try to forget," he said.

"And," he added, "I'll try to forgive—even Jack. But, mother, I will never see him again, at least not until my regiment returns from the war."

"Willie, are you awake?" his mother cried.

"I am awake, mother, and what I am going to tell you is true."

Then he told her about his meeting with Fey Fraser and his strange prophecy.

"The ravings of a madman, Willie. Surely my boy has more sense than to listen to such a poor, daft man as that!"

"He is very, very old," said Willie, as if talking to himself; "and very old people may catch glimpses of things that we cannot fathom or see; voices may whisper to them that we cannot hear.

"'The sunset of life gives them mystical lore,
And coming events cast their shadows before.'"

* * * * *

Mrs. Saunders was silent, and when Willie looked up he noticed that the tears were falling a-down her cheeks. He must be the comforter now, and right manfully he buckled himself to the task.

He spoke of all the good that foreign travel, or mixing with strange peoples in strange lands, was capable of effecting in a well-trained mind; and he spoke of the bright side of a soldier's life, of the pomp and panoply of war, of the honour and glory attached to it, and of his certainty of rising in the regiment he should choose, even should it be but to wield the sword of a brave sergeant. Then he told her the time would soon, soon fly, and that he would come home, when he did come, for good, and never go away again, and that then they would be happier than ever.

His mother only wept, still silently wept.

"If, mother," he said, seeing that all other arguments failed, "if, dear mother, I go abroad, I may forget my grief; I may live it down. If I stay here at home, and brood over it, as sure as the sun will rise to-morrow, mother, in a year or two at most I shall be in the grave. I am not a boy now, mother. I might have been a boy two days ago; I am now a man. But I will not be a soldier, though to me it means life, without your consent. I see a life of happiness yet in store for me if I go. If I stay I only see——"

"What, Willie?"

"A coffin and a grave!"

Willie's mother dried her eyes now.

"You must go, dear boy, and I will pray for you."

"Spoken like my own brave mother," said Willie; and he kissed her hands fondly and reverently.

"And now," he said, "let us change the subject. Let us talk of something more pleasant than even war."

They sat for hours beside the fire, Willie building castles in the air, his mother listening, sometimes sighing, it is true, but oftentimes smiling; and before they both retired that poor mother was at least beginning to be reconciled to the inevitable.

* * * * *

On Willie's bedroom mantelpiece he found a letter that had come that afternoon in his absence.

It was an invitation to spend a fortnight with a friend in Inverness.

"I'll go," said Willie to himself. "Yes, I shall go to-morrow morning. I dread to meet Jack. In after life I may be able to forgive him; but if we met now, oh, I fear what would come of it!"

CHAPTER V.

SERGEANT McKINNON, OF THE GALLANT 93rd.

WILLIE SAUNDERS did not leave home next day. He busied himself in packing his things for his fortnight's sojourn in the Highlands of Inverness.

His faithful collie, Bruce, never left him for a moment, trotting after him when he left the room or went out into the garden, and lying beside him in the house watching the preparations for the journey.

"I cannot take you, Bruce. You must be a good dog, and stop at home to watch over my mother."

Bruce wagged his tail, as if in acquiescence; but he sighed, and looked very sad. He was but a young collie, barely yet a year and a half old, but wondrous wise nevertheless, for the Scottish collie possesses sagacity and reasoning power that is almost human in a measure.

When Willie had packed his box he laid himself down beside the honest dog on the rug, and placed one arm around his shaggy neck.

"Don't you grieve, dear doggie," he said, talking

just as if Bruce could understand every word he said. "Don't you grieve, because, although I am going away, it will not be for very long—only for a fortnight, or a month at most, this time, Bruce, and it will enable you, doggie, to reconcile yourself to my absence. Because, dear boy, my next journey will be a very much longer one, for I'm going far, far across the sea to fight for my Queen and my country. I shall go away, Bruce, only carrying a gun and a bayonet, but I may come back—who knows?—with a sergeant's sash around my waist and a sergeant's sword by my side. And all the time I am away, Bruce, you will keep near to my mother, and guard her safely for me till I come back again."

Bruce had got one of Willie's wrists hooked to the rug with a bonnie white paw, and was lovingly licking his hand with his soft pink tongue.

Willie patted and kissed his bawsent brow, then slowly rose to go and seek his mother and tell her he was all ready.

* * * * *

Now Willie's parents had given him money enough to take him as a saloon passenger in the steamer from Aberdeen to Inverness, but as in a short time he would have to rough it as a private soldier, he determined to begin roughing it at once. So he took a steerage ticket.

It was late at night before the steamer arrived from Leith, for the wind blew high and was dead ahead. But Willie had found himself a bundle of canvas in the goods' shed on the quay, and rolling his plaid around him, went to sleep as soundly as if he had been in his own bed at home.

So sound asleep was he indeed that he did not hear the first nor the second steamer bell. A sailor, however, came to find a box, and discovered his whereabouts.

"Hullo! matie, are ye gaun wi' the steamer? Man, you'll need to hurry. She'll be aff in five minutes. Here, I'll carry your box for the price o' an ounce o' tobacco."

"I'm going to carry my box mysel'," said Willie; "but here's the price o' the tobacco a' the same. Ye deserve that and mair for waukin' me."

And with the box on his back Willie marched over the gangway, and forward to the steerage.

This was no such easy task, for the deck was covered with sheep, and through these he had to force his way.

The steerage was a lively place, but certainly not a very pleasant one. However, our hero went below. It was right in the bows of the vessel, with a table athwart-ships in the centre, and lockers all round. There were human forms huddled up on these lockers, and Willie thought he would throw in his lot with them, so he snuggled up in a corner, and having nothing now on his mind soon went fast asleep again.

It was a good thing for him he slept, for the wind had gone round to the north-west by west, and was blowing about a gale dead off the land. He had been often to sea, however, and so was not troubled with *mal-de-mer*. It was five o'clock in the morning before he awoke, only to find that the vessel had broken down, and being unable to make much sail, had been blown a long way out of her course.

"Half-way to Norway mebbe," said the steward when Willie asked him where they were.

"Dinna believe him, laddie," said a Highland soldier, whose dark tartan and buttons indicated him as belonging to the old 93rd, "dinna believe him. Stewards and sailors o' a' sorts are born leears.

"Here," he added to three of his comrades who lay asleep on deck with their heads pillowed on their canvas bags, "here, you lazy chiels, are ye gaun to sleep a' day? Get up and let's ha'e a dance."

He kicked one; that one awoke and kicked his two neighbours, and soon all three were up, and wide enough awake. They had whisky and oat-cakes, then shouted for the piper. It was evident enough those soldiers had no intention of letting down their hearts.

They danced ram-reel * after ram-reel to the sound of the bagpipes, but they soon tired of this.

"Is there no lassies about?" cried one.

Then first one bundle pulled itself up off the lockers, then another, and another. They were lassies certainly, but very sleepy-looking.

"Hurrah!" cried the soldiers. "Come along, my dearies. Play up, piper. Gie's the 'High Road to Linton.' Hooch!"

The lassies laughed, but they danced all the same. And so the ball once begun was kept merrily up till breakfast-time. The dancing had not spoiled anybody's appetite.

---

* A reel in which men only are dancing.

But by this time the repairs below were completed, and by-and-by the ship's head was turned westward, and she went paddling on her voyage to the capital of the Scottish Highlands.

The sergeant of this gay party of soldiers was a stalwart young fellow, apparently not much older than Willie himself; but he was as brown as the back of a fiddle or a well-burned brick.

Willie was glad indeed to make his acquaintance, which he did at the breakfast-table, and they afterwards went on deck together.

They were very glad to be permitted to go on the bridge between the paddle-boxes, for the odour from the sheep and pigs below was by no means over-pleasant. Here they sat them down.

Although the storm had died away, there was still a bit of sea on, but the motion was considered by Willie rather pleasant than otherwise.

Sergeant McKinnon lit his short and well-coloured meerschaum.

"You're not used to life in the steerage, I can see," he said, after a few puffs.

"Well, the fact is," said Willie, "my father gave me money to pay saloon fare, but ——"

"You spent it. Just like what a student would do. Oh, I know them well!"

"Oh, no, it wasn't that! and I am not a student, only as I am going to be a soldier I thought the sooner I learned to rough it the better."

"A soldier are you going to be, sir?"

It will be observed that the worthy sergeant now

added the "sir." He thought he was talking to a cadet or junior officer.

"What regiment are you going to have a commission in?"

Willie Saunders sighed.

"Alas!" he said, "no such luck for me as a commission; I am going to enter the ranks, sergeant."

The sergeant turned to look at him.

"Now look here, young fellow, I liked your appearance the moment I saw you foot the floor.* You have a grand physique, and a handsome, happy-go-lucky sort of a face; but you're a gentleman's son; I could see that from a glance. And you've quarrelled with your folks. That much I can guess. Well, take my advice, lad; go home like a man, and ask them to forgive you. You will never repent it. The army, or rather the ranks, are not for the like of you."

"Sergeant McKinnon, you are awfully kind and good, but your advice comes too late. I have made up my mind: I *am* going into the ranks. Either that or I shall die. No, I have not quarrelled with father; it is worse than that."

"Fallen in love, and been jilted?"

"That's it."

"Poor boy. God help you!"

Sergeant McKinnon extended his hand, and Willie Saunders knew he had made a friend.

"A fellow feeling makes us wondrous kind."

---

* Dance.

"I too have been through the fire."

"Have you been in love, and—and—— "

"Jilted. Give it the right name, my boy. Women are wondrous beings."

"And you got over it?"

"Years and years ago. Do *I* look like a love-sick swain now?"

"No, that you don't."

"Well, lad, I'm glad I've met you. Of course you will join the gallant 93rd?"

"It must be a Highland regiment," said Willie; "but whether yours or not I cannot say. It is like this, you know, I want to join a regiment that will soon go on foreign service. It will kill me to stop at home."

"Bravo! That is ours. I have heard that we are soon to be ordered off to China. You'll have learned the goose-step before then."

Willie laughed.

"I know that already, and all the drill a single man can be taught. My mother's father was a Major McGregor. He died two years ago, but he dearly loved a soldier's life, and there is very little he did not teach me. He used to have Peter McKay and me always at sword-stick too, and I never saw a better swordsman than Peter."

"And pray who is Peter?"

"Well, Peter is simply our cow-bailie, an honest, good-looking, strapping lad of twenty, or nearly. He has been with us all his life."

"I suppose he is fond of you?"

"Ay, and I of him."

"What's your name?"

"Willie Saunders."

"Does Peter know you are going to 'list?"

"I didn't tell him."

"Well, *do* tell him, and ask him to come with you."

"That I will," said Willie.

"And now, sergeant," he continued, "you are going to Inverness to recruit, aren't you?"

"True enough."

"Have me as No. 1?"

"Not to-day, lad; not to-day. I want you to think well over the matter. If I hadn't taken a sort of a fancy for you, I should have seen to you and enrolled you at once, but I won't. A week may work wonders. Come to me at the end of a week, and I'll put you to rights. Meanwhile, think.

"The army is rough on youngsters like you," he added, "that have never been over their own glen-head, but I doubt not you'll come to like it."

"I know I shall if there be plenty of fighting."

"Lord love the laddie; you'll have more of that than you can wag your stick at. But don't imagine that war means honour and glory for the man in the ranks."

"What does it mean then?"

"Mean?" said Sergeant McKinnon. "It would take an hour to tell you what all it means. It means implicit obedience to begin with. A man must *jump*"—the sergeant spoke the word as quickly and sharply as if he had been on parade—"he must jump at the word of command, as if a pin were stuck in him.

When he gets an order he must think of nothing but the word *obey*. He is a mere machine, or rather part of a machine; nay, he is even less than that. A watch has wheels, and wheels have cogs. Your private soldier is but one of the cogs, and must do his duty when his turn comes just as regularly and just as unthinkingly. Do you follow me?"

"I believe I do."

"Obedience then, lad, to the sergeant, or corporal even, above you is the first duty of the private."

"Yes; my grandfather has told me so."

"Well, if you mean to rise in the army—and you see I have—you must be clean and orderly in all your habits; temperate too to a degree, and always pleasant and cheerful, without being servile or sycophantic even to the officer. An officer, if he be a gentleman, hates a lickspittle.

"Now, Willie Saunders, you may think it is easy to be all I tell you. And so—apart from home pleasures and temptations—in times of peace it is; but, lad, during a campaign—ah! then is the time of trial. When you're tired, sleepy, hungry—starving perhaps—weary and war-worn, then I can tell you it takes all the courage and strength of mind the bravest man possesses, to always yield implicit obedience with willingness, alacrity, and cheerfulness."

"Yes."

"It isn't in the field so much that this is so difficult. I've seen men half dead with fatigue, sore-footed, and hardly able to lag along, change into the brightest and briskest lads you ever saw when the enemy suddenly hove in sight, ay, and fight like heroes for hours under fire. But obedience comes hardest when a man is tired, and has not the excitement of fighting to stir him up. Your officer may be tired then, mind you, and querulous also, and it is hard enough to obey such a man at such a time with cheerfulness. But *if* you do, he will not forget it, nor will he forget you.

"No, lad, all the honour and glory likely to come your direction during a campaign is precious small. You must just be content to imagine you have it, you must love your flag for your flag's sake, and the regiment because you are in it, and because its prestige has been handed down to you to maintain. Then, you know, there is always the old country to think about, and the friends at home. You want to return to them, if ever you return at all, with an untarnished name, and with a face you can hold up before the world.

"You know, I dare say, Willie Saunders, that ancient Spartan mothers used to give their shields to their sons before they went to battle——

"'Here is your shield, my son,' a mother would say. 'Return *with* it, or return *on* it.'"

"Yes," said Willie, "but we have not such mothers now."

"Dear lad," said the sergeant, "you are going to be a soldier. Well, let this thought ever lead you on to duty, the thought that you *have* such a mother, and a very exacting one she is. That mother is your country."

"Thank you," said Willie, "I shall ever try to remember that."

"Now one word more. You are going to join the 93rd.

I know and feel you are; that is, if you join the army at all."

"That I certainly shall."

"Well, I hope to have you in my company."

"I shall be delighted."

"But stay. Here you and I are talking together as equals. In the service, on parade, or on duty, I may often seem exacting, stern, and all that. You 'll believe, nevertheless, won't you, that I am not unfriendly?"

"I will."

"Well, shake hands, lad; I hope there is a bright future before you, or——"

"A soldier's grave."

The sergeant laughed.

"You 'll get a good deal of your poetry and romance knocked out of you, my boy, before you 're long in the ranks. And perhaps just as well. Duty is what we want most of, you know. Duty, duty, duty! And I feel sure from the looks of you that you won't forget that. The grandson of a MacGregor will not disgrace either himself or the colours he fights beneath.

"But mind you, Willie, I don't want to banish all romance and poetry from your nature. A soldier, and especially a Scottish soldier, has always an element of that deep down in the bottom of his heart. We Scotch are soldiers born, you know, and who would not fight for a land like ours. You mind what Scott says—

> "'Land of brown heath and shaggy wood,
> Land of the mountain and the flood,
> Land of my sires, what mortal hand
> Can e'er untie the filial band
> That knits me to thy rugged strand.'

"Yes, Willie, a true Scotsman is nothing if not patriotic, and it seems to me that patriotism and poetry are so far from being incompatible, that they very often go hand in hand."

"I think, Sergeant McKinnon," said Willie, laughing, "that the goddess of poetry was not very far away when you were born."

"Perhaps not, lad, perhaps not. But even in my short time in the service I've come through enough to scare poetry clean away."

"Well, sergeant, I suppose poetry won't fill the porridge-pot."

"No, nor will she help to staunch a bleeding wound or extract a bullet; but song and poetry have often helped to keep the spirits of our soldiers up, and incite them to many a gallant deed.

"Just the night before the great battle of Inkermann, Willie, our soldiers might have been heard singing in camp. And hear what the poet says about this—

"''Twas strange, in that dark hovel drear,
With war's impending horrors near,
Those homely Scottish tones to hear,
    Or list the vocal flow
Of sad but sacred home-love blent
With chivalrous and bold intent,
And thoughts on deadly conflict bent,
    And battle's wildest throe.

"'Blame not the uncouth melodies,
   From Nature's holy source upheaving,
That, mingled with the keen wind's sighs,
   Regret and grief alike relieving.
No recreant will that soldier prove
   Within whose valiant breast
The gentle thoughts of woman's love
   With warlike ardours rest.'

"But come, young man, I've made you sad; so we shall change the subject. See, there is land on the lee bow. In three hours' time we will be safe in Inverness. Did it ever occur to you, Willie, that a sailor's life is a happy one?"

"No; but I think it takes a man with a happy-go-lucky kind of nature to be a sailor."

"True. Well, a soldier, you know, who sees a good deal of foreign service, sees life in every form, on the ocean as well as on the land. But I must go below now. I've got to look after Tommy Atkins, you know. Your private soldier who never means to be anything else but a private soldier, is very apt to take all out of life he can, and this isn't always the best thing he can do for his health. Ta, ta, Willie Saunders, I'll see you again. Mind this, Fort George is the head-quarters of Sergeant McKinnon for a few months; but you may tumble across him on the streets of Inverness with a whole wisp of coloured ribbons fluttering from his bonnet."

"Ta, ta!" said Willie; "and there is one thing I feel pretty sure of ——"

"And what is that?"

"I'll tumble across Sergeant McKinnon somewhere."

Then the sergeant went below.

*   *   *   *   *

Willie's friend was a second cousin, a clergyman, who lived in a beautiful strath not far from Loch Ness.

He was very pleased indeed to see his young friend. Indeed, he gave him a hearty Highland welcome, and just did his very best to let him have a really good time of it.

He tried nevertheless to dissuade him from going as a soldier, but Willie only smiled and said nothing.

Very quickly did that fortnight fly away; then Willie Saunders stopped another week, to enjoy a little more trout fishing in the lochs. The scenery all around here was wildly, grandly beautiful. But as the minister was too stout to walk far, our hero had to take his fishing excursions by himself, accompanied only by the parson's collie. Being alone therefore he began to think too much, and all his old love for Annie Lindsay, as well as his bitterness against Jack Morrison, seemed to return with double force.

So one evening he told his cousin that next day he meant to go to Inverness and seek out the bold sergeant.

"Ah! well, my boy," said his cousin somewhat sadly, "it is your fate; so go, if you must, and mind you return safe."

"Yes," said Willie, "*with* my shield, or *on* it."

*   *   *   *   *

Willie bade his cousin a long farewell next day, and took the steamer at Inverfarigaig to Inverness, along the loch and the lovely canal.

When he arrived in the town he found that the steamer from Aberdeen had not yet come in, and was not expected for hours.

There is little difficulty in spending a few hours pleasantly enough in the beautiful capital of the Highlands, but Willie Saunders went down in time to meet the boat all the same.

Almost the first person he saw in the bows as she came in was his father's honest cow-bailie, Peter McKay.

Peter was waving his Scotch bonnet, and seemed delighted to see his foster-brother.

"How are you, Peter?"

"Man!" said Peter, "I'm better now; but sich a nicht I had!"

"Was it stormy?"

"Man, I dinna ken. I lay on deck under a bit o' tarry sailcloth, and my head on a coil o' ropes a' the time. Sick? Man, sickness is nae name for it."

"But you're going to be a soldier with me?"

"Rather!"

"Well, come and feed, for you do look rather green."

A good dinner put life and courage in Peter once more, and he told Willie, as the two went trudging along the street, that he now felt bold enough to fight the French or Russians either.

"Ha! my boy," cried Sergeant McKinnon, coming suddenly round the corner, with many a gay ribbon fluttering in his bonnet. "So we meet again!"

"Yes, sergeant, and right happy I am. And this is Peter McKay. We are both ready to join."

"Spoken like heroes! Come on; we'll soon make you soldiers!"

The piper came up at this very moment. McKinnon took four ribbons from his pocket, and fastened them to the young fellows' bonnets; the pipes struck up, and away they marched.

And before they had gone half a mile—and this was to McKinnon's lodgings—the sergeant had hooked two more recruits, almost as tall and handsome as Willie Saunders and Peter McKay themselves.

No wonder the sergeant felt happy.

But Willie bargained with the sergeant for a few days' grace, that he might run home and see and bid farewell to his father and mother, and dear old Bruce, the collie.

This was willingly granted, and a rendezvous at Aberdeen barracks was appointed.

Just one week from this date Willie and his foster brother were *en route* for Dover.

They had begun their soldier-life in earnest.

CHAPTER VI.

OFF TO THE WARS.

THE time flew on.

Willie Saunders and his foster-brother, Peter McKay, had been soldiers for nearly a whole year, and all this time they were stationed at Dover. It was a somewhat monotonous life for Willie. He would much sooner have been ordered abroad at once to India or to Persia, where there was a chance of seeing some active service.

However, this was not to be. His friend Sergeant McKinnon told him he need not expect it.

"We don't send Johnnie Raws out for foreign service," he said, smiling at Willie's enthusiasm and desire to be what he called a soldier in downright earnest. "Stick to your drill, my lad. Think about it on parade. Study it when off. Dream about it at night. You've got the makings of a good soldier in you. Don't forget all I tell you. I am your father and your mother both, mind you."

Well, what better advice could he have had? He followed it.

His officers soon saw that Willie Saunders was no muff. That he had the "grit" in him, as Captain G—— phrased it.

One day, about four months after joining the regiment, Willie's name happened to be mentioned at the mess-table.

"He is a gentleman's son," said one. "I could tell that whenever I saw him."

"Ah," said another, "they, as a rule, make deuced bad soldiers."

"Well," said Captain G——, "that all depends. Many a gentleman's son enlists because he has gone thoroughly to the bad. His father cuts him off with a shilling."

"Yes," said a lieutenant, "and having taken the shilling from the father, he turns it into two by taking one from the Queen."

"That's it," said G——; "and it is this sort of youth that makes a bad soldier. It is impossible for him to reclaim himself all at once, and, as often as not, he deserts. But Saunders hasn't the look of a fellow of this sort."

"No," said the lieutenant; "and I have heard that it was a love affair that drove him to enter the army."

"Well, anyhow," continued Captain G——, "as I said, he has got the grit in him; and he doesn't want to have an easy life of it either. I'll give you an instance. Just to try him, you know—for I wouldn't have a gentleman as my servant for all the world—I called him into my room one day last week. 'You are a smart lad,' I said, 'and you keep yourself and all your accoutrements tidy and nice. I wouldn't mind having such a young fellow as you to be my servant. Will you come?' Well, boys, you should have seen how his face changed from joy to sadness. He positively grew white at first, and gasped a little. Then he grew red. But he did not answer at once. 'What is your reply?' I said. He spoke now, and to the point too. 'Sergeant McKinnon told me,' he said, 'and I've heard my grandfather, who was in the army, say the same, that a soldier's first duty was to obey. If you command me to be your servant, sir, I will be so, but——'

"'But what, my lad?' 'I'd ten hundred thousand times rather be in the ranks,' he answered. I simply said 'Good!' and there was no more about it."

Not long after this Willie found himself promoted to corporal.

Well, one day early in April of that awful year for India—1857—Willie was coming along one of the principal streets of Dover. He had been for a long walk with his foster brother, and was returning towards his quarters when he met Sergeant McKinnon. The sergeant seemed joyfully excited about something.

He turned sharp on his heel, and entering a quiet inn, where he seemed to be known, beckoned to Willie and Peter to follow him.

The landlord's daughter nodded and smiled to the sergeant, and hastened to show the three of them into a tiny but cosy room.

"Just three glasses of bitter, Ellen," said the sergeant. "Now, Willie," cried McKinnon; "you'll have your wish at last. Guess what the news is!"

"Got the route?"

"That 's it."

"Hurrah!" shouted Willie. "Peter, aren't you glad? Now we'll have a chance of seeing what war really means."

"I hope you 'll like it, boys," said the sergeant. "But war is something you soon may tire of."

"War!" cried Ellen, entering with the beer at that moment. "Who talks of war?"

"Ellen, lassie," said the sergeant, as she stood beside him still holding the tray in her hand, "you won't forget the gallant 93rd, will you?"

She grew as pale as death.

"Oh, Fergus," she pleaded, "say that you are only joking. Say it isn't true. You 're not going?"

"Ah, Ellen, the best of friends must part! Yes, we 've got the route. We 're going to China. You 'll soon hear the bagpipes playing 'Farewell to Lochaber.'"

Poor Ellen! a very pretty English girl she was, with a slender willowy figure and large wondering blue eyes.

These eyes began to fill with tears, as she now gazed incredulously at Sergeant McKinnon.

McKinnon had a splendid full-toned baritone voice of his own, and he now commenced singing that sad Highland lament, which has sounded like a death-knell in the ears of many a loving wife and maiden, as husband and sweetheart were marching along the crowded streets to join their ship for foreign service—

"Farewell to Lochaber and farewell to my Jean,
Where happy wi' thee I hae mony a day been;
But Lochaber no more, and Lochaber no more,
We 'll may be return to Lochaber no more."

There was something in the song and the way in which the sergeant sung it that was irresistibly pathetic.

Ellen had hardly heard the last wailing line ere she burst into such a fit of weeping and sobbing as Willie Saunders had never before listened to.

Sturdy McKinnon sprang up and took the poor girl in his arms, while Willie and his foster brother rose and stood by the window looking out, or pretending to, at the early spring flowers in the garden.

The grief of Ellen was for a time distressing to witness, and it told a tale too, it told even those two young soldiers that the girl dearly loved the dashing Highland sergeant. But he managed to soothe her at last, assuring her that although the regiment really was ordered abroad, as all regiments must be at times, it might not start for months yet, and when they did go it would not likely be for a long time, as they were only going to China. The Highlanders would, he said, make short work with Johnnie Fookoo, and would then be ordered home, and after that——

Well after that, Willie and his companion heard no more, for their sergeant had lowered his voice, but what he told poor Ellen no doubt had the desired effect, for when the lads looked round after a time, she was standing by his shoulder and smiling hopefully, while he held her soft white hand in his.

"Oh," she said, "it will be a woeful parting, but I'll count every day and hour until you return. Oh, Fergus, you'll come safe home, won't you, and you won't run into any kind of danger, will you?"

"Highland soldiers never do," said Fergus smiling.

"And you too, poor boys. Oh, won't it be nice when I see you all again! Take care of your sergeant, boys," she added with a bonnie blush. "Mind he is my sergeant as well as yours."

"I assure you," said Willie Saunders, "we will take all the care we can of our sergeant, Miss Ellen, and bring him safely back to his country and to you."

From the first moment of their entrance into this house, there had been no attempt on the part of this poor girl to conceal the affection she had for Fergus McKinnon. Her's was the sweet abandon of love, but the abandon of complete innocence. To her Fergus was the greatest of all heroes. Who could help loving such a man, so handsome, so dashing, so brave? Why should she be ashamed of innocent, heartfelt love like this. On the contrary she was proud of it, and glad rather than otherwise that people should know she loved him, and that he was *her* Sergeant McKinnon.

Willie Saunders was gazing at her wonderingly and somewhat sadly. He was thinking then of home. He was thinking of the Lodge at the glen-head, and that last night in the moonlight with Annie Lindsay by his side.

What a different world would this have been for Willie, had sweet Annie Lindsay only loved him with half the love that Ellen bore for Fergus.

Ellen was not slow to observe the pathos of that far-away glance, and with a woman's instinct she was quick to read its meaning.

"Just look at that poor boy," she said kindly. "Oh, I can tell easily that he has left a sweetheart in bonnie Scotland."

Willie Saunders heard no more. He muttered some incoherent words, then hurried from the room. Had he stayed there another half minute he would have burst into tears just as Ellen had done, and this would not have looked very soldierly.

Many times during the next month did Willie and his foster brother drop in of an evening to the cosy little Albyn Inn, and from her soft and gentle manner towards him, our hero felt perfectly sure that Fergus McKinnon had told Ellen something of his sad story.

* * * * * *

That was a busy month indeed for the gallant 93rd. It was busy in many different ways, for there is much to be done in a regiment that is being sent abroad almost unexpectedly. I must do the Sutherlands the credit of saying, however, that if it had been actually necessary they could have been all ready to embark in three days' time.

However, many men were unfit for foreign service; these had to pass the doctors and be sent to hospital or discharged; then there were men whose time was expired, or soon would be, these also must go. So that the ranks of the 93rd got considerably thinned one way or another, and must be made up to their full strength, the corps numbering when complete, well-nigh twelve hundred all told.

The extra strength to fill up the gaps was obtained from draughts of men from the other kilted regiments, especially from the 79th, the 92nd or Gordon Highlanders, and from the 42nd or "gallant forty-twa," usually called "The Black Watch."

* * * * * *

Sad enough was the farewell of the 93rd to Dover, for the soldiers—or Scotties, as they were called—both men and officers, had made many friends during their stay in the town and in the country round about.

There was no lad however in all the brave regiment more sorry to part with his lass, than was Fergus McKinnon to bid adieu to gentle Ellen Grey. And hers was a grief that words cannot easily describe, so this farewell I must pass over.

But the sergeant told Willie Saunders afterwards, that, although he did all he could to keep up the poor girl's heart, he had a presentiment that he should never hold her in his arms again, never again gaze down into her sweet face.

"Well," he said, laughing lightly, though I am sure the laugh did not come from his heart, "it is a soldier's fate you know, Willie. I suppose I shall be killed."

Willie himself could have been granted leave to run home and see his mother, but did not request it. The truth is that every bush, brake, and brae in the dear old glen, every woodland and tree, would have brought back reminiscences of his boyhood, that he was trying for a time to forget. Oh, only for a time, he assured himself on this point. After many years he would return, he trusted, and his now aching, "voidsome" heart would be healed—he hoped.

But what he would have dreaded most of all was a meeting with Annie, for his old love would be re-kindled, and the consequences would be assuredly fatal to his prospects in life.

So he made up his mind not to go home.

On the other hand both his mother and father made up their minds to come and see their boy before he left the country. Not at Dover, but at Portsmouth, at which sea-port the greater portion of the regiment were to embark.

Here at Portsmouth a great honour awaited the 93rd, they were reviewed by Her Majesty Queen Victoria herself, and by the good old Colin Campbell, afterwards Lord Clyde. How the 93rd loved this splendid soldier, none knew save those whom he had so often led to victory.

The soldiers loved their Queen, but I can assure you, reader, that the greatest part of that wild huzzaing was for the soldier himself, and our Queen, God bless her, knew it, and did not feel one little bit jealous.

Sir Colin took a fatherly leave of the old Sutherlands. He would never see the lads again, he thought, never again see their sable plumes nodding in the wind, never more see their tartans wave, or hear their battle-cry, or the skirl of their warlike bagpipes.

He was getting old, if not old already, and all he longed for now was those few years of well-earned rest which all soldiers are entitled to, betwixt the camp and the grave.

But little did the gallant Sir Colin know, or the men to whom he spoke, how, when, and where they were all to meet again.

CHAPTER VII.

"WE'LL HAE NANE BUT HIGHLAND BONNETS HERE."*

THE last tears were shed, the last farewells were spoken, and the transport that bore the bulk of the regiment was far away at sea.

England, with its long, white chalky cliffs, had been left days ago. The *Mauritius*, a steam troopship in which were the bulk of the regiment, had sailed from Portsmouth about the second week in June, and was already across the dreaded Bay of Biscay.

There was nothing very dreadful about the Bay on this occasion, however; the bo's'n assured Fergus McKinnon that in weather like that which they were now enjoying they might cross in a dinghy boat.

The weather began soon to get sensibly hotter, however, and by the time they reached the beautiful island of Madeira the heat was almost tropical.

But delightful breezes blew and cooled the air, so that the voyage was very pleasant indeed.

---

* Pronounced "hay," not "ha."

Awnings were spread fore and aft, whenever this was possible, and did not interfere with the sailing of the ship; for whenever a good and fair wind blew it was taken advantage of, so that coals might be saved; our Government, whether Liberal or Conservative, holding the same views precisely as regards coals in the service. They buy and supply us with the cheapest and worst for economy's sake, and tell us not to burn them if such extravagance can possibly be avoided. Thus, then, in the matter of fuel, a Liberal Government becomes Conservative, but a Conservative Government is never Liberal.

Although under sail the *Mauritius* did not make a very fine show, it was very pleasant when fires were banked. There were then no smuts blowing about the deck, nor cinders as big as hailstones lying on the white saloon tablecloths.

Well, soldiers are soldiers even at sea, and a transport is not really a man-of-war. Bravely though our army officers can fight and rough it on shore, when on board a trooper they do not object to have their little comforts, so they were even permitted to lounge in chairs under the awning, and listen of a forenoon to the dulcet music of the band, while they dreamily read their novels or magazines. Fancy, if you can, a naval officer in a deck chair. But such an anomaly was never seen or heard tell of.

I was myself brought up with a round turn once by Commander McHardy of the *Penguin*, a gunboat in which I served. I was very young in the service then, and had one forenoon seated myself for a moment on the skylight.

The captain, as McHardy was called by courtesy, was on the bridge.

"Quartermaster!" he shouted, "bring the doctor a chair."

I took the hint, and went below.

But poor McHardy was a bit of a martinet. One day, for example, I was going on shore on the African coast in one of our own boats. When about half-way, as the sun was broiling my skull, I ventured to elevate my umbrella.

But suddenly astern of us, from the quarter-deck of our saucy little craft, came the stentorian hail:

"Boat aho—oy!"

"Ay, ay, sir."

"Who is that officer with an umbrella up in a British man-o'-war's boat?"

Collapse of the umbrella!

Collapse of the officer also!

Neatness and tidiness were the rule of the day and night too on board the transport. Not a rope's end was ever seen out of its place, not a sheet uncoiled, the decks were kept as white as piano keys, never a tuft of rope yarn was left lying about, the guns were polished black as ebony, the lanyards were little coils of snow, everywhere the woodwork was polished, and the brasswork, if only that on the top of a belaying pin, shone like burnished gold.

I need not say that both soldiers and sailors were always neat and clean, and a prettier sight than a Sunday morning inspection, it would surely have been difficult indeed to have imagined.

But after all the soldiers had little else to do save to

eat and drink, to lounge, to smoke, to read, and to tell stories.

But after dark a crowd of cheery souls, both soldiers and sailors, would always be found at the forecastle-head, smoking the calumet of peace and swapping yarns.

Sing-songs too were got up, and some of the officers did not consider it *infra dig.* to visit the men in their quarters or mess-places, and do all they could think of to make things easy and comfortable for them.

Although a sergeant of the status of Fergus McKinnon must not as a general thing keep company with the rank and file, or with those but a grade higher, still our young hero Willie Saunders was a friend—moreover no one was likely to overlook the fact that Willie was a gentleman albeit only a corporal. So the sergeant and he were very much together during the passage of the *Mauritius* to the Cape, when duty permitted such intimacy.

It was from Fergus that Willie one evening received the following brief account of the career of Scotland's favourite general, Colin Campbell.

It was given more in the form of a conversation than anything else, and there were more listeners around the stalwart sergeant than Willie and Peter, but it was so dark it would have been difficult to have told who was there, or whether they were soldiers or sailors.

One thing was unmistakable enough, every man, whether Jack-o'-tar or Tommy Atkins, was smoking.

"Poor Sir Colin," began Fergus, "I fear we will never see him more. Who has a light?"

Several hands were advanced towards him, and the sergeant soon lit a large cigar. He seldom if ever smoked a pipe on board, but he never bought a cigar on shore or afloat. This is only another way of saying that McKinnon was well liked by the officers, whether naval or military.

"No," he continued, "I don't think we'll see Sir Colin again, and we all liked, ay, we loved him. I mean every man who ever fought under him."

"That's true," said more than one voice.

"Ah! I can hear," said Fergus, "though I can't see, that there is more than one man of the old 93rd not far from my elbow; well if I say what isn't true, they are welcome to contradict me or to put me right.

"But brave Scotch Colin was a pretty strict disciplinarian, though he dearly loved his soldiers, and would often go a long distance out of his way to see the sick and wounded. Just one fault had Colin."

"A fault?" said a voice.

"Ay, a fault, lad, but it was one in the right direction. He was, in a manner of speaking, too brave or too foolhardy; and I for one never saw an officer more cool under fire than he, nor more cool either in the thick of a bayonet charge, when pistols rang or cracked, when cold steel met cold steel, and men clutched men in the throes of death!"

"Hear! hear!"

"But what makes you think, sergeant," said Willie, "that we will never see him more?"

"Because," said the sergeant, "there is a limit to even the life of a lucky soldier. I knew Sir Colin more intimately in the Crimea than did a good many men. I was very frequently in his company, and I had grown so that I could almost tell what he was thinking about by looking at him; for mind you, men, though the old soldier's face be a pretty stern one, it is wondrously expressive. Sir Colin is getting old, not so much through years, mind you, as from exposure. He is war-worn, and he is just a trifle weary. He needs rest."

The sergeant paused for a moment, puffing so vehemently at his big cigar, that the light from its tip illumined the faces of his listeners around him.

"You may think me boastive, boys, and perhaps I am, but I am proud to tell you that I believe I was the last man—I don't say commissioned officer—of the 93rd that the General spoke to. It was the day after the review, and I was passing the door of the Fountain Hotel, when I met Sir Colin.

"Much though I loved him, I would not have dared to have spoken. I would have saluted and passed on, but he stopped me.

"'McKinnon, isn't it?' he said, 'used to be an orderly of mine in the Crimea. Well, I'm glad I tumbled across you. Good friends we used to be.'

"'Yes, Sir Colin; and I make bold to say I wish you were going to China with us.'

"Sir Colin laughed. 'Be just like old times, wouldn't it?' he said. 'But, ah! my lad, it isn't to be. Look at my grey hairs. However, my good wishes and my prayers will ever be with the brave old 93rd, that fought so bravely for me and our country at Balaklava!

"'Good-bye again, McKinnon. If you do return, and if I am alive, don't pass my door. The old soldier will always be glad to see you. But ——'

"'But what, Sir Colin?'

"He gave me his hand. It felt thin and cold in mine, and I could see some moisture in his eyes as he quoted just two lines of a bonnie old song—

> "'A boding voice says in my ear
> We're parting now to meet no more.'"

Again the sergeant pulled hard at his big cigar for a few moments.

"Let me see," he resumed. "Sir Colin is getting on in years. He must be in his sixty-fifth year. Yes, for he was born in the month of October, 1792. He belonged you know, boys, to the good old though not numerous clan of the McLivers.* But his mother was a Campbell, and when he entered the army in 1808 he adopted her name.

"He was just as brave when a boy of seventeen as he is now; for we find that he not only gained credit by his conduct in the face of the foe in the Peninsular War and during the sad expedition of Walcheren, but we know for a fact that he was the leader of a forlorn hope at the assault on San Sebastian. Lord Lynedoch officially declared that Captain Colin Campbell, while lieutenant of the 9th foot, behaved with conspicuous gallantry and intrepidity at the storming of the convent redoubt in the advance of San Sebastian, and afterwards at the assault upon that fortification, on both of which occasions he was severely wounded; also in a battle near Irun, during which the enemy was compelled to retire from a strong position they held on the Bidassoa.

* Pronounced Macleevers.

"At this time Colin Campbell was but twenty years of age, and it is related of him that in order to participate in the glory of that battle he deserted from the hospital.

"This of course was duly reported by the surgeon-in-chief to his commanding officer. It would have been a great breach of discipline even had he been almost well, but his wounds were very far indeed from being healed. Such conduct as this could not be overlooked, so he found himself hauled up—'planked,' as you sailors call it—and severely reprimanded; but there was a rider appended to this reprimand which must have quite taken out the sting of it, for he was told that but for his gallant conduct in the field his *mis*conduct would have met with a far more heavy punishment.

"Concerning his deeds of prowess and daring in the field of battle, Sir Charles Napier, some years after this, while presenting new colours to the gallant 98th, of which Campbell was now one of the chief officers, referred as follows: 'Yonder,' he said, 'stands Lieutenant-Colonel Campbell, and right well do I know that, if need should be, the soldiers of the 98th would follow him as boldly as did those gallant men of the glorious 9th, who fell fighting around him in the trenches of San Sebastian.'

"I am not a book, boys, else I could give you the whole history of brave old Sir Colin; but if I were a book I should need to be a volume as bulky as a big ha' Bible to tell you all his life or recount to you all his gallant deeds in, for example, the American War of 1814, the West India War, the Chinese War of 1842, and the Sikh War of 1848. After the latter war he was made a Knight Commander of the Bath. Sir Charles Napier himself it was who wrote to Colin telling him of his promotion 'for deeds done during this war' and for his steady coolness and military precision as a commander of the forces, and adding that no man ever wore the distinction who had won it better.

"Well, boys, he certainly won that distinction well on many a hard-fought field, for in this Sikh War, as he himself phrased it, he had the good fortune to be present in every engagement or affair during the whole campaign wherever there was anything to do, even to the pursuit of Dost Mahommed as far as the fatal Kybor Pass.

"Poor Sir Colin! Even at this time, although he was but fifty-seven years of age, he had begun to weary of warfare and long for rest. Fact is, lads, he was tired; but although he suggested retirement altogether from a life of activity—a life on the war-path ——

"'Why,' he told a friend, 'should I desire to remain any longer on the active list? There are better men than I am in the army, and my carriage stops the way. Honour and glory is all very well, but I have had enough of even that; and now I believe I have enough money one way or another to save my family from privation and smooth in some measure my own pathway to the grave, I want to go; I want to enjoy now some of the blessings of peace. I know all about war that is worth knowing.'

"Well, this seems to me, lads, more like the peevishness that is begotten of physical wear and tear and mental anxiety than anything else. We have all of us felt somewhat like it after a campaign, and thought that we should never, never care to fight again or seek for glory in the camp or tented field; and then we have been surprised to find, after a few weeks of rest and furlough, that we had a whole jugful of go left in us yet, that it wasn't possible to expend in any other way than by activity in the field.

"Sir Colin's sword was not to be sheathed yet—not by a long chalk, my lads—and he permitted himself to be persuaded to remain some years longer in India, engaged in what is possibly the hardest and most fatiguing of all kinds of warfare, namely, frontier or border work. And those wild hill tribes in the Afghanistan glens and straths gave him plenty to do and plenty to think of. About the beginning of 1853 he joyfully told a friend after mess one night that he would soon be in England now. 'I feel like a schoolboy,' he said, 'going home for the holidays, but, dear me!' he added, 'how the time has flown, and I am four years older since my last big grumble. Ah! well, they won't ask me to stay in India any more. I bid adieu to it for ever, and to warfare too.'

"'You will long to be back in camp, I do believe,' said his friend, laughing.

"'It will be in my dreams then,' said Sir Colin. 'No, I shall not be idle altogether. I shall cultivate flowers, perhaps, and grow Scotch kail and things.'

"Hullo! I must light another cigar. Splendid smokes

these; they are Captain C.'s pets. But I suppose you are tired of my yarning about good Sir Colin?"

"No! no!" from several.

"Well, the bold and daring Sir Colin did not have a very long time to rest and grow Scotch kail and things after all, for in 1854 the war broke out, and our Scottish hero burnished up his rusty sword once more. Perhaps he had been pruning bushes with it. But if the blade was rusty the hand that held it and the brain that directed it were as active as ever. He assumed command of the Highland Brigade. We all know what Campbell did in the Crimea, and how bravely he fought. We 93rd men have no occasion to be ashamed of Balaklava, or the thin red line of Highlanders that withstood the hosts of the enemy."

"Hurrah for Colin Campbell!" cried a man.

"Ay, lad, hurrah! indeed. And it has always seemed to me that the great soldier's example and cheerfulness of manner were in themselves alone equal to a small army. 'He had unbounded confidence in Lord Raglan,' says one of his biographers, 'and towards the latter end of the Crimean campaign, during the very worst times of that weary winter, the experienced old soldier never took a gloomy view of matters. He was quick to recognise Lord Raglan's great difficulties. He was quick to see that the work cut out for him was none the less heavy and hard from the fact that Britain had embarked on the serious operation of invading the Crimea after a peace that had lasted forty years, with her army greatly reduced in numbers and with administrative services calculated only for peace work or colonial requirements, and with moreover a total want of that organisation which alone can ensure success in war.'

"But for all this I say Sir Colin Campbell took nothing but the most hopeful view of things in the trenches, and in spite of discontent and murmuring, which by the way he never would listen to or permit in his hearing, he felt confident that success would finally crown the endeavours of the allied armies.

"Nor was he mistaken.

"People said we made peace too soon, and that the Russians had neither been humbled nor punished enough. I am but a simple sergeant, boys, but my opinion is that we Highlanders, and Englishmen too, can look upon this peace as a peace with honour, and look back to that long and bloody war as one that redounds to the courage and pluck of every man who ever drew a claymore, wore a kilt, or donned a Hielan' bonnet. And, as Wattie Scott says—

"'Ne'er in battle-field throbbed heart more brave
Than that which beats beneath the Scottish plaid.'

"I mind well the words of Sir Colin," continued the sergeant, "as he took leave of his brave John Hielan'men before embarking for his native land.

"'Good-bye, lads, good-bye,' he said, and as reverentially as if we had been his superiors did he lift the feathered bonnet he had asked and obtained permission of Lord Raglan after Alma to wear for the rest of the campaign, instead of the cocked-hat of a general. 'Good-bye; my warfare is over at last, for I feel that I now am old. Nevermore then shall I be called upon to serve my Queen and country. Nothing will now remain to me save the memory of my many campaigns, and the memory of the enduring, hardy, unselfish soldiers with whom I have been associated, and whose name and glory will live in the hearts of their countrymen for ever and for aye. Good-bye, lads, good-bye, but though you may see me not again, go where I may, the thought of you shall accompany me, and cheer my few remaining years with the glorious recollections of the hardships and dangers we have endured and confronted, hand in hand, shoulder to shoulder. And never will a bagpipe sound near me without carrying my thoughts away back to those bright days, when I was at your head wearing the bonnet that your courage gained for me, and those honourable decorations on my breast I owe to you and you alone. Good-bye.'"

"The battle of Alma was gained almost wholly by Highlanders, was it not sergeant?" said Willie Saunders.

"Ay, lad, ay, it was *the* battle of the Gael, for after the Light Division had taken a redoubt, it was retaken by the enemy. Then was brave Campbell's time to shout the war cry of the old Montrose, 'On wi' the tartan.' The tartan did rush on, and with a will too, and the Russian columns were soon shattered and scattered in flight. Oh, it was a great, a glorious day!"

"You were there, sergeant?"

"I had that honour, thank heaven.

"But it is in a letter, I think to Colonel Vincent, that Sir Colin himself says: 'The gallant 42nd continued their advance, and, by my orders, were followed by two other Highland regiments, who formed in echelon as soon as they gained the left brow of the Alma. On

"The street Arabs in a wild rush had clambered up behind Sir Colin Campbell's carriage." p. 97.

gaining the height, we found the foe that we had driven from the redoubt endeavouring to reform upon two large masses of Russian troops, that were advancing over the plateau to meet the attack of the 42nd. The men were too much pumped to think of charging, so they opened fire as they advanced in line, at which they had been well practised, and finally drove with terrible slaughter not only the fugitives from the redoubt before them, but the two large masses of men that had been advancing to check their onslaught.'"

"Where were the Guards at this time?" asked Willie.

"They weren't in it," said the sergeant, "nor anywhere near it. That I can testify, and we have Sir Colin's own printed words to prove it. 'During these operations,' he writes, 'the Guards were far away to the right, and quite removed from the fight. It was a fight of the Highland Brigade.'

"Yes, boys, the Guards, when they saw the grand final rush, began to press forward to share in the glory and capture; but Sir Colin cheered on his men, shouting aloud, 'We'll hae none but Highland bonnets here.'

"Sir Colin Campbell's return to Glasgow, his native city, after the peace was a hero's triumph. He was a kindly soul and dearly loved even the street Arabs, for when these in a wild rush had clambered up behind his carriage, and were waving their grimy bonnets over his head, the good old man did naught but smile, and would not permit the police to remove them."

"But I'm sayin', sairgent," said Peter McKay, who spoke but seldom, "Was there no' a sang written aboot the Alma?"

"That there was, Peter," replied the sergeant, "and if you men will join in the chorus I'll sing it where I stand."

"We'll hae nane but Highland Bonnets here."*

"Alma, field of heroes, hail!
Alma, glorious to the Gael,
Glorious to the symbol dear,
Glorious to the mountaineer;
Hark, hark to Campbell's battle-cry!
It led the brave to victory,
It thundered through the charging cheer,
'We'll hae nane but Highland bonnets here.'

Chorus—We'll hae nane but Highland bonnets here,
We'll hae nane but Highland bonnets here,
It thundered through the charging cheer,
We'll hae nane but Highland bonnets here.

"See, see the heights where fight the brave!
See, see the gallant tartans wave!
How wild the work of Highland steel,
Where conquered thousands backward reel!
See, see the warriors of the North
To death or glory rushing forth;
Hark to their shout from front to rear,
'We'll hae nane but Highland bonnets here!'

Chorus—We'll hae nane but Highland bonnets here,
We'll hae nane but Highland bonnets here,
Hark to that shout from front to rear,
We'll hae nane but Highland bonnets here.

---

* This song was written by Alex. Maclagan, and inscribed to Sir Colin Campbell.

Air—"The Campbells are Coming," but sung more slowly, with force and action.—G. S.

"Braver field was never won,
Braver deeds were never done,
Braver blood was never shed,
Braver chieftain never led;
Braver swords were never wet
With life's red tide when heroes met,
Braver words ne'er thrilled the ear,
'We'll hae nane but Highland bonnets here.'

Chorus—We'll hae nane but Highland bonnets here,
We'll hae nane but Highland bonnets here,
Braver words ne'er thrilled the ear,
We'll hae nane but Highland bonnets here.

"Let glory rear her flag of fame,
Brave Scotland cries, 'This spot I claim,'
Here will Scotland bare her brand,
Here will Scotland's lion stand,
Here will Scotland's banner fly,
Here Scotland's sons will do or die,
Here shout above the symbol dear,
'We'll hae nane but Highland bonnets here.'

Chorus—We'll hae nane but Highland bonnets here,
We'll hae nane but Highland bonnets here,
It thundered through the charging cheer,
We'll hae nane but Highland bonnets here."

That last ringing chorus was joined in by many of the sailors, and by several young officers who had come forward.

"Bravo, McKinnon, bravo!" cried the officers, and the clapping of hands was something to be remembered. But it was scarcely finished before the sergeant had betaken himself below.

McKinnon was brave.

But—McKinnon was shy.

CHAPTER VIII.

WILLIE AND JACK.

WHILE the good ship *Mauritius* goes ploughing on her way, southward ho! before the merry trade winds, and calm and peace seem to dwell in every heart on board, I must take the opportunity of harking back a little way in my story, and returning to the glen where Willie Saunders was born and reared.

We must even go as far back as the night of Annie Lindsay's birthday-ball.

Annie had engaged herself to Willie for more than one other dance that evening; but one was to be something special, viz., the gay, grand old Reel o' Tulloch. Much earlier that night poor Willie had looked longingly forward to this dance, and for more reasons than one. First, because he wanted to take the shine out of that 'Varsity fellow, who thought he could dance because he could glide through a dreamy waltz; and, secondly, because he felt certain that ere that dance took place, he would have a claim to Annie Lindsay's hand that no one else in the room could boast of.

But, alas! and alas! before the time for the reel came that scene by the moonlit cañon had taken place, and Willie had gone—fled.

The time had come, but the man had not.

Annie waited for him anxiously while the musicians were tuning up, then did a thing which it is quite unusual for a young lady to do; but the circumstances in this case were exceptional. She went to look for him.

She looked in the conservatory. He was nowhere there. He was nowhere on the lawn. Where could he be? Could he have gone back to the rustic seat under the drooping birchen foliage, she wondered. Fearfully she crossed the bridge, trembling a little as she gazed for a moment over it down to where, far beneath her, the linn roared white in the moonlight, then hurrying on to find that the seat was empty.

As she regained the bridge a dreadful thought got possession of her mind that for a moment almost caused her heart to stand still. Could he, oh, surely he could not have thrown himself over the bridge? And yet there was a possibility, for never in all her life would she be likely to forget the look of anguish that came over his face when she refused to become his affianced bride. She was so confused now that she hardly remembered what she had said to him, what she had answered him, what she had told him. Had she said that she did not love him? She hoped she had not, because—because—well, because she did, just a little.

No, no, Willie could not, would not have done anything so dreadful. He was too good and too brave for that! She hurried away from the bridge all the same; for voices seemed to be mingling with the roar of the linn, and repeating themselves in her bewildered brain.

Once more on the moonlit lawn, going wearily back towards the conservatory, with drooping head and a load of fear and sorrow and doubt at her heart that words cannot express.

Ha! she has a happy thought. He may have gone home. Well, she could easily ascertain; for he wore a plaid, and he always carried a hazel crook or Highland alpenstock.

She ran briskly now round to the hall door. It was ajar. She pushed it open and went in.

There was many a plaid there and several crooks, but Willie's crook and plaid were gone.

The fear left her heart now, but the sorrow remained.

He had gone. He had left her in anger, and she would never, never see him more. Of this she felt convinced.

All gaiety and joy had departed. She went back to the ball-room. She suffered another dance or two, but complained of being tired and weary.

When the ball came to a conclusion at last, and all the guests had gone, Annie made haste to get to her own room.

She threw herself on the bed without undressing.

When the morning sun shone in through her window Annie was sound asleep, still undressed, but her pillow was wet with tears.

When day after day went by and Willie came not, she—Annie Lindsay—knew the cause of his absence; and when her parents began to wonder at his seeming neglect—a neglect so unusual in him—then she told them all.

The evening after the ball Jack Morrison had ridden up to the glen-head to call at Balaklava Lodge.

"I had half-expected to find Willie here," he said. "I can't make it out at all. He seemed to disappear all at once from the ball-room that night, though I made sure we would walk home together.

"I called at the Raven's Nest and saw his mother. She appeared a little distressed about something, but all she knew I'm sure she told me; namely, that Willie had not appeared to be over well, and that he had gone a long way over the hills to try to dispel a headache."

"I think," said Mrs Lindsay, "he must have been indisposed, and that too somewhat suddenly, for he went away and said good-bye to no one."

"Ah!" said Jack smiling, "indisposition would account for it then, for he naturally thought that if he came to say good-bye he would be prevailed upon to stay on.

"The worst of it is," continued Jack Morrison, "I'm off to Aberdeen on business of the very greatest importance, and won't be able to see Willie for two whole weeks. Remember me most kindly to him. I've written him a note to say that I'm going to the Granite City, and that when I come back I hope to give him a glad surprise."

I must mention here, parenthetically, that Willie Saunders had received this letter, and had instantly torn it in pieces and thrown it behind the fire.

"Glad surprise, indeed!" had been his words. "I

know what his glad surprise is; and this after a lifetime of pretended brotherly affection!"

And the bitterness of Willie's heart was increased tenfold for a time.

"And may I ask," said Colonel Lindsay, "what takes you to Aberdeen, Jack?"

"Oh, I don't mind letting *you* into the secret, only keep it dark, you know!"

"As dark as Erebus!" said the soldier.

"Well then it is this, I want to see a bit of the world. I don't want to be mewed up at an old farm-steading all my life, even though it is to be mine when poor dear father wears away. Don't you see?"

"Well, Jack, I follow you so far, but I don't quite gather from what you have said in what particular way you are going to gain your *desideratum*."

"That's what I'm coming to. I saw an advertisement in the *Aberdeen Herald* for the services of a young man—it said young gentleman of good education—to proceed to India to enter a magistrate's office. The salary offered is very good, and the position, it seems to me, excellent. The candidate must be young—I'm not old; he must be tall and strong—I'm not a dwarf; and just feel that biceps, Colonel Lindsay, and look at that hammer of a hand. He must be a good Latin scholar and write well—I've taken many a prize for classics, and I write a clear and readable fist, you know. Finally, he must be of good moral character and healthy. Well, sir, the minister of our parish will testify that I never stole a horse, and as to being healthy, why, my looks should tell them that; and if there be any doubt about the matter, let them just place a one pound tender, juicy rump-steak, smothered in well-browned onions and flanked by mealy potatoes, before me, and the doubt will vanish like snowflakes in a river. I tell you what it is, Colonel Lindsay, I'm the winning candidate. You just wait a week or two, and see."

"Well, I wish you all the success in the world, my lad; but what does your father say about it?"

"The fact is, sir, I haven't told father yet. And I don't mean to till I am sure of the appointment."

"But you won't go away against your father's wishes, Jack, surely?" said Mrs. Lindsay.

"No, Mrs. Lindsay; that I will not. But when daddy sees how anxious I am to get a peep at the world in a laudable way, and all the rest of it, I feel sure he will have no objections. Only, remember, the secret is all with you as yet."

"I'll keep it faithfully," said Lindsay and his wife.

"And so will I," said Annie sadly enough.

* * * * *

There were over twenty candidates for that situation to go to India, for the emoluments were good, and there was a fair chance of the successful competitor rising to a position of some standing in India.

Jack Morrison went away and stayed away for a whole week and over. He certainly made as good a show physically as anyone, but there were brighter and cleverer youths applied for the vacancy, so Jack came home again somewhat heartless and hopeless.

However, nothing would be decided for some weeks. Two things happened in one day some time after this. Willie Saunders returned home, and, strangely enough, on the same day came a long, official-looking blue envelope addressed to John Morrison, Esq., &c., &c. John Morrison, Esq., was Jack.

Jack was elected.

"Hurrah!" cried Jack; and off he bounced to find his father.

Jack thought he would make sure of his daddy first, and did, for the lad was very eloquent in pleading his own cause. Then the mother had to be won over.

She was grief-stricken.

But as Jack's daddy represented that it seemed really to be Providence, and that it must be for Jack's good, and moreover that they ought to be proud of their son rather than otherwise, Mrs. Morrison slowly yielded.

Away went Jack now, with his letter in his pocket, up to Balaklava Lodge, riding on his sturdy brown cob. Jean was this cob's name, and no one knew her way about better than she did. Jean had belonged to a doctor before Jack got hold of her, but he had developed her considerably. You see, the young fellow was fond of animals, and he had found out one interesting fact concerning the mare that many people who ride horses would do well to take a hint from, namely, that she knew nearly everything that was said to her. For example, she knew the names of places. Jack would smooth her ears kindly before mounting.

"Jean," he would say, "we are going to Boortree to-day." Or it might be Knockando, or Balaklava, or any other place within ten miles. After telling her this Jack would mount and away Jean would trot, and after a time she never made a mistake. Arrived at the house or farm, Jack jumped off, hitched the reins loosely to the pommel by a plan of his own, and went about his business. Jean looked after herself.

To-day, however, Jack was so full of life and joy and energy, that trotting would not meet the requirements of the case, and Jean must gallop.

Arrived at Balaklava lawn, Jack leapt nimbly to the ground, and bolted in through the lawn casement window. No one was in the room except Annie, who came forward smiling to meet him.

Jack caught her in his arms and fairly hugged her.

"Wish me joy, Annie," he cried, "I'm appointed over all the other candidates. Hurrah! I don't know how to express my triumph and delight. Have I *really* disarranged your frills and frizzliebobs and furbelows? Never mind, sissie dear, your big brother Jack—for mind you I feel just like a brother to you—will bring you such a lovely shawl from India, and if you're good he'll—— Hullo! here comes your father. Wish me joy, Colonel Lindsay, I'm accepted."

"Accepted!" said the Colonel, looking first at Annie, then at radiant Jack. "Accepted! Why this is the first time I knew there was anything between you two."

"Ha, ha, ha!" laughed Jack. "Well that *is* good. Why it isn't Annie that has accepted me—I never thought of asking Annie—but Bitters and Co., Limited. Read that."

Jack thrust the long official envelope into the soldier's

hand. The soldier stuck his *pince nez* on, and read the letter, then he held out his hand.

"I do wish you joy, my lad, with all my heart. Bitters and Co., Limited. Strange name!"

"Yes; but there will be nothing bitter about the situation, and no limit to my fun and enjoyment out in India. Would you like a few tiger skins, Annie, or a white elephant, or any little thing of that sort? If so, I'll send it like a shot."

He stopped all the afternoon, and started to ride home a little before sunset.

He was coming trotting easily along from Balaklava Lodge, singing to himself, while the sun big and red sank low towards the western woods, flooding all the glen with a strange purple light, and shimmering across the loch in a broad band of crimson.

Jack had been singing to himself, and Jean had leant one ear back to listen, for she was very fond of music, as most horses are. I don't think that at that moment there were two more as happy young fellows as Jack Morrison in all the glen. But this happiness of his was doomed to be damped before he was many minutes older, and that too in a most unexpected way.

"I'll just ride on to Raven's Nest," he had said to Jean. "Raven's Nest, old girl, you know it, don't you?"

Jean moved her ears and nodded groundwards with her nose, as if to say, "Give me a slacker rein, and I'll have you there before you can say stirrups."

The road down which he was riding came only from Balaklava, so that anyone meeting him could not help knowing where he had been. A little farther along it struck the main highway leading through the great glen, making a bend to the left just here.

And it was just at this junction, or a little way beyond it, that, greatly to his delight, Jack saw Willie Saunders coming straight towards him, Willie and Bruce.

Willie made a slight or momentary halt when he saw his quondam friend, as if uncertain what to do, but immediately after came straight on.

Jack, with a little cry of surprise and joy, jumped right off his mare and held out his hand.

Young Morrison, though quite as tall, if not taller, was not so strikingly handsome in face and bearing as Willie Saunders. He looked what he was and nothing more, a happy-go-lucky, guileless young farmer. And the smile that now illumined his innocent almost boyish face, and flickered around his sparkling eye, was a really genuine one.

"Ha! Willie, you truant," he cried, "I was going straight to the Nest. I've got something to tell you that will surprise you. Rejoice with me, Willie, I'm going to be —— Why, Willie, what is the matter?"

Willie only looked at him with cold and haughty surprise. Jack started as if shot. Indeed he seemed almost turned to stone.

"Willie!" he gasped, "that—look—to—*me*."

Bruce, the honest, bawsent-faced collie, had rushed up to welcome and fawn upon Jack, and in the bitterness of his heart Willie smote him lightly with his cane.

The poor dog uttered a whine rather than a cry, a whine of disappointment, wonder, and surprise.

But his master only turned his back and walked on.

Bruce looked back at Jack Morrison, and sorrow the deepest was expressed in every lineament of his sagacious face.

"You can see it isn't my fault," the dog had seemed to say. Then he trotted on after Willie, his tail low towards the ground, and his very head bent down with sorrow.

When fairly out of sight, with trees between him and Jack, he stooped down and kissed the dog's neck.

"There! there! Bruce, my own dear dog," he said, "I am not angry with you. No, no, no.

"We won't be long together now. May Heaven forgive me, my faithful Bruce, that I even made pretence to strike you. Strike *you*, Bruce! And friends so few in this cold world. No, no.

"And I pray too," he had added, "that God may forgive me for treating poor Jack so. But I cannot, could not help it. Yet that look of his I shall never, never forget."

Then Willie had sunk down upon the green bank, and covering his face with his hands seemed for a time quite broken down with grief, while, sorely puzzled by all this, Bruce stood close by his side. His canine nature could not fathom or understand, but he knew his master was in trouble and sorrow, and he could lick his hands, and this he did with much concern in his brown eyes, and very, very fondly.

* * * * * *

It had been but a few days after this that Willie Saunders met the sergeant at the rendezvous in company with Peter McKay and joined the gallant 93rd.

Book II.

The Mutiny in Full Swing.

"But we will drain the life-blood where we stand
To save our children:—fight ye side by side,
And serried close, ye men of youthful pride,
Disdaining fear, and deeming light the cost
Of life itself in glorious battle lost."

CAMPBELL

Book II.

CHAPTER I.

"YOUR BIG BROWN BROTHER JACK."

STURDILY steaming onwards south and south went the good ship *Mauritius*, and life on board went on much the same.

But it seemed to have become a standing joke both fore and aft to ask one's neighbour the question:

"Any signs of the *Belleisle?*"

The *Belleisle* was a sailing ship, a strong old seventy or eighty gun ship, and one that had made her mark in the hull and masts of many a foe in the brave old days of Nelson. And this craft had started about ten days before the steamer with the other three companies of the 93rd.

"Good morning," the doctor would say to the sailing master, "seen anything of the old *Belleisle?*"

"Good morning," the soldier officers would say, when they came into breakfast, "sighted the *Belleisle* yet?"

The fact of the matter is that the captain of the

Mauritius had told the first lieutenant, who had told it in confidence to the paymaster, who had whispered it to the clerks, who had "blabbed" it to the gun-room stewards, who had given it to the marines, and therefore to all the ship's crew, sailors and soldiers, that *he*, the captain, was not going to permit that jolly old tub of a *Belleisle* to reach the Cape of Good Hope before him, although they had handicapped him by giving her a ten days' start.

"We'll come up to her south of the line, you'll see," he said. "Come up with her hand over hand, and overhaul her about ten south. Mark my words for that."

The *Mauritius* lay in with letters at Madeira, and everybody asked that question, "Seen the old *Belleisle?*" And when they reached the Cape de Verdes the self-same question was repeated or something like it, "Any-body seen the old *Belleisle?*"

But lo and behold for once in his lifetime, if only for once, the bold captain of the *Mauritius* had reckoned without his host, and they never saw the old *Belleisle* till they steamed into Simon's Bay in the dusk of the evening, and heard the bugle-call of the 93rd sounding cheerily over the water. So the old *Belleisle* had won the race.

But the old *Belleisle* was very glad indeed to meet the *Mauritius,* as she brought the last letters and the last news from home.

It was now the 12th of August, 1857, and sad indeed was the news that had awaited the *Belleisle,* and was now communicated to the *Mauritius.*

The terrible Indian Mutiny had broken out, the Sepoys had revolted, had murdered their officers and every European (so said report) they could lay hands upon—men, women, and helpless children.

Though it turned out to be only too true, the news was not at first credited. Only it had the effect of changing the destination of the gallant 93rd. Instead of sailing for China therefore, both ships were ordered to take additional drafts of men that had been intended for the squadron in the far eastern seas, and to make the best of their way forthwith to Calcutta and the Ganges.

* * * * * *

When Willie Saunders bade farewell to his native glen, and went south to join his regiment at Dover, one of his last requests to his mother—and a very earnest one it was—referred to his unfortunate attachment to Annie Lindsay, and his strained relations with Jack Morrison.

"I am going away, mother dear," he said; "it is partly because I want to see the world, to see other faces than those in our glen, and other hills than those that hem it in. But I am also going away because I want to forget. Dear mother, you must help me to forget, and whatever should happen at Balaklava Lodge, or to Jack or Annie, I must know nothing at all about it. Do you promise, mother?"

"I promise, boy," said Mrs. Saunders, and right faithfully she had kept her promise.

Then as Willie had no correspondent at all in the glen save her, the glen was virtually dead to him, and had been so for a whole year.

If he thought of Jack and Annie at all, they rose up before his mind's eye as a wedded pair, living perhaps at Jack's father's, or even at the Lodge. What cared Willie now? To think of Annie would be a sin, though his love for her had darkened his life, and why should he think of Jack since he could not yet forgive him for what he considered his rank duplicity. His main object in life for a whole year back had been to forget. But often and often of late in his dreams by night, when far away on the lone, dark sea, he met Jack Morrison; and always he was the same, always standing silently by his brown mare's shoulder, with that big red hand of his extended, and that look of wonder and sadness on his innocent almost boyish face.

Now, reader, I do not know what you may be, but brought up as I have been in the silence of a far northern part of the country, and coming as I do of a race of Celts, I am just a trifle superstitious, and to some extent a believer in dreams. However, I do not desire that my beliefs should influence yours in the slightest degree.

It was somewhat strange, nevertheless, that just two days before the *Mauritius* steamed into Simon's Bay he should dream once more of his old friend Jack, a dream so vivid and startling that he awoke trembling and bathed in perspiration.

Jack Morrison was not standing by his mare's shoulder this time, but under a palm-tree, not a tall one; it was but little more than a bush, and there were others near it, but the glare of tropical sunshine outside the green of these trees was so great that Jack appeared to be in a cave. Yet a broad stripe of light revealed his whole form and countenance. He was kneeling beside something that the dreamer scarce could see, but it looked like a doubled-up or slain corpse.

Jack's arms were extended as if in supplication; his face was worn and white, his eyes sunk deep in his head, and a thin line of blood seemed trickling down from a wound above the temple.

"Willie, Willie!" pleaded Jack, "come out and help us."

Willie Saunders slept no more that night, and he was almost afraid to fall asleep next night, lest the same terrible vision might once again present itself.

But it did not.

But now comes the strange part of this dream-tale. Among the letters brought by a steamer from England a day before the *Mauritius* sailed was one in Jack's well-known hand.

At first Willie felt half inclined to tear it up and throw it away. "Why, he said to himself, "should I open up old sores that are just beginning to heal over?"

But then he remembered his dream—"Willie, Willie, come out and help us!"

He went farther forward with the letter in his hands and leant over the bows. If there was anything in it to displease or annoy him he meant to drop it into the sea.

Much to Willie's surprise the letter was dated from India, and seeing the address his heart gave an uneasy throb.

"Heaven help me," he thought, "is Jack out there, and Annie too, murdered by this time perhaps."

There was no likelihood of Willie's throwing away the

letter now, he would read it to the end, however bitter that end might be.

But March 31st, 1857, was the date of the letter, and Agra was its postal town. It must have been delayed long in transmission.

"Dear Old Friend," (it began)

"I know you will be surprised to hear from me after the strange and unaccountable way we last parted. I would not be writing now, dear old man, but for the fact that something has only just occurred that tends to clear matters up between us, and explains to me your treatment of me when I met you, as I rode down the glen from Balaklava. Though it was unfortunate that you did not give me a chance to finish my sentence, and tell you that I wished you to rejoice with me over a success I had in Aberdeen in obtaining a splendid appointment in India, and which I had deferred mentioning to you till I was certain, still, Willie, I do not wonder at you cutting me dead as you did, under the belief that I had deceived you and acted the part of a man who is more a fiend than a friend. But I had not done so, I never made love to Annie Lindsay, I never breathed a word of love to her, though I have always looked upon her as almost a sister. Nor did she ever love or care for me otherwise than as a friend or brother.

"But, Willie, you were haughty with me that day. There seemed to blaze in your eyes all the bitterness of hate.

"Do you remember how you even struck poor Bruce, because the dear fellow fawned on me as usual?"

Willie Saunders groaned aloud at this reminiscence, and his eyes grew misty with tears.

"So, Willie, although I could not understand your conduct nor understand you, I fell back on my Highland pride and tried hard to forget you.

"I even stopped people in the midst of a conversation if they ever mentioned your name.

"And now as to my reason for now writing you. It is this: I have just received a letter from a young lady in Scotland who used to live in our glen. It seems that you had, innocently enough no doubt, given her some cause to think you were not indifferent to her. But your evident regard for Annie Lindsay, which, on the evening of the ball you took small pains to hide, stirred up in her mind the demon jealousy, and with a friend of hers she formed a plan to be revenged on you, and this was carried out in the conservatory.

"It was a brutal and a cruel act, and I wonder much that anyone could have done it. I enclose her letter to me, which you will see is a full confession. She is evidently penitent, and full of remorse and grief that the words she meant you to hear in the conservatory should have had the effect of banishing you from your native land, and of destroying the brotherly love and friendship that has existed 'twixt you and me since

> "'We baith did run aboot the braes,
> And pu'd the gowans fine.'

"Willie, Willie, I know already that the cloud is dispelled, and that we are true friends again as of yore. I feel as I write the warm grasp of your hand, and see the happy smile upon your face. Friends again! Oh, how happy I am!

"A word about myself farther on, but first a word about Annie. Believe me then, lad, when I tell you that I feel certain she cares for you. I would be the last to raise in your honest heart one single ray of hope that was likely in future to be quenched in disappointment; but, Willie, I know nothing of woman's heart if Annie's is not all yours. But you must pardon me for adding, Willie, that you are a laggard in love, though I'll wager my head you will prove no dastard in war. Why, man, didn't you press your suit, instead of going off with your heart in your mouth to become a soldier?

"Enough then, I have given you hope. Write to the lassie, whose letter I enclose. Be a Christian, and forgive her. Write to *me*, and write to the Lindsays, *one and all.*

"Now just a word about myself. I will tell you far more when next I write.

"I am in India, you know. India is the jolliest place out by a very long long chalk, Willie, and it seems to suit me all to pieces. My work is responsible work, but it is not hard. I live with my employer, who is a magistrate; but I have plenty of time to read and keep my journal, and plenty of time for sport. I have already killed a tiger or two, and have sent Annie the skins, to show the prowess of this big brown brother of hers. Yes, I'm brown; indeed, brown is no word for it. In a contest for colour bricks wouldn't have the ghost of a chance beside either my cheeks or my brow.

"Hullo! here comes a servant with an order for me to start up country at once on an important mission. So

I'm off. I shall have a whole cavalcade of servants and horses, and five faithful Sepoys to guard me, though the country, despite some ugly rumours concerning disaffection, is as safe as our dear old glen.

"Good-bye, Willie. Isn't it jolly just that we are now as good friends as ever, and that the ugly dark cloud that hid us from each other has blown quite away?

"God bless you, Willie!

"Your big brown brother,

"JACK."

The letter almost fell from Willie's hands as he finished reading it.

"What a fool I have been!" he said, "and what a brute to Jack! Yes, yes, dear brother mine, the cloud has gone. We are to each other now as we were in days of yore—brothers still!

"And Annie—dear girl!—is it possible that Jack could have read her heart better than I? Is it possible that she cares for me?"

The thought was a very pleasing one.

But next moment Willie's face changed. He looked at the postmarks on the letter. Why, poor Jack must be in the very thick of the Mutiny!

Then he thought of his dream—"Willie, Willie, come out and help us!"

"Oh, Jack, Jack!" he exclaimed half-aloud, "what if we shall be too late? What if you are already among the slain? Oh, Jack, my brother, my brother!"

CHAPTER II.

LIFE ON INDIAN SHORES.

WE must once more leave the gallant ships *Mauritius* and the old *Belleisle*, and betake ourselves to Indian shores. We know well that all that sailors can do will be done on board to speed the passage, and that, arrived on shore, all that brave soldiers can do will be done to rescue beleaguered garrisons, and bring health and safety to helpless women and children.

Here we are then "on India's coral strand," as the poet calls it. It is towards the end of autumn in 1856, and the Mutiny has not yet broken out. Jack Morrison has just come out from England, and is here by the sea, where he remains for a few weeks before going up country, at the house of a brother of the magistrate to whose office he will soon be attached.

How different is everything here from that to which we have been accustomed in Scotland north! Here no crimson heath or purple heather clothes the hills, no scarlet poppies peep up through rising corn, no dewy-eyed bluebell, no modest primrose, glints through the grass's green by covert or hedgerow. But a bluer, brighter sky gleams over us; above us burns a fiercer sun, the groves of orange and citron and plantain look foreign though beautiful to the eye; the forest trees themselves are strange; strange forms of insect life fill the air with musical hum, and brilliantly-plumaged birds flit from bough to bough. Those birds may be lovely, one thinks; but why do so few of them sing, as do our linnets and larks at home? I can tell you the why, reader. Up in yonder tree hides many a hawk and bird of prey, so the little birds must sing their love songs so low that only the birds they are addressed to can hear them—even the snakes and reptiles that lurk beneath the fairest flowers would find them out if they did not woo in silence.

Out yonder towards the south and east, if we cast our eyes, we shall look upon an ocean far brighter and more pellucid in its waters than any we have ever dreamt of; and in tiny ripples its wavelets are now breaking musically upon a snowy beach of coral sand. Were the brightness of the day to tempt us to bathe we might swim or wade for miles from the land without getting beyond our depth, and if naturalists or lovers of nature we could hardly help wishing we might live for ever in that bright and sunlit sea. For down there beneath lie submarine gardens more beautiful by far than Arab's dream of paradise. Describe them, did you say. Would that I could, and yet they rise up before my mind's eye even now as I write, and I have but to shut my eyes to see them once again, their brightness scarcely dimmed by the lapse of years; see them, as I often have, as I leant over the gunwale of my skiff lying entranced mayhap for hours.

But the English language is singularly destitute of words truly descriptive of beauty, and I, at all events, can find none that are capable of giving a stranger to these regions an idea of even half the loveliness that waves on coral sands 'neath Indian seas. "Waves" is just the word, for every branchlet, every twig, every stem and flower, ofttimes clad in more than rainbow brightness of colour and sparkling with light, seems instinct with half-animal power of life and motion, and even in weather so calm that there is not so much as a ripple upon the ocean's breast, we may see them gently moving to and fro.

But beautiful though these gaily-tinted coral algæ be, let us hasten back to the beach, nor tempt a swim in the deeper water; for where the shore suddenly shelves, where we lose sight suddenly of our sea flowers, and the water grows dark around us, we may catch glimpses deep down, of monstrous forms that may haunt our dreams for many a day.

So we hasten back to the shore, and here in some cool grotto await the day's decline. And now come gentle breezes, fanning our heated brows, and almost wooing us to sweetest slumber. But even at eventide scenes of beauty are still before us. Look! Away over the ocean yonder, towards the distant and now fading horizon, a solitary light gently rising and falling on the billows. 'Tis a homeward bound steamer, perhaps—a little world in itself, afloat on the deep —filled with its own fears, cheered with its own hopes. Care and sorrow, joy and gladness, all are there—a little city on the sea. Let us pray God to speed her, and turn our eyes towards the east. There, from an emerald-tinted sky, gleams out the evening star—the star of love, the bright-eyed happy, gloaming star. Behind us, if we look, low towards the ground, we shall see many other stars—less bright, it is true, but restless, moving, gliding, flitting, dancing around every bush, and wheeling in fiery flight among the feathery palm trees. Fire-flies these.

But there, we have stayed long enough out on the beach; for, sweet and cool as the evening breeze may be, the night winds in these latitudes often bear clammy death upon their wings. Walk inland then, for from above the distant forest-clad mountains the moon is already shedding her silvery beams over the land and over the seas. The pathway is broad, but brown not green, as our woodland walks at home are wont to be. Perhaps we stop soon to wonder what lies yonder right in our path. It is as large and round as a small footstool, dark and glistening in the moon's rays. We have room to avoid it, and we do so, wisely, for its bite is deadly. It is the black snake, or water-snake, coiled up and asleep. By-and-by he will measure all his length on the ground, creep off to find a frog or lizard, and then back to his evil cave in some dark and damp recess.

Yes, there are sounds enough in the forest here to frighten any novice. The yelping bark of the jackal, the sullen, roaring boom of wilder beasts than he. Hark! What was that spirit-like shriek? Is it a warning cry? Again we hear it—"Go back! Go back! Go back!" Yet is it but the voice of a harmless bird.

And strange birds often emit more terrible ear-splitting

sounds by night in jungle or forest than all the wild beasts that dwell therein.

The sudden, uncanny yell, for instance, close in the bush beside you, is not the war-whoop of painted savages, but the voice of a bird. So too is that wild, unearthly laugh that ever and anon rises swelling on the night air. The silence of a few minutes may be suddenly broken by screams and shrieks from some dark thicket, as of a poor mortal in pain or agony—shrieks loud, prolonged, and dying away in mournful cadence. But these also proceed from birds holding their nocturnal revels.

I have given you, then, a brief peep at life by the sea in the province where Jack Morrison spent his first few weeks. All was fresh and new to him, but all was very delightful. He felt indeed as if he had taken a new lease of life, and, if the truth must be told, he felt too that he would rather laze and lounge than work.

But life is made for work, especially young life. And so Jack was not altogether sorry when he left his southern home, and started up country to take up his appointment, and perform whatever duties devolved upon him.

And when we next meet Jack he is standing in the compound of a large and beautiful bungalow. A hale and hearty man in the very prime of life is shaking hands with him. In the doorway of the bungalow stands Mrs. Mayne herself, while two beautiful children, a girl of ten and a boy about eight, are playing in the gardens with a tame mongoose.

Mr. Mayne, I need hardly tell the reader, was the magistrate Jack Morrison had come out to serve, and the bungalow was situated on the outskirts of Agra.

"Well, Mr. Morrison, we are truly glad to see you, and will try to make you as happy as possible. Come in out of the glare. The servants—and we have plenty of them—will see to your traps."

Jack advanced towards the porch, lifting his hat to the lady as he did so.

"My wife, Mr. Morrison; Mr. Morrison, our new secretary, my dear."

"We are plain people, Mr. Morrison, although, as you see, we have a very large house, and beautiful gardens, and servants galore, as you say in Scotland. Indeed, my wife often says we have too many; but, you see, every one of them has his duties to perform, light though they may be, and the very man who brushes your boots will not be allowed to place them on the mat at your bedroom door; the servant that places water in your room would scarce demean himself by emptying your shaving water. Well, you see, we can afford them, and the fellows are faithful, and very fond of us."

Jack had been shown into a large room with green waving jalousies or blinds before the great open casement windows, but coming in out of the bright sunshine for a time he could see nothing. Gradually, however, he began to observe things as if in a sort of twilight, and presently his sight was quite restored.

The apartment he could now observe was furnished with great elegance and luxury, but everything almost was Oriental, with the exception of course of the musical instruments. That piano, for instance, had come from a celebrated London maker, that harp was an Erard.

The walls were painted and gilded instead of being papered, and Jack, fresh from England, thought it strange to see unsightly-looking small lizards—gheckoes—crawling thereon stalking flies or moths. The rugs that lay everywhere on the polished floor were chiefly skins of wild beasts, of tigers, lions, leopards, and hyænas. Skins lay about too on sofas and ottomans, while many a huge bronze vase stood here and there, the use of which was at present a mystery to the new-comer. There were books in profusion, and arms apparently from every country under the sun.

A huge punkah depended from the roof of the room, moved by invisible hands, and the odour of orange blossom was everywhere.

"Will my secretary drink or eat?" said Magistrate Mayne.

"I think, sir, I would rather drink now."

"Wine? We have the best to be had. We have even beer. How would that suit? No? Well I shall let Saka here prescribe for you."

Saka was a tall and very handsome brown-skinned native, who wore a dress of clean white linen and a gilded turban. His dark hair hung in massive ringlets down behind, and depended quite to his waist. Saka retired for a minute or two to give orders, and soon returned marshalling in no less than three dark-skinned little native boys, each bearing a tray, which he held in front of him quite on a level with his head.

"Ice?" cried Jack. "What a luxury!"

"Oh, we never want ice! We have it with every meal."

"And between meals too," said Mrs. Mayne with a pleasant smile.

Mrs. Mayne was dressed with almost a studied negligence, but she was possessed of a beautiful figure and an intellectual face, and her every movement was graceful. She looked extremely good-natured too, and it was evident that she was not only proud of her husband but very fond of him also.

"What strange fruits," said Jack. "I don't think I shall attempt to eat any but the small ones."

"Why, my lad?"

"Well, because I am sure I do not know how to eat the large one. I should be afraid to cut that big thing, for example. It may be hard and need slicing, or it may be pulpy and require a spoon. No, I shall study the anatomy of all of these in private, then I shan't make a mistake."

But there were fruits there that Jack could tackle, as he termed it inwardly, and the iced syrup-water was truly delightful. It not only cooled and refreshed him, but calmed his nervous system, and caused him to feel perfectly at home.

By-and-by, accompanied by their ayah, a delicate-looking but pretty Indian girl, the children came in.

"There you are, then?" said a voice in a distant corner. It seemed that of some cracked-voiced old lady. "So there you are. Delighted, I'm sure! Delighted. Delighted! Give us a nut."

It was only a parrot, though one of a species Jack had never seen before.

The boy lay down with his mongoose in his arms on a lion's skin. A mina in a cage began to sing plaintively and sweetly, and Jessie, the girl, stood shyly by her father's side, with her hand in his, looking at the new arrival.

It occurred to Jack then that he had never seen a happier or more contented family in his life. And subsequent events did prove that every member of it was devoted to all the rest.

* * * * * * *

"Now, Mr. Secretary," said Mr. Mayne that day after dinner, as Jack sat opposite to him making anatomical experiments on various kinds of fruit that he had never seen before, "I am going to propose that you live here with us in our large house. If, however, you would prefer to have a small bungalow of your own there will be no difficulty about the matter."

"I shall take your advice, of course, sir, and do whatever you may consider best."

"Thank you. Well, I look at it from perhaps a somewhat selfish point of view. You see we are virtually living all alone here, and although our life is a very pleasant one, still, except when strangers drop in, or we give a little durbar, as Jessie grandly terms our garden parties, we don't see a deal of society. What I miss most is somebody to chat with and exchange ideas with after dinner. Mrs. Mayne is a capital hand at exchanging ideas," he continued, smiling, "but she prefers dress to politics, and a copy of a *Lady's Pictorial* to the *Law Times.* You see?"

"I follow you, sir."

"Well, if you are living in the house, you would help to make life more shortsome, as you call it in Scotland."

"I'll do my best."

"From your own standpoint, however, the place possesses some advantages. You see you are here as my secretary, though your position is really not much better than that of a head clerk."

"Good enough for me," said Jack.

"Nonsense, lad, nonsense! You must be ambitious. Why, you may be Governor of Agra yet, or even Governor of India."

Jack laughed lightly, and stuck his knife into a mango.

"Ah! there is no laughing about it. When I say 'must be' I mean 'must be.' Well, it may surprise you to know that I knew Colonel Lindsay long ago, and when I got his letter, so highly recommending you, I said to Mrs. Mayne, "I hope that Morrison has a pleasant face and manner, if so he shall stay in the house, and I'll do all I can for him."

Jack blushed a little, and bowed over his mango.

"I'm pleased with your looks, boy, and I'm pleased with your manners, and if you stay here ——"

"I shall with much pleasure."

"You will be always at hand to consult with or to consult me. But this isn't all; there are dozens of good appointments to be picked up in India, but mind you this, these appointments are becoming in a great measure competitive. Letters of recommendation and pleasing manners, willingness to work, good health, and all that are all very well in their way, but you want *knowledge* as well."

"Certainly."

"Very well, I have as capital a library as anyone of my status in India can possess. It is at your service, if you care to study, and all knotty points I shall be most pleased to smooth over for you."

"A thousand thanks, I'm sure."

"Now if you have completed your investigations in natural history, as far as fruit is concerned, let us go to the drawing-room. We all study music here. Do you play anything?"

"The fiddle. A little, that is."

"Good! I play the piano, so does my wife. Jessie is a capital harpist for her age; and Teddie is content as yet with the tambourine or triangles. Come!"

CHAPTER III.

A CLOUD NO BIGGER THAN A MAN'S HAND.

SIX weeks had passed away, and that too right pleasantly. The more Jack knew of his life and duties the better he liked them; the more he knew of the Maynes the better he loved them. Mr. Mayne was always brusque, jolly, and straightforward. He was a man indeed who carried his heart on his sleeve, and if you didn't like it, why you were not compelled to; you could turn your head the other way, and not look at it.

Mrs. Mayne was always good-natured and pleasant. She had the utmost confidence in her large retinue of servants, and they all seemed to like her. The little ayah, indeed, appeared to worship the very ground she trode on.

Jessie Stopford Mayne—she always would throw in the Stopford, with emphasis too, when asked to tell her name—continued a trifle shy and thoughtful, but was upon the whole often a charming little companion to

Jack in his rambles, which otherwise might at times have been somewhat solitary.

Teddie came too. A little romp of a rascal he was. When asked his name he told you boldly enough "Teddie Mayne," and added, "Without any bothering Stopford!"

When Teddie got tired walking during a ramble he mounted "cockertycoosie" on Jack's broad shoulders. This didn't interfere with the young man's progress in the slightest degree; but as Teddie always insisted upon taking the mongoose up also, and spreading it longways in front of him and half-way round Jack's neck, Jack sometimes felt uncomfortably hot at that particular spot.

Jessie often came to keep the secretary company when he was hard at work in his writing-room. But this was no hindrance to him, but rather gave him the sensation of companionship.

"Go on with your work, Mr. Morrison," she would say. "Don't mind me. I'll just curl up in a corner with my dollies, only sometimes I'll look at you."

But Mr. Morrison had by this time become "Jack" to Mr. Mayne, and this was much more pleasant, even in office, than the stilted, stand-offish "*Mr.*"

Mr. Mayne, despite the colour of his hair—for India and Africa often bleach the locks of quite young men—could walk well, and could ride well also. Duty often called him far away across his district, and even entailed visits to distant towns or cities, such as Muttra, Meerut, or Delhi.

On these excursions Jack always accompanied him, or nearly always; and they had, moreover, a fairly large retinue of armed retainers; for even at this early date—

January, 1857—a cloud, though no bigger than a man's hand, was rising on the eastern horizon, and there was a calm in the air that might or might not presage a storm.

Not everyone could see this little cloud, and but few of those who did so considered that it boded anything worthy of a moment's uneasiness.

It is evident that Lord Dalhousie was not of this easy-going party, for when he resigned his Governorship in the beginning of the year he thought it right to speak a word of warning to his countrymen in India. "They were not to fall asleep," he said, "for at any moment, and even when least expected, a storm may burst and violence be committed of a nature too dreadful to contemplate."

Lord Canning, the new Governor-General, believed that danger existed, as we may gather from the speech he delivered at a dinner given by the Court of Directors before his departure to take up his appointment.

"May my office be one of peace," he said. "Peaceful I wish it to begin, peaceful to end. And yet I cannot conceal from myself the seeming truth that in the sky of India, blue, calm, and serene though it now appears, a tiny cloudlet may arise no larger at first than a man's hand, but which growing larger and larger may threaten at last to burst in fearful storm and overwhelm us with ruin."

* * * * *

I wish my young readers now to take with me a glance at India as it then was, before the outbreak of the terrible

Hindoo Koosh
Kashmir
Ladak
Himalaya Mountains
PUNJAB
Baree Doab
Bhawolpoor
DELHI
NEPAUL
Scinde
RAJPOOTANA
Lucknow Oude
Benares
Burhampoor
Raneegunge
Barrackpore
CALCUTTA
Cutch
Gulf of Cutch
Kattiwar
MALWA
Indore
CENTRAL
Nagpore
PROV
Candeish
Berar
ARABIAN
SEA
BOMBAY
Hyderabad
BAY
of
BENGAL
Mysore
Gulf of
Manaar
CEYLON

MAP OF INDIA.

storm that Canning told the British nation might possibly arise.

From my own experience of school life I happen to know that history, if couched in big words and technical phraseology, is just about as distasteful to boys in general as politics itself, or any of the "ologies," and as to dates I am quite of their way of thinking, namely, that the best sort are those you can eat, not those you have got to remember and may get "ploughed" for.

But those who have read my writings will have perfect confidence in my not pestering them with anything disagreeable or dry-as-dust, and indeed I believe that after all the best writers of history are not your blue-faced, prim, prigmatic men who delight in long sentences and ponderous verbiage, but men like the great Macaulay and Dr. Russell, whose works have about them all the charm of a well-written romance, although while reading them we know and feel there is truth in every line.

The first glance I want you to take of India then, dear young readers, is a glance at the map itself. I have had one specially prepared for this book. And a word in confidence. I have made it an easy one. I don't think you will find the name of a single place or river or bay therein that is unnecessary.

Glance at the boundaries. Thibet in the north and east; farther to the west is Kashmir, where the pretty shawls and things come from, you know. West of that again is Afghanistan, where our British soldiers have so often covered themselves with glory. Then run right south from Afghanistan through Beloochistan and you tumble right into the Arabian Sea. That insures you of a wet jacket anyhow, but then the water is so delightfully warm, and the sky above so blue and sunny, that there isn't the slightest chance of your catching a severe cold.

Only now that we are in the sea we may as well order a boat or a beautiful and expensive yacht. The expense does not signify, because we won't be called upon to pay.

Ah, this is truly delightful! No better way of studying a map and seeing a bit of the world can be devised. And this yacht we are now on board of is a second *Sunbeam.* Just look how taut and trim she is, how saucily the masts rake, how neat the rigging, and how nattily the men are dressed.

The sun is hot to be sure, but there is an awning spread, and as we lounge on the clean white deck in our chairs we can keep cool enough as we listen to the string band, by sipping iced sherbet and using a fan.

We sail south with a trifle of east in it. We hug the shore, that is we go as near to it as we safely can, but are never close enough to pitch a ball of spun-yarn on to the beach. That is the Gulf of Cutch away up yonder on the lee bow, but we shan't go in, but continue our voyage by the green coast of the province of Kathiawar. India, you will observe, is all divided into provinces, and although I don't insist on it, still it would do you no harm now, nor in after life, if you could acquaint yourselves with the names and bearings and boundaries of these. For instance, we often hear of Assam about tea-time, or when we go to our grocers to order the wherewithal to make the cup that cheers, but does not inebriate.

"Where in all the world is Assam?" a question we've heard.

"Oh, somewhere in India!" the answer.

This would not do for me if I were your teacher. But here is my map; find it, please.

Southward still in our yacht. But now the land recedes, and presently we see none at all. Have we altered our course? Oh no, we are but sailing past the entrance to the Gulf of Cambay! I could tell you a story about this bay that would make your flesh creep. Not to-day though.

And here we are at Bombay. We all knew from our very infancy that Bombay was on Indian shores, but lots of us did not know it was on the west coast. At the time of the Mutiny Bombay was a walled town, but the walls have since been pulled down—a good thing too, for they were practically useless, and they kept the air out. Fresh air was much needed in Bombay, especially in the old town.

We leave the harbour and city of Bombay, the former crowded with ships of all nations under the sun, and go silently sailing along by the coast of Malabar till we reach the most southerly point of India or Hindustan, and double the Cape.

What stories and tales crowd into my memory as I look upon the mere outline of that Malabar coast—stories it would take a whole long lifetime to write.

But here we are in the Gulf of Manar, and heading away north and east now, because it is no part of our purpose to touch at Ceylon. That great and lovely island lies on the east and south of us. Perhaps you and I, reader, may visit it together some day in a voyage of the mind. But now that we have doubled the Cape we have formed some conception of the vast extent of even the west coast of our splendid Empire of India, and the eastern shores are quite as long. On the coast of Coromandel, that sailors so often sing about—for indeed there is a musical ring about the very name—we find the city of Madras. Higher up, a very long way, is the city of Masulipatam, which was once destroyed—about twenty years ago I think—by a great storm and sea-wave, thirty thousand lives being lost in one terrible night.

But northwards we sail, and now we reach the mouths of the sacred river Ganges, and Calcutta itself, which lies but a little way south of the tropic of Capricorn.

If, instead of sailing up to Calcutta, we should change our course and sail directly east, we should come to Chittagong. In there, you know, is Burmah, where the rubies come from, and where the sacred white elephant was said to live. We conquered and annexed the country, found the ruby mines, and captured the white elephant, which wasn't white after all, and Burmah is now British territory. We can't go any farther east without going right out of my map, so we will return to Calcutta, and leave our yacht there. Yet I trust our little cruise has not been altogether unprofitable.

If you please we will now go up the Ganges, but first and foremost just take one wide bird's-eye glance at the provinces of India as a whole.

There are a few of them that you ought to, and *must* know the situation and bearings of.

Sind lies away in the west, to the north of Cutch. It is a very historic country.

Rajputana is very large, and to the east and north of Sind. You have often heard of this country.

The Central Provinces are easy to think of and to bear in mind. So too are the dominions of the Nizam.

But Oudh, or Oude, is a province of which I want you to take particular notice, because I shall probably have to mention it more than once in my story.

And now, if starting from Calcutta, you follow the course of the great river Ganges, beginning with the Hoogley, one of its mouths, you will have no difficulty in finding out or spotting, as you may term it, the principal towns in and around which the great rebellion raged its fiercest and its cruellest.

I do not want to cram your beautifully elastic memory with the names of all of these, but you must look out Dinapur, Benares, and Allahabad. You will note that about here the river Jumna joins the Ganges. Glance up the Ganges, and you will easily find Cawnpore, where the fiendish massacre took place. To the east of this lies Lucknow, while a long way to the west you find Gwalior. Having stumbled upon Gwalior, you can take train to Agra, where Jack Morrison's home was. Some distance north is Muttra; still farther north of that is Delhi. And having found this, you will have no difficulty at all in getting the bearings of Meerut, the station at which the Mutiny really commenced.

India taken altogether is therefore, you will observe, a land of immense areas. Says Major-General Sir Owen

Burne*: "The single Lieutenant-Governorship of Lower Bengal is as large as France; Madras exceeds Great Britain; Bombay equals Germany; the North-Western Provinces and Oude cover as much space as Great Britain, Belgium, and Holland; the size of the Punjab is that of Italy; while the native States put together have an area equal to Great Britain and Ireland, Germany, and France combined."

The population of India at present, reader mine, is over rather than under 300,000,000, and our beloved Queen is Empress of the whole.

The Sepoys are the native-trained soldiers. It was these who mutinied, about one hundred thousand of them, and these were joined of course by riff-raff of every description, from towns and villages and country hamlets, among whom were the fiendish prisoners let loose from the gaol, all burning for revenge and loot and murder grim.

Of the Bengal Native Infantry—seventy regiments in all—forty-five mutinied, twenty were disarmed, three were disbanded, and only six remained true to their salt. Sir Owen Burne says: "The bulk of the vast population of India may be conveniently divided into Hindoos and Muhammadans, inasmuch as these two classes inhabit in greater or less numbers every one of its provinces, and figure almost exclusively in the events of the Mutiny. The typical Hindoo is quiet, industrious, and tolerant in religious matters unless provoked to excitement. As a soldier he is obedient and patient, although warped by

* *Rulers of India*, the Clarendon Press.

those caste prejudices which have always given the Brahmans special control over comrades and subordinates. These qualities were strongly marked in the mutinous Sepoys. The Muhammadan on his part is by nature restless, fanatical, and ready for any adventure that may come to hand. In Northern India he is, as a rule, a born soldier, and even in the south he still retains in some measure the martial instinct which inspired his forefathers."

We, in governing this great country, as the General points out, "laboured under the disadvantage of being separated from these Muhammadans and Hindoos by blood, religion, and character, and had to contend against the almost insuperable difficulty of ignorance as to the under current of public feeling."

The storm did not break without warning.

"Months before the actual outbreak of the mutinous Sepoys, an idea had taken hold of a large number of persons within range of Hindoo and Muhammadan influence, that a crisis in the world's history was near at hand; that great events were pending, and that the British Government was bent on departing from its ancient principles of non-interference with the customs, traditions, and religions of its Indian subjects.

"Englishmen were warned by native friends to be on their guard, and written prophecies were spread broadcast through the land, foretelling the downfall of British power after the centenary of Plassy.

"Notwithstanding these indications of ill-feeling and imminent disaster, the attitude of the people of India generally during this eventful period was one of neutrality

. . . the principal assistance given to the rebel Sepoys came from a small number of disaffected nobles and deposed officials, who, in their turn, found support only from the lawless and restless spirits of their neighbourhood, no longer restrained by a powerful government.

"The Mutiny was thus primarily a military rising, aided and abetted to a limited extent by a proportion of the hereditary criminal classes, and confined in a great measure to the Sepoys of the Bengal Regular Army.

"At this particular juncture, too, the proportion of British to native troops in India was dangerously small. The warnings given by Dalhousie had been neglected, and owing to the paucity of European troops the principal arsenals and military posts of India—notably that of Delhi—were garrisoned by disaffected Sepoys."

You have seen, reader, in your time, no doubt, patches of withered furze on a hillside that a single lighted match applied to would set in flames from end to end. To such furze we may liken the Indian Army in the latter end of 1856 and beginning of the terrible year of 1857, ripe for the fires of rebellion, only awaiting the one little spark that should set all ablaze.

That spark was kindled, and all too soon.

CHAPTER IV.

DUM-DUM AND THE STORY OF THE GREASED CARTRIDGES.

EVER hear the story of Dum-Dum and the greased cartridges, reader? It is a very brief one, but very suggestive.

Once upon a time, long before you were born, I suppose, Dum-Dum, a military station or garrison about eight miles from the city of Calcutta, was the head-quarters of the Bengal Artillery, and had been so for many years. Here most of the officers of that distinguished army corps had received their first real military education—their initiation in the mysteries of the art of war. But finally the artillery were removed high up the country to Meerut, and Dum-Dum garrison became a manufactory and store-house, or series of store-houses, for small arms; and as, some time before the mutiny, the Enfield rifle was beginning to supersede the old Brown Bess, so famous in the history of this country, Dum-Dum became also a school of musketry to instruct soldiers and their officers in the use of the new weapon.

When I myself first joined the service, though it was many years after the Mutiny, this Enfield was still in use among our red Marines; and well do I remember that this muzzle-loader had five motions to the introduction of the cartridge.

(1) You tore off the top of the cartridge with the finger and thumb of the left hand, which encircled the rifle at the end of the muzzle; (2) you poured in the gunpowder; (3) you reversed the cartridge, inserting that part of it that carried the bullet; (4) you tore off the loose protruding paper; and (5) you used the ramrod to send the bullet home.

I remember that in my first brush with the Arabs, a Marine who was sitting next to me in the boat, when the order was given to load with ball-cartridge, forgot in his excitement motion No. 4. He tried to get home the bullet, paper, and all, and so stuck his ramrod in the gun. He and I got it out with great difficulty, and I loaded the next time. An assistant-surgeon thus became musketry instructor to a red Marine; but then I knew all about it, having been for years a full private in the Aberdeen Volunteers.

There were at Dum-Dum, as there are at all garrisons, as well as on board P. and O. mail-boats, low-caste working men called Lascars. In fact, I do not think that these men are supposed to have any caste at all. I know that Hindoos and Mahommedans alike look upon them as but half a remove above the brutes.

Well, one broiling hot day in the month of January, 1857, a poor Lascar, who had been working naked almost, till his mouth was parched and his body dripping with sweat, met a high-caste Sepoy carrying a lotah* of cool water. The Lascar approached the Sepoy, addressing him in words of which the following is a mere paraphrase:

"For the love of heaven, let me have a little water to drink, for I die of thirst!"

The Sepoy lowered his brows, and drew himself up to his full height. He drew himself away too from the Lascar as if he had been a loathsome beast.

"Give *you* water to drink from my lotah! Perish the thought! Think you I would break my caste by having my drinking-vessel contaminated by the lips of a low Lascar? Away!"

"Ha, ha, ha!" laughed the Lascar, now aroused to anger by the haughtiness of this gay soldier, "what need it matter to you? But a little longer, and *you* will have no caste at all. How then?"

"What mean you?"

"I mean what I say."

He was turning away, but the Sepoy now eagerly detained him.

"Explain!" he cried, "explain!"

"Why," the Lascar replied, "the British Government are using the fat of swine and cows to grease the new cartridges for the Enfield rifles. These will soon be served out to the whole army. You will have to touch the accursed fat† with lips and teeth. How then about your caste? Ha, ha!"

---

* A drinking-vessel made of brass.

† The Sepoys bit off the tops of their cartridges instead of using their fingers.

"You lie, you dog."

"I speak the truth."

Away went the tired and weary Lascar, the Sepoy gazing after him aghast. Would he return and confess to having been joking or lying?

But the Lascar disappeared without even looking round.

Now there was but slight foundation for what the Lascar had said. Nevertheless his words formed the torch, that commenced the most awful military conflagration and revolt that ever took place in the world.

The Sepoy hurried off to his mess and told of his adventure with the Lascar to his fellows, and it would be difficult indeed to describe in words the horror with which the story was received.

They thought that the British Government had long tried to introduce Christianity into their midst, and being but partially successful they had devised this mean expedient, whereby, while pretending to place in the hands of the Sepoy a new and more destructive rifle, they could entirely destroy his caste. That was their belief now.

I may tell you, reader, that such destruction of caste would signify to a Sepoy that he was to be deprived of all spiritual happiness and comfort in this world, and doomed to the loss of all hope for the next. The Sepoys, or Indian soldiers, were made up of Hindoos and Mahommedans alike. And to both these the pig is an unclean animal while the cow is sacred.

The story of the greased cartridges spread throughout India with the speed of wildfire, and it was turned to good account by the preachers of sedition all throughout the North-West Provinces.

It was not long before this, remember, that Oude had been annexed to the British territory and its king of course deposed. He was at this time living at Calcutta, and had friends there and everywhere else, for he still retained the hope that his house would yet be restored to the throne. His agents, it goes almost without saying, made the very most of the tale of Dum-Dum and the greased cartridges.

There are two names you cannot help hearing when reading of the mutiny, nay, even three, as Solomon says.

I. The terrible Nana Sahib. This fellow was an adopted son of deposed Maratha Peshwa—petty kings in India who had no issue were in the habit of adopting sons—Nana Sahib was allowed to inherit his adoptive father's personal effects, and also a large estate that lay near to Cawnpore, but had been refused the continuance of a pension, and on this account he now became one of the most active agents in the spread of disaffection and mutiny.

II. The titular King of Delhi. This man was naturally enough our bitter enemy. He and his family lived at Delhi, in the ancient palace of the Moguls; there he himself did all a lazy man could to stir up strife and fan the flame of insurrection, while for years his bold sons had been preaching sedition throughout the land.

III. The Ranee of Jhansi. Her husband had died without an heir, and, rightly or wrongly, I cannot say which, the British had quietly annexed his territory.

Tantia Topee is another name you may have heard of.

He was a great friend and companion of Nana Sahib, and probably the best and ablest general in the rebel army.

This fiend incarnate had been brought up in the same house as Nana Sahib, so that there is no wonder that he took up arms for him, even at the very first outbreak of the terrible Mutiny.

This Tantia Topee is said not to have been brave or daring. I think this is wrong. At last, however, he seems to have been a convert to the opinion that discretion is the best part of valour, and that

> "He who fights, and thus gets slain,
> Will never live to fight again;
> While he who fights and runs away
> Will live to fight some other day."

Anyhow, Tantia Topee's nine months' flight from Gwalior, after the capture of that city, was quite a masterly one, and as it is quite historical I trust I shall have space briefly to tell you the strange story in a future chapter.

It would seem, from what I have just told you, that the origin of the Mutiny was in some degree the outcome of a political conspiracy, at the head of which were the King of Oude, the King of Delhi, and Nana Sahib, all three candidates for kingdoms.

There seems to be truth in this. We find Lord Lawrence, while making a speech to a large assembly in Glasgow, in the year 1860, giving utterance to the following opinions:

"The annexation of Oude had nothing to do with the Mutiny in the first place, though that measure did add to the number of our enemies after the Mutiny commenced.

"The old government of Oude was extremely obnoxious to the mass of our native soldiers of the regular army, who came from Oude and the adjacent province of Behar, and with whom the Mutiny originated. These men were the sons and kinsmen of the Hindoo yeomen of the country, all of whom benefited more or less by annexation; while Oude was ruled by a Mohammedan family, which had never identified itself with the people, and whose government was extremely oppressive to all classes except its immediate creatures and followers.

"But when the introduction of the greased cartridges had excited the native army to revolt, when the mutineers saw nothing before them short of escape on the one hand, or destruction on the other, they and all who sympathised with them were driven to the most desperate measures. Then all who could be influenced by love or fear rallied round them. All who had little or nothing to lose joined their ranks, all that dangerous class of religious fanatics and devotees who abound in India, all the political intriguers who in peaceful times can do no mischief, swelled the number of the enemy, and gave spirit and direction to their measures.

"Besides, India is full of races of men who from time immemorial have lived by service or by plunder, and who are ready to join in any disturbance which may promise employment or loot.

"Oude was full also of disbanded soldiers who had not had time to settle down. Our gaols furnished thousands of desperate men let loose on society. The cry throughout the country, as cantonment after cantonment became the scene of triumphant mutiny, was, 'The

English rule is at an end. Let us plunder, kill, and enjoy ourselves.'

"The industrious classes all over India were on our side, but for a long time feared to act. On the one hand they saw the few British in the country shot down or flying for their lives, or at the best standing on the defensive and sorely pressed; on the other side they saw summary punishment in the shape of plunder and destruction of their houses dealt out to those who aided us. *But* when we evinced signs of vigour, when we began to assume the defensive and vindicate our authority, then many of those people came forward and identified themselves with our cause."

* * * * * *

Jack Morrison's life continued to be a very pleasant one at the house of his kindly employer at Agra. In fact it seemed all one long picnic. He had long ere January, 1857, become thoroughly acclimatised, in fact he had become an East-Indian out and out, for not only had he become accustomed to the climate, but to the creepie-creepies also. Do not smile, reader, please; I can assure you that while an ordinarily healthy European or Britisher may become inured to the heat of the weather, and to the climate generally, in about six weeks, it takes one a year or more to get used to the creepie-creepies, be they deadly or simply annoying. The heat of the summer combined with the attacks of insects, costs us many a British life in India, for it is the insects, be they mosquitoes or bugs, that keep one awake at night, and without good sleep one cannot long remain well in a tropical country. Snakes are bad enough, and they may be met with in one's garden or compound often enough, or in the thatch, but for the simple reason that they are more numerous, if not so deadly, the loathsome centipedes are even worse. Cockroaches are troublesome, but the flying bug is a dreadful nuisance; he gets into everything, into your milk and your sugee that you are having for supper, and into your hair or moustache if you are going to a ball, when, if you are unfortunate enough to bruise him, a shampoo, and a good one, is the only thing that will remove the revolting smell he emits.

Then we have lizards of all kinds, and flying things and crawling things too, so that on the whole I think my hero Jack was a true man to get over his fear of them, and to be able to sleep as he often did, and had to, without a mosquito curtain.

With the commencement of the year came ugly rumours of an impending crisis, but it did not affect the spirits of anybody at Mr. Mayne's bungalow. Not even the story of the greased cartridges. The subject indeed was scarcely ever mentioned. We cannot wonder at this if we remember that even among the European population of Meerut, until the very day that the Mutiny burst over the station like a bolt from the blue, people were laughing and talking and jesting about each other's fears or doubts, holding garden-parties, going to church, marrying and giving in marriage. And yet Agra itself became some time after this one of the centres of the awful Mutiny.

"Jack," said Mr. Mayne one day, "I'm going to give you a treat."

This was in the month of April.

"Well, sir," said Jack, "you have given me so many already, that I should feel ashamed to have any more."

"O, but this is a special one. I want you to go to Muttra and to Delhi."

"O! papa," cried Teddie, "you mustn't send Mr. Jack away. Jessie and I and Goosie can't spare him—'deed, indeed we can't."

Jessie came, in her fond, half-shy little way, and stood by Jack with her hand in his.

"If you please, dad," she said, "couldn't Teddie and I go too?"

"No, darlings; but I'm sure Jack will bring you something very nice from Delhi."

"That I will," said Jack.

"When will you be able to start?"

"To-morrow morning."

"Bravo! And the treat is this, that I'm going to make you travel, not on horseback, but in a palkee" (palanquin).

"How luxurious."

"Yes; you may imagine yourself an Indian rajah. You know you told me you were going to write a book about your Indian experiences. Well, palkee travelling will form a chapter."

"I'm sure you are very kind."

"Heard any more word about the expected outbreak?" said Mrs. Mayne.

"Nothing fresh, dear. Only the old, old stories repeated over and over again. Why Jackson, the indigo merchant, told me only to-day that he seemed to hear already the low muttering of thunder on the horizon that ever precedes a terrible storm. 'Very likely,' I replied; 'but, Jackson, we often hear such mutterings, and the storm never comes.'"

It was in the forenoon that Mr. Mayne had spoken to his young secretary, and the latter spent the rest of the day getting ready.

But towards eventide he went out for a drive with the children, and the everlasting mongoose. Jack never forgot that evening. The sun was brightly blue; a purple haze half hid the greenery of the country; the weird-like beauty of all around was very impressive.

Teddie was full of prattle about all the fine things he expected that Jack would bring him from Delhi; but poor Jessie seemed listless and low, and more than once the tears trembled on her eyelashes, when Jack drew her nearer to him and spoke kindly to her.

They got back to the compound and the beautiful house just as the sun had set, for twilight is very brief indeed in these latitudes.

That night after dinner, and after Jack had kissed the children and wished them good night, Mr. Mayne and he sat long out in the verandah, looking at the bright moonlight that bathed and beautified everything, and even dimmed the light of the fireflies that danced and flitted from bush to bush.

The country all around was very still, and if now and then the murmur of the distant city seemed to wax louder, or the yap-yapping of a jackal fell upon their ears, there were few other sounds to break the solemn, the impressive stillness. So silent indeed was the night that they could now and then hear the rustle of the wings of a tailor-bird, that had built its nest betwixt two broad leaves only a few yards from the verandah.

"Well, Jack," said Mr. Mayne at last, "if you won't have another cigar, I think you had better go to bed. I have given you your letters and all your orders, so there will be no bother in the morning. Good night, dear boy."

"Good night, sir."

Jack got his candle, and went gliding away through the drawing-room and vestibule to his beautifully-furnished and home-like bedroom.

Little did he think that this would be the last time that ever he should sleep in that room, or that the very roof above him would soon be given to the flames.

CHAPTER V.

THE OUTBREAK OF THE FEARFUL STORM.

THERE is perhaps no more pleasant way of travelling in India than that by palanquin. It is however unusual to adopt such a method for long journeys, and the distance from Agra to Muttra is about thirty-three miles. But then Mr. Mayne thought that having worked very hard, Jack had really earned an easy holiday, and in the "palkee" he certainly would have time to look about him and to think as well.

He had a good retinue of armed servants, as well as those who relieved each other every hour in bearing the palanquin along. And these servants were on horseback.

I wish I had time to describe fully, to linger over as it were, that delightful palkee journey to Muttra and far beyond in the direction of Delhi. Jack travelled only in the early morning and in the evening, indulging in a siesta during the very hottest part of the day. It must not be imagined however that he permitted himself to be carried all the way. He was too young and strong for that. He felt life in every limb, sturdiness and strength in every sinew. But he was the sahib for the present, and to have walked much instead of lounging with Oriental indolence in his beautiful palanquin, would have been to lower himself in the eyes of his Sepoy servants and his Lascar bearers as well.

Have you ever seen a palanquin, reader? Perhaps not, but you must have seen illustrations of the old Sedan chair. Well a palkee might be called a Sedan sofa, that is, instead of sitting as in the old fashion chair-conveyance, you lie in a palkee at full length. There is an opening prettily curtained and upholstered at each side, and as the bearers trot along with you, you can gaze with half shut eyes at the lovely panorama that is drifting past on either side. Woods and wilds, hills and dales, rippling streams and roaring cataracts. Sometimes you are winding along on a steep mountain side, with, far beneath you, the precipice that bounds a deep defile through which perhaps there goes meandering and winding along a silvery thread of a river with green banks at each side, but so far beneath you that meadows or gardens look no larger than tablecloths, and human dwellings like tiny dolls'-houses—so high indeed may the brae below you be that tall trees point up to you; you would have to fall a long way before you even touched their tops, and birds that you know to be eagles or vultures seem no larger than flies.

Now and then you cross a rustic bridge, and terribly insecure some of those appear. High above rocky cañons they may be, and you look from your palkee window, right down upon a white and foaming torrent that spends its whole existence in trying to dislodge or wear away the black boulders that lie here and there in its midst. At times you are passing over wide and arid wastes, and anon through jungles so dense and dark you cannot but believe wild beasts and horrid snakes abound, but even these are beautified here and there with a wealth of trailing and climbing flowers that dazzles the eye, and seems to steep the senses in a languorous pleasure that is born of their bright colouring, their strange and wondrous shapes, and the perfume from them that fills the air around. In such spots as these there is no lack of bright winged birds, butterflies like floating painted fans, and droning beetles of every size and form. As you pass along you cannot help saying to yourself "What a glorious place for a picnic!" and probably there rise up before your mind's eye visions of happy picnics spent long ago in your own loved native land. The scenery that surrounded those could not compare with this in grandeur, but ah! the picnic is ever to be remembered nevertheless, and you sigh as your palkee passes on, and some other picture in this grand panorama is spread out before you.

I think, indeed I am sure, that Jack Morrison sometimes fell asleep as he was borne along, nor do I wonder, for the weather was heavenly, just sufficient breeze to send a soft whisper through the trees that, mingling with the hum of insect life, and the twittering song of birds, was enough to lap the soul in somnolence.

Did the thought ever occur to Jack during this journey that there might after all be some truth in the strange rumours that filled the city air of Agra, that murder and mutiny were already raising their gaunt forms, and preparing to strike, that here was he—a Christian and therefore "an infidel dog," according to his guards and bearers—alone and unprotected, except by the very men who would perhaps gladly see every European floating dead along the Ganges to form food for slimy eels and alligators? Yes, such thoughts did cross his mind more than once; but in his well and luxurious-furnished palkee he carried revolvers—not that these could have protected him very long, though he would have fought to the last, and sold his life dearly. But as soon as such thoughts arose Jack did all he could to banish them, as unworthy of him, and a crime against the gentle, kindly fellows who formed his guard. If the thoughts did not leave his mind at once, he reached for a book, and commenced to read, and as likely as not reading ended in sleep. This sleep was something of such a gentle nature that he could hardly believe he had dropped off at all, till one of his men came smiling up and restored to him his book that had fallen out of the palkee, with some such remark as, "The sahib have sleap for two hour, but I not disturb till he have waked."

At Muttra he stayed for several weeks. The Europeans here were very kind to him, and besides there was much to be seen. The city of Muttra is very large and very picturesque, especially as viewed from the river Jumna. It is a city of palaces and temples, it is the Mecca or the Jerusalem of the Hindoos. The temples are not by any means very imposing structures, or rather, I should say, the temple may be but part and portion of a house or shop; but if you can secure entrance to the temple's interior, which is as much like a small theatre as anything else, then the dim religious light, the curtained alcoves, the elevated stage, the shrine, the wild, unearthly, but sometimes pleasant music—all these may impress the mind; but after all it is only a form of heathen worship.

The main street of this great city is imposing in the extreme, and seems indeed to be the work of fairy fingers.

There are many beautiful gardens about Muttra, but there are many loathsome places in it also—the home of the wild dog, the swine, and men of the lowest caste.

But Jack left Muttra at last with many a kindly word and wish ringing in his ears, and pursued his way onwards for Delhi.

* * * * *

We must leave Jack Morrison for the present slowly moving northwards, while we go further north and west than even Delhi.

And here we find ourselves at the great military station of Meerut, which you can easily find on the map, reader.

At this place at the time of the outbreak were stationed two regiments of Native Infantry, the 11th and 20th, besides the 3rd Native Cavalry. This was a large contingent of natives; but it must be remembered that the British had for their protection, if need be, a battalion of the 60th Rifles, besides Horse and Foot Artillery and a regiment of Dragoons.

The station at Meerut was a very large one, and was divided in two by a deep ditch. On the north side of this ditch were a number of officers' bungalows, and then came the barracks of the European infantry and the cavalry barracks, with the English church between.

When you crossed the ditch you came to acres of bazaars or streets, and at quite a long distance from these were the native lines.

The best authorities agree with me in stating that the plan of Meerut was a mistake, and that so great a distance should not have existed between the British and the native soldiery.

Be this as it may, Meerut became the scene of the first outbreak of the great Mutiny.

It will soon be seen, however, that this was neither planned nor premeditated, and that it was really the story of the greased cartridges that hurried affairs onwards.

And here is the best place to say that long before the outbreak a somewhat strange thing had happened at Mr. Mayne's bungalow. This was, I think, early in February. On coming in to breakfast, Jack Morrison, who had been first down, found that a little native cake, or choopattie, had been placed by each plate. Jack thought it was some little game of Teddie's; but when Mr. Mayne himself came in and saw these, he evinced some slight degree of displeasure.

"How came these things here?" he said, "and why?" he asked a servant.

The servant shrugged his shoulders.

"I not know why," he answered, "but one good man bring him."

"Well, take them away."

The servant obeyed, just a little sullenly.

When he had gone, and Jack was alone with his master, he said anxiously, "You do not think they were poisoned, sir?"

"No, no, no, Jack, not that; but I have been told that before an outbreak these choopatties are distributed. It was well to have them removed, for Mrs. Mayne is nervous, and so too is poor little Jessie."

That same week news had come to Agra of the distribution of choopattie cakes all over India.

And the following evidence given by a native will explain the mystery, while showing at the same time how it had been planned and intended that the Mutiny should be carried out.

"A night was to have been fixed on which, without risking anything, the whole of the European officers were to have been killed and the treasuries plundered. The magazines were to have been captured wherever possible and blown up; but it was never intended to injure women or children. Nearly all the men in the different regiments were of the same mind on this point. It is not the Brahmins and great men that have destroyed helpless children and poor ladies. It was the intention to kill your men, but it was villagers and savages who destroyed your women and children. Nana Sahib, though always a worthless fellow, could never have ordered the murder of women and children. Had they no mothers or sisters? Had they no heart for them? I heard of what happened with sorrow. We object to your raj (rule). It is true that under it all men have peace and freedom, such freedom as we never enjoyed before, but *we sorrow for our caste.* I am speaking of Brahmins.

Brahmins love good food and ease. The Company does not give it for nothing, and we wish for a return of that raj which will enable us to retain it.

"The choopattie cakes in question were a jadoo (a charm), which originated with Dassa Bawa, who told Nana Sahib that he would make a jadoo, and as far as these magic cakes should be carried, so far would the people be on his side."

Well, when the story of Dum-Dum and the greased cartridges reached Meerut the excitement was very great, and although the officers tried to assure their Sepoys that there was scarcely a word of truth in the tale, confidence was not restored nor was the excitement allayed.

On the 24th of April Colonel Smyth, who commanded the native cavalry, ordered a parade and a distribution of cartridges, which the men were informed need not be bitten with the teeth, but torn with the fingers. Only five men, however, would receive them. The others sullenly refused.

It was nonsense, they said to each other, if not to their officers, to tell them that the cartridges could be torn instead of bitten. If they possessed those cartridges at all, custom would assert itself, and in moments of forgetfulness they would bite the end off. Then would they be defiled body and soul, and all caste be at an end.

Colonel Smyth ordered a court of enquiry to be held on these men, and in the end a court-martial condemned them to ten years' imprisonment.

Colonel Smyth, it may be observed, was a somewhat

hard and strict service man, and therefore very far indeed from being popular.

Meanwhile the growing storm asserted itself in a new phase, and incendiary fires were almost of nightly occurrence.

The sentence of the court-martial was on the 9th of May rigorously and ruthlessly carried out.

The morning broke fair and beautiful, but soon heavy and ominous clouds began to darken the sky and hide the sun. There was a boding gloom over the whole of this great military camp. This, however, did not prevent all hands, ladies gay and children merry, from turning out to the general parade.

The felons were marched into the centre, and here their uniforms were roughly stripped off, and although they shrieked for mercy, for sake of their wives and children, blacksmiths riveted the chains upon their arms and legs, and they were led away shouting curses, loud and long, upon the British, and upon Colonel Smyth in particular.

Ladies put their fingers in their ears to keep out the sound of those fearful curses, and innocent children wonderingly asked their mothers what it all meant.

Had Smyth gained a victory? The sequel will answer the question.

All that day the Sepoys were unusually obedient to command, and even the most tender-hearted women admitted that though the punishment was a sad one it was just, and must do good.

On the Sunday everything seemed as usual on the

European side of the ditch; but foul mutiny was being preached and hatched beyond.

The chaplain was preparing for evening service at sunset when one of his female servants begged and prayed of him to stay at home if he valued his life.

The clergyman laughed at her, and drove off to church. He soon found, however, that the woman's warning was not the result of a delusion, for as he approached the sacred edifice he could hear in the distance the sharp rattle of musketry fired in volleys, and sparks and smoke and flames arising from burning houses, and rolling away to leeward on the evening breeze.

Whether or not the Sepoys had intended to strike a blow that night I am not certain; but if so the church parade of the European soldiers precipitated matters, and the cry was raised that the Rifles and Artillery were on their way to disarm the native troops.

On hearing this startling yell the Sepoys ran quickly back from the streets towards their lines.

Wild war had commenced in earnest.

The native cavalry naturally were the first to take action. Had they not stood on the parade but a day back, and seen their companions rivetted with chains, and led off to gaol without their being able to strike a blow on their behalf, and that too amid the jeers of the Europeans, the ladies even smiling their approbation of the terrible injustice?

Hurrah! They would be revenged.

They spurred on their horses now at a mad gallop towards the gaol, locks and bolts gave way before them, doors were smashed and fell in pieces, and soon they reached their comrades' cells, and relieving them of their chains brought them forth to the fresh air and to freedom.

The Infantry had armed themselves on reaching their lines.

Several European officers had rushed thither in the hope of pacifying them, among them being Colonel Finnis, the commander of the 11th.

He was shot almost at once, but not, it is believed, by his own men.

The thirst of the mutineers for the blood of Christians was only stimulated, Holmes tells us, by the slaughter of Finnis.

The convicts let loose from the gaols, and fraternising with the native police, and the increasing swarms of budmashes, joined in the bloody work. Gangs of these marauders, armed with swords and clubs, roamed about the station, hurled showers of bricks upon every European that crossed their path, burst into peaceful dwellings, murdered the inmates, and poured forth again laden with plunder; and the terrified witnesses of this dreadful scene heard mingling with the roar that leapt up from the burning houses, the savage voices of Mahommedans shouting "Ali! Ali!"

But why, it may be asked, did not the white regiments at once fly to the rescue of those poor victims? The answer seems to be that the commander of the British forces, General Hewitt, whose age could be his only excuse—for he was both infirm and old—seemed quite to lose his head, and did nothing

Wilson, the Brigadier, might have acted more quickly and energetically than he did.

Even the mutineers themselves felt certain that the British would speedily be upon the scene of action, and so raised the cry, "Quick, brothers, quick! To Delhi! to Delhi!"

When therefore Wilson reached the lines with his Artillery there were few Sepoys left to engage, and these quickly betook themselves to the jungle, whence they could defy General Wilson to dislodge them.

Meanwhile the mutineers were flying in the direction of Delhi, sure enough in their own minds that they were being hotly pursued by the British troops.

But though the night was now bright and clear, with moon as well as stars shining above, Wilson neglected to follow them up, and thus left Delhi to their mercy.

That was a fearful night in Meerut.

Says Holmes: "The baffled Europeans encamped on their own parade-ground, but did nothing to assist the suffering people for whose protection they had been retained, though the sullen roar of a thousand fires might have warned them to be up and doing."

It is pleasant to know, reader, that although the European troops, or rather their incapable leaders, did nothing to save the lives of the poor civilians who were being murdered—in some cases even burned alive—there were faithful servants among the natives themselves who behaved far more like heroes.

One of the servants for example, Golab Khan to name, saved his master Greathead and his wife from a fearful death. When the ruffians broke into his house, armed with their blood-dripping knives, they had taken refuge on the roof, and their burning building would have become their funeral pile had not Golab enticed the murderers away under pretence of showing them the hiding-place of his master.

Nor was this the only instance of heroism.

Craigie's own Sepoys posted themselves outside his bungalow, and protected his wife from the savagery of the horrible mob.

Lieutenant Müller of the 11th besought General Hewitt to permit him that night to ride alone to Delhi and warn the inhabitants of the approach of the mutineers. His request was refused point-blank.

"Give me," cried Captain Rosser of the Dragoons, "but a few guns and one squadron of my regiment, and I will pursue the Sepoys and stop their retreat."

"No," was the reply, "we cannot spare the men. Meerut must be held."

And yet, reader, it is the opinion of the greatest authorities on the Indian Mutiny, that Hewitt might easily have sent one half his Europeans for the defence of Delhi. A blow struck at once, and struck hard, has saved many a kingdom ere now.

The same gallant officer, Müller, mentioned above, had justice done, however, on a mutineer who had cruelly slain a brother officer's wife. Single-handed he tracked him to his lair, made him prisoner, and marched at the revolver's point to the camp, and there he was summarily tried and hanged.

General Hewitt then, it will be seen, to say nothing of Brigadier Wilson, seemed perfectly paralysed by the outbreak at Meerut, and even next day remained inactive, passive.

And when daylight had returned terrible indeed was the scene presented to view.

Meerut was wrecked, everywhere stood the blackened ruins of what had but a day before been smiling bungalows, and in the gardens and compounds lay piles of broken furniture, pictures, and all the charming nick-nackery that helps to make home so homely. And, alas! among the ruins could be seen many a knifed and mangled corpse, their sightless eyeballs seeming to stare upwards at the morning sky.

CHAPTER VI.

FIGHTING AND MASSACRE AT DELHI—HOW A BRITISH BOY DID HIS DUTY.

I HAVE no desire, in this o'er true tale of mine, to paint any of the sad scenes and the incidents that occurred during the terrible Mutiny in language too graphic. I wish but to tell the plain unvarnished truth, and not even the whole of tnat. But it is a tale that all British boys and girls should be told at least once during their lives, if only to prove to them how brave our British men and women can be; nay, but I will go further and say that in some places, such as Lucknow and Cawnpore, there was almost a holiness in their heroism and in their unselfish display of courage and endurance, which, if one attempts to portray, he finds the language at his command is far too feeble and inadequate even to trace.

In the last chapter we left the British general at Meerut, although commanding bold and courageous troops, completely paralysed at the great misfortune that had fallen upon the military station, though not a man under him but would, with the greatest alacrity, have gone in pursuit of the flying rebels and meted out to them such a punishment as would have caused Sepoys all over India to think twice ere they deserted their flag, and might have gone far to extinguish the rising flames of mutiny before it could reach the *summus mons* of our power and sway in India. And we left the rebel Sepoys not yet satiated with blood and slaughter, but flying fearfully onward to Delhi in the silence of night, their rear guard often stopping to listen for the footsteps of pursuing cavalry.

And what a whirlwind of blood and cruelty that was, now sweeping on to burst upon Delhi. It is sad indeed to read of villages in the far and beautiful interior of Africa being captured at the dead of night by Arab hordes of slavers, their old men and women ruthlessly murdered, their helpless children speared or tossed into the raging flames, the young men struck down and borne bleeding coastwards, never to see their homes again. But here at Delhi matters seem to us to have been infinitely worse, because the defenceless whites were our own dear people, bearing our names and having all the customs and traditions, the language, the love, and the religion of our own dear native land, and because the tragedy enacted was on a far, far larger scale.

Delhi was even then a large and well-fortified city, high up on the banks of the Jumna, with its walls and ramparts, its gates and fosses, its king's palace, its public buildings, and its maze of bazaars and narrow streets.

It stands about forty miles from Meerut, but nevertheless the mutineers had accomplished the whole of that long journey during the dreadful night of the 10th of May. Indeed, one might say that the blood of their innocent victims was hardly dry on their hands and fingers ere they were once more waving their murder-steeped knives and tulwars in Delhi itself.

Everyone in the city was taken completely unawares. If anyone had an inkling of what was about to happen, and of the terrors that soon would reign in the devoted city, it must have been the Sepoys themselves; but even they could not have known of the complete and easy victory their brethren in arms had accomplished at Meerut, for morning parade passed by and they gave no sign, and their officers, talking, laughing, and chaffing, were sitting at breakfast.

The day had begun at Delhi as usual in every way. The bazaars were crowded, the merchants there were excited, but only in the same bullying or wrangling way they ever are when driving a bargain. In the low caste slums swine and wild dogs ran about quarrelling over the offal; strange, gaunt birds, with an immensity of bill—the adjutants—went stalking about performing their duties of scavenging; and the swarms of blue-bottle flies had already cleaned up the blood in European abattoirs. Here and there, tossing her proud little head aloft, a sacred cow might be seen walking alone by herself, or staying for a minute or two here and there to feed on the fruit of the bread-nut tree, while religious devotees piously touched her brow and then their own, muttering words of prayer as they did so.

And high over all, the sun shone hot in a blue and almost cloudless sky, his beams reflected from many a mosque and dome and from the broad waters of the Jumna itself.

But listen. While the magistrates or judges are busy trying cases, and trying to understand the bearing of speeches thereon made by many a gesticulating and excited witness, suddenly messengers arrive to report that a cloud of dust is visible on the high road from Meerut, and that armed men on horseback are sweeping onwards to the city.

Before word could be sent to the cantonments, where Graves was General, and to the magazine to warn Willoughby, the Lieutenant in charge, the Meerut mutineers had already succeeded in entering Delhi.

I can only compare the sudden inrush of these murdering fiends to that of a Highland mountain stream, which, after a storm among the distant hills, comes down in roaring spate—a perfect wall of brown water, madly tumbling on and on, bearing before it, and mixed with its froth and spume, trees and branches, boulders and sods, and even drowned cattle or sheep.

The chief body of the insurgent band effected an entrance at the Rajgat gate.

This gate might easily have been defended had the Sepoys inside been true to their flag.

Far from being so, they threw off their allegiance at once.

They opened the gate to the Meerut men.

They fraternised with them, welcomed them wildly

tossed their arms high in the air, even foamed at the mouth in the madness of their excitement.

Backwards now rush these Sepoys.

The carnage, the murder, the fiendish cruelty and fire, have commenced in earnest.

Brave Captain Douglas, who was in charge of the palace guards, has been trying to urge these men to remain faithful and true; but his appeal, and that of Fraser the Commissioner, are alike in vain.

While the terrible work is going on, and tragedies are being enacted at every European house or bungalow, Douglas, fearfully wounded by leaping into the moat, is borne by natives into the palace and into his apartments. But Fraser still attempts to harangue the mob in a courtyard. Alas! he is cut down at last, and the guards, the very men that ought to have protected him, stab him to the heart.

Now upstairs the murderers rush, with awful yells and shouts, to the room where the sorely wounded Douglas lies weltering in his blood, surrounded by his distracted friends, among whom were the chaplain and two ladies.

In vain they try to barricade the door; it is forced in, dashed in, and next minute all inside are slain, and the room presents a sight that it is best to draw a veil across, lest it should haunt our dreams at night.

All this was done, and a dozen deeds far more cruel and vile, by the first party of horsemen that had arrived. Then the infantry from Meerut came pouring in and joined them, and the work of death received fresh impulse.

Still another portion of the mutineers attacked the

public buildings. The manager of the bank here, shoulder to shoulder with his wife, made a gallant stand, but both were soon overpowered and slain; and all Christians, no matter to what country they belonged, fell beneath the knives or tulwars of the mutineers.

The church itself did not protect them, for this was stormed and desecrated.

As to the Eurasian Christians and converts, who lived in the low part of the town, although they barricaded their lanes, and did all they could to defend themselves, they were butchered everywhere as if they had been pigs. A few, however, were taken prisoners, but only to meet with a far worse fate. They were immured in stifling, slimy, vermin-haunted dungeons, and after starvation and ill-treatment for five days, they were hauled forth and executed amidst the shouts and jeerings of the mutineers, who afterwards pitched their bodies into the Jumna.

A very affecting and tragical episode connected with the first portion of the dreadful attack upon Delhi is thus related by Holmes, though taken from Cave-Browne's report:

"In the telegraph office hard by the church a young signaller was standing with his hand upon the signalling apparatus. The mutineers were almost upon him, and more and more plainly he heard them yelling as they swept along. Still he went on with his work.

"Click, click," sounded the instrument, click, click, click, click; while nearer and nearer came those awful yells.

"Flashed up the wires to Umballah, to Lahore, to Rawal

Pindee, and to Peshawur, this message warned the authorities in the Punjaub: 'The Sepoys come in from Meerut. Burning everything. Murdering all whites and Christians. Todd dead. Many others. Must shut up.'"

The mutineers burst in, the last click died away, and in the performance of his duty the signaller was slain.

It must not be supposed, however, that no defence was made. As soon indeed as Graves, the Brigadier-General at the cantonment, had received the message from the magistrate he commenced to act, and as speedily as possible Captain Ripley marched with a portion of his regiment to the Cashmere Gate, the rest was to follow up with two guns under the command of Major de Taisser. But at this gate they were met by a body of the rebel troopers, and no less than six of the officers of the 54th fell under their pistol fire. The Sepoys of this regiment, when ordered to fire, fired in the air, then at once rushed up and bayoneted their Colonel.

All the force now at the command of Brigadier Graves was a few companies of the 38th, 74th, and a score or so of artillerymen.

The cantonments, I should have said, were fully two miles to the northward and west of the city, so that much of the mischief was done before De Taisser's guns came on. The murderers fled at their approach, and the guns were placed at the main guard.

Hard work indeed had the Brigadier to keep his mutinous men in charge all that terrible afternoon, during which they waited, but waited in vain, for assistance from Meerut.

A brave young Briton volunteered to ride to that city for assistance. Had he succeeded doubtless it would have been denied him. But woe is me! he was speedily discovered and killed by the mutinous 38th.

Meanwhile Graves was not idle. He had collected all the women and children he could find and placed them in a small room in the flagstaff tower, a room which, we are told, was even smaller than the Black Hole of Calcutta.

"There huddled together," says a writer, "was collected a great company of every age and class, frightened children crying and clinging to their not less frightened ayahs, women weeping and bewailing the deaths of husbands and brothers, while others were bearing up against heat, discomfort, and anxiety, and busily unfastening cartridges for the men.

Graves and his company could only guess the awful work that was going on in the interior of the city.

I have mentioned Lieutenant Willoughby, who was in charge of the magazine. A more gallant young fellow—he was little more than a boy, and a shy and youthful-looking boy he was—surely never stepped in shoe leather.

His post was one of the utmost difficulty and danger but not for one moment did he flinch from it.

His guards he knew were but waiting the chance to join the other mutineers. And his whole European force were in number—how many think you, reader? Why only eight.

Now listen and hear how a British boy can do his duty in the hour of trial and emergency.

Young Willoughby had barricaded the outer gates of

the magazine, and then determined to wait with patience the reinforcements which he, like the Brigadier, thought would surely soon arrive from Meerut.

Was that barricade sufficient to keep out the murdering mutineers? Alas, no! They could at any moment crash through it, and assassinate all within, and their hesitation was no doubt owing to the fact that their king feared as yet to join the rebels.

That young hero, however, determined that when, or if they did break through, they should meet with a warm and terrible reception.

There grew a tree in the yard of the magazine, and from this tree a train was laid to the powder store, and a brave man—Conductor Scully—volunteered to fire this train from the tree as soon as Willoughby should give the signal.

That was act first in this fearful tragedy of defence. Act second commences when the King of Delhi, certain at last that no help could come to the British from Meerut, and feeling joyful with the prospect that his dynasty would now soon be restored at last, joined the mutineers, and demanded the surrender of the magazine.

The little garrison answered never a word. That is they did not answer immediately, and the mutineers, with dreadful shouts and yells, prepared to storm the place. Ah! then came the answer—an iron hail from the mouth of every gun.

No guns were ever better handled despite the fact that the men who worked them—that brave little band of Englishmen—were exposed to a rather hot fire of musketry from the mutineers.

For hours young Willoughby fought on. For hours he hoped and hoped that assistance would come. But he saw now that the end could not be far away.

One last longing look he took down the Meerut road. The afternoon sun was blazing over the woods. Slowly and sullenly flowed the river past the bastion, but no help or faintest sign of help was visible. The time has come, and the last act of the tragedy arises before our mental vision.

We see the youthful, boyish form of Willoughby silhouetted against the evening sky, we see him wave his hat.

It is the signal, and Scully fires the train. Next moment the whole city is shaken to its very foundations by the roar and thunder of that terrible explosion, and amidst dust and *débris*, and masses of timber and masonry, over a thousand mutineers are hurled high in the air—arms, legs, and heads drop here and there a few moments afterwards in the most distant streets and bazaars, and scores are killed outside by the bursting of shells.

In the dread silence and awful confusion that followed Willoughby escaped, and also Lieutenants Raynor and Forest, with Conductors Buckley and Shaw, and Sergeant Stuart.

Poor Scully, the man who had so bravely fired the train, was dreadfully wounded, and fell and died by the tree.

I wish I could tell the reader that brave young Willoughby lived, as did the others who escaped, to wear the Victoria Cross. He did not, however, for he was afterwards murdered while going towards Meerut.

The sound of the explosion startled the Brigadier and those with him at the gate. For a time they could not understand whether it were caused by accident or not. But they found out all too soon.

And now the 38th at the main-guard threw off every vestige of their pretended allegiance, and at once commenced to shoot their officers.

Three fell dead at the first volley, two more leaped from a bastion, but when the rest were about to follow them fell upon their ears the screams of the women.

Could they desert them, do you ask?

I will answer the question by another.

"Did Englishmen or Scotchmen or Irishmen *ever* desert women and children in distress?"

Reader, the answer to my question is the answer to yours.

CHAPTER VII.

THE FLIGHT FROM DELHI—STRANGE ADVENTURES OF JACK MORRISON.

THE truth concerning the fearful explosion spread like wildfire, and with it came the news that the king of Delhi had thrown in his lot with the mutineers.

The raj of the British was at an end then, the prophecy was true, and the rejoicing among all classes of the community was now ecstatic. But a terrible way they took to give expression thereto. There was no disguise now. Every Sepoy at once threw off the cloak of allegiance to his old flag. These mutineers were a band of brothers, a band of furies, and religious fanaticism knew neither bounds nor limits. The cry that resounded through every street or bazaar was, "Kill, kill, kill." And in every case murder was combined with the most revolting cruelty, and followed by wholesale plunder.

To save the women, however, was now the endeavour of the European officers. The poor creatures gazed fearfully down into that awful ditch of three and thirty feet depth, and shuddered as they clung to their would-be rescuers, but these were busy making ropes of their clothing and belts, and now as shot began to fall around them there was no more hesitation, and men and women made the dangerous descent. Then there was the ascent to be made on the other side; and, after struggles to which terror lent strength, all were got to bank.

The women and children were also got out of their hot and horrible prison in the Flagstaff Tower. When the Brigadier had reached the cantonments with these the Sepoys of the 74th deserted, after gruffly warning the British to fly if they valued their lives.

* * * * *

They were advised to fly. Fly they must, for already they could see the sparks and flames leaping up in clouds of smoke from their burning bungalows, the homes in which but a day before they had been so happy, and hear the howling of the savages who, thirsting for Christian blood, had already taken up the pursuit.

They had one friend left, only one, and this was the darkness. So with night closing around them the unhappy fugitives took their way towards forest and jungle, leaving the bands of mutineers to wreck their vengeance upon the cantonments.

It is hardly possible to conceive of a more dismal plight than that these poor people now found themselves in. Men and gentlemen there were among them who, if left to themselves, might have made a bold push for somewhere; but hampered as they were in their flight by the women and children — many of them had been delicately nurtured and reared in the lap of luxury—all they could do was to trust in God to protect those in their charge in every way they could, and when the worst came to the worst sell their lives dearly and die.

It would take volumes to describe one half the sufferings those fugitives endured, not only physically but mentally; for by the villagers, who at times gave them food or water begrudgingly, they were looked upon as inferior animals, but little raised above the beasts of the fields.

It goes without saying that the majority of them succumbed to their sufferings.

We read of their being driven to hide in jungles or morasses from the bands of despicable villains that the Mutiny had let loose to wander over the country in search of adventure and plunder; of their being robbed by these, and even tied to trees to be beaten and scourged; of their being entrapped by villagers with promises of assistance, only to be ill-treated and stripped of the best portions of their clothing; of their being exposed nearly naked to the blazing sunshine and the burning winds; of their ranks being thinned while fording rivers; of their being devoured by alligators, bitten by snakes in the jungles in which they hid, falling dead by the wayside of exhaustion and starvation, in some instances being left by sorrowing friends under the shade of trees to die.*

But there is just one ray of sunshine to lighten this dark picture, though only in parts; for those who at last, weary and worn and dejected, managed to escape, had to

* HOLMES and many other sources.

tell of instances of real kindness at the hands of some of the natives, of their having been hidden for weeks from those who sought their lives and tenderly nursed and fed.

There is something good in human nature after all, reader, and the very blackest pages of our history reveal this fact.

* * * * *

We must return for a short time to Jack Morrison, whom we left journeying on towards Delhi. What a pleasant and happy life he had led for weeks past, in this tour of his. Contrast it, if you will, with that which the fugitives had to lead in their headlong flight from the same city.

Well, one is a picture of peace, the other of war, in its most awful form.

But clouds soon began to rise on Jack's horizon. One day while halting for refreshments in a small mud village, situated amidst the most charming scenery, he noticed a half-naked budmash creep out of his hovel and address Jack's servants, all of whom, with the exception of the Lascars, had been Sepoys, and had served in the regular army.

This budmash was neither over nice nor over polite in his remarks. He talked too fast for Jack to understand what he said, for his knowledge of any dialect of Hindoostan was very limited. Nevertheless there were many words understood by him: those made his heart beat high with a nameless dread.

The budmash talked not only fast but most excitedly, and his words were received at first with signs of incredulity by the servants, then with interest, and at last they appeared to catch a deal of the excitement evinced by the speaker.

This fellow finally turned towards the palkee, drew his dirty hand across his throat, and spat upon the ground.

The story he had told the Sepoy servants was a garbled account of the outbreak of the mutiny at Meerut and at Delhi.

What was to be done? Could the story be true? Considering everything, and the confidence Mr. Mayne had all along exhibited in the peaceful state of the country, he came to the conclusion it was not. His servants, however, looked doubtful as he gave them the orders to proceed as if nothing had happened. They shook their heads, however, as they glanced back to the spot where the evil-minded budmash still stood raving excitedly, making gestures that meant murder if he could have had his will, and spitting on the ground.

That same afternoon, however, it became all too apparent that what the budmash had said was virtually true. Towards sunset they were journeying quietly onwards along the rough, foot-beaten path, when suddenly, at a bend of the road, they were confronted by a band of cavalry Sepoys. They were about fifteen in all, and under the command of a jemadar. Those men had probably come from Delhi, and had taken part in the mutiny and massacre there. Be this as it may, their presence created something very like a panic in the ranks of Jack's little company.

As for the Lascars, they dropped the palkee forthwith, and fled incontinently to the woods.

Jack sprang out as quickly as he could, sword and revolver in hand.

At the same time his Sepoys were peremptorily ordered to give up their prisoner.

"But prisoner he is not," was the bold reply; and from that moment Jack was confident his fellows would be true to him.

The attacking party, or rather their sergeant, now called on Jack to surrender.

"I am the bearer of a message to Delhi, and I am going on there," was Jack's reply. "If you or your men dare to stop me you will rue it."

"Delhi is no longer the residence of the vile dogs of British. They are all slain, they and their pigs of women and children. Surrender!"

Now Jack Morrison was, as we already know, a powerfully-built young fellow. And he had also learned the art of self-defence by fists alone. Moreover he was a fairly good swordsman.

Oh, there was no nicety about Jack's swordsmanship. He possessed not the easy grace of a *maître d'armes*. You may have seen a Scotch peasant threshing corn with a flail. That was the style Jack went in for. And there is something to be said for it after all. More than once have I seen our sailor Jacks or blue-jackets beat down the guards of Arabs in this flail fashion, and break their heads at the same time.

Thinking that his victory would be an easy one, the jemadar had dismounted.

"Surrender, you beast?" cried Jack. "Take that."

It was a beautiful left-hander, straight from the

shoulder, and landed "skrunch" between the jemadar's eyes. He went down as if shot.

Two more saddles were emptied in a moment. Emptied by five shots. Two to five, and that isn't bad practice.

Now Jack cleverly mounted the jemadar's horse. From being a mere infantry soldier he suddenly became a cavalryman, and a dashing one too.

His men had retired a little way, but seeing how gallantly their young master went for that band of murderers they fired a volley, and with a wild shout came on at the charge.

The battle was decided almost at once, and those who did not fall fled.

Three of the attacking party were killed outright. Four were wounded; while so quick had been the onslaught of Jack's men that not one was hurt.

Their blood was up, however, and quickly dismounting, and before Jack could interfere to prevent them, they had dispatched the wounded men.

"How could you be so cruel? I am cross and angry."

"Sahib must not be angry. These men are murderers; deserve all they got. Now we fight for you once, we fight for you *always.*"

That these men deserved their fate Jack Morrison soon had sad and fearsome evidence.

They had not gone above two miles—after leaving the palkee where it was, exchanging it, we may say, for three horses, for the Lascars did not return—ere they came upon a sight that almost froze the marrow in Jack's bones.

Here on the road lay three women, two children about

"The battle was decided almost at once, and those who did not fall, fled" p. 186.

the ages of Jessie and Teddie, and two men, evidently all British, and all dead and fearfully mutilated. The men were almost naked, the women partially so, and wearing the loose cloaks of the dead officers, who had evidently struggled hard to protect them, as their bodies, covered with blood and dust, and the trampled condition of the pathway amply proved. Two or three of the attacking party had been killed, and one horse lay over his dead rider.

With thoughts that may be better imagined than described, Jack begged the assistance of his Sepoy servants, and together they dragged the bodies into the jungle, placed them side by side, and covered them with leaves and branches. A strange burial, but sufficient—ants and other insects would do all the rest.

It was necessary now, however, for Jack to consider what he should do. To go further in this direction would be folly. However he knew his bearings well, for on horseback he had travelled all over the country.

Instead, therefore, of going back upon Muttra, which he considered would by this time be in the hands of the mutineers, he decided to take a bridle path to the right. This, he remembered, would lead him towards the river Ganges, and there was more than one small town on its banks to which it was unlikely the Mutiny had yet spread. He knew merchants who lived there, and who, he felt certain, would give him safe convoy down the river as far as Cawnpore, which was doubtless held by British troops.

He explained to his Sepoys what he intended to do, and they quite approved of the scheme.

The pathway was very narrow, and as no wind could reach it owing to the trees, it was also insufferably hot.

But it was to all appearance safe.

Safe and silent—as silent as the grave to-day. The very lizards and insects seemed to feel the heat, and beautiful birds sat in the shade of green boughs with open bills panting.

They had not gone above a mile till they heard dogs barking in the distance.

"'T will be as well, sahib," said Jack's chief man, "to keep away from the village."

He pointed in the direction from which the barking came as he spoke.

Jack signified his assent by a nod, and still riding in single file, they now entered what was a jungle indeed. So dense was it that they were frequently obliged to dismount and lead their horses. This was a safe plan for another reason, because snakes hung from many of the branches. Very pretty snakes some of them were, but very poisonous nevertheless. It is disagreeable, to say the least—and I speak from experience—to find something that you have taken to be a branch of a climbing flower-stem dart quickly round and hiss in your face.

About a mile farther on they came to a stream, what we in this country would call a river. However, it was easily fordable, and now the jungle became an open wood, and the party remounted.

Jack was getting tired now, and a halt was called for rest and refreshments.

The woods around continued very silent, and so soft

was the ground beneath the trees that a footstep could not be heard.

Suddenly one of the spare horses neighed, and all the party immediately started to their feet and grabbed their pistols.

No need, however, to be alarmed. The ragged and wretched-looking figure that came wearily towards them was far too weak to hurt anyone, even had he been a foe. But he was only a fugitive, an Englishman of the name of Frank Wood.

"Thank God," he said as he extended his thin yellow hand to greet Jack, "you are a countryman and a friend. My sister may live. Oh," he added, and the tears born of debility and suffering ran down his cheeks, "how brave poor Lily has been!"

"But where is your sister?" cried Jack.

"A little way from here, hidden in the bush. I went to look for fruit, and God in his mercy sent me in your direction."

Lily was soon one of the party. Not more than sixteen was she, but so haggard and worn that she looked thirty, only her soft brown eyes retained their brightness. But her hair was tangled and roughly bound up with the root of a trailing plant.

She smiled through her tears as Jack took her hand.

Then Frank Wood told all the terrible story of Delhi, and—as far as he knew it—of Meerut also.

"We must save ourselves now," he said, "as best we can, and I think your plan is a good one. But I believe I can improve upon it."

Jack had already told him of his own recent adventures

"First and foremost," the stranger said, "we must hark back some distance, for we must rob the dead."

"Rob the dead?"

"Yes," and Frank smiled faintly, "we must rob the very Sepoys you and your brave fellows so conveniently killed. You see," he explained, "we can never hope to escape as Englishmen."

"I see now."

"Sahib," said Jack's chief man, "what this English officer speak is true. But no time to lose. I will take me two fellows and ride back and bring the dress. Else more Sepoy may come up the main road from Delhi and quickly take away the clothes."

"I can trust you," said Jack; "go."

In less than an hour he was back.

"And now to make up," cried Wood almost merrily. "Lily, you must imagine we are going on the boards of our little theatre at the cantonments. Mind you, Morrison, I and Lily can talk and look like natives, but you must be dumb."

"I can assist the mem-sahib," said Jack's head man. "I can do her hair-dress."

"Alas!" said Lily laughing, "I know what that means, I must have it all cut off. And poor aunt used to admire it so."

Again her eyes filled with tears. The aunt had been murdered.

In a very short time, however, Lily's head-dress was finished, and then she retired into the bush to exchange her own rags for the clothes of a young Sepoy. Luckily they fitted her, then her brother stained her skin and

Jack's with the juice of a nut, and soon the disguises of all were complete and as perfect as could be expected.

That night they slept in the forest, but they did not retire till far on towards morning, for the moon shone very brightly, and they wished to make the best of their way eastwards and south towards the river.

The sun had risen, and all the woods around them were one noisy babel, with the voices of birds and beasts and the sound of insect life.

Not far off was a little brawling burn, and here Lily and her brother performed their ablutions, while Jack went a little farther off.

Washing, however, removed a considerable portion of the stain from their faces, and this had to be replaced. After this they sat down to breakfast, which was a substantial one, for Jack's Sepoys had not lost any of the stores.

It was then that Frank Wood told Jack of many more harrowing scenes that he and his brave young sister had been witnesses to in Delhi and during their flight.

One portion of his sad story he almost whispered, it was concerning a tragedy that had taken place. Poor Mrs. S—— had killed her two children while raving mad, then shot herself with her husband's revolver.

"Ah! lucky for the husband he did not see it," said Frank Wood.

"He was absent then?" said Jack.

"Yes; he was dead. His wife from a window had seen him clubbed and murdered in the street."

No wonder the poor lady had gone mad.

CHAPTER VIII.

JACK AND HIS PARTY FLY TO LUCKNOW—HENRY LAWRENCE.

THIS was indeed a strange flight, but a far more fortunate one than that of most of the other fugitives.

Luckily for Jack and his companions the Sepoys remained faithful and true, else, at any moment, they might have been overpowered and slain.

They travelled as much by night as possible, and gave most of the villages a wide berth.

Sometimes, however, they were compelled to enter a small town or village after cautiously reconnoitring it, to obtain additional supplies of food or water, or even to enquire the way.

In hardly any of these, however, did they find Sepoys. They were mostly carrying on the work of death, destruction, and robbery in the larger towns.

The party cantered dashingly into the villages, and as often as not demanded an interview with the chief man or little rajah! Some of these little rajahs thought themselves individuals of no small importance.

But they did not scare bold Frank Wood nor his sister, and Jack could not help admiring the plucky way in which—in the name of the King of Delhi—Frank demanded food and refreshment, and *didn't* pay for the obligement. The Sepoys, Jack's servants, were all eagerly questioned as to the doings in Delhi, and the young Scotsman was quite astonished at the coolness with which they spun their yarns, graphically describing to the wondering villagers all the glories and splendours of the new court that surrounded the old King of Delhi.

After hearing such stories as these the villagers were proud and pleased to let the jemadar—Frank Wood—have anything he desired, and seemed sorry when the party once more rode on.

Several times, however, Jack had found himself the object of very undesirable scrutiny in some of these villages, and more than once it had been hinted that he was a European in disguise.

The fact is, honest, gentle Jack did not bear himself with the easy grace of a dashing Sepoy, and his eyes were as brightly blue as the sky above him. This was a drawback that nearly ended in a disaster. They had crossed the canal, and had nearly reached the banks of the Ganges, determining now, as their fortune seemed to favour them, to push on to Cawnpore by land instead of venturing on water as Jack had first proposed, and that too by the main trunk road, for they had now become somewhat foolhardy, owing to their success.

It was near sunset. The day had been peculiarly

bright and cool for the season, though clouds lying low on the southern horizon presaged a gathering storm, which soon might burst upon them with a fury that is unknown in more temperate climes.

They had struck the great trunk road that forenoon, and resolved to stick to it if nothing untoward should take place. And now, save for the low singing of some birds in the groves and thickets near to them, there was scarcely a sound to break the silence. Jack was riding by Frank Wood, his sister but a little way behind, and after him came the Sepoy servants. It was getting near halting-time, and as the horses were rather fatigued but little progress was being made.

Jack and Frank were talking too loud for safety's sake, for woods as well as walls have ears.

Suddenly they became aware that a strange horseman was by their side.

Jack and his friend glanced uneasily round, but the newcomer, who had evidently been in the forest, so that they had really met him, saluted Jack with a smile and the words "Salaam Sahib."

The fellow's horse seemed fresh, and he immediately after gave him his head. He trotted on at a fair pace, but as soon as out of sight, at the bend of the road, it was evident from the sound of his feet that the horse had been put to the gallop.

A consultation was hastily held.

It was evident enough that the fellow had suspected that all was not right, perhaps he even knew all the truth. What should they do? To go on meant getting into a trap. That mounted Sepoy was doubtless one of a party, and was reconnoitring. But to go back was worse. So Jack said, for, like most Scotsmen, he considered retrogression somewhat unlucky.

At all events they must take to the forest, and keep well out of sight.

This they now did, and after riding on some distance with great difficulty, for the boughs hung close overhead, they found themselves in a thicket, and here they determined to wait.

The sun went lower and lower down towards the west, and they were beginning to think after all that their alarm had been needless, when suddenly the sound of distant hoofs fell upon their ears.

In a moment, after looking to their arms, every Sepoy sprang to his horse's head, and Jack and his companions, did the same. Their object was to prevent the animals from neighing, for, although completely hidden, they were in dangerous proximity to the road.

Nearer and nearer the galloping horsemen came, and soon were abreast. The horses of Jack's party evinced great restlessness, but soon it was all over, and the danger was past.

Frank now ran out of the bush to look after the squad. They were mutineers without doubt, who had come probably from Cawnpore, and were scouring the country in pursuit of human game, or to stir up allies to their cause. In number they could not have been less than fifty.

"Thank God," said Frank, embracing his sister, "that danger has been averted."

They now boldly took to the road again. This was

risky certainly, but to lie in the forest all night might have been even more so.

There was no more thoughts of halting for a time.

They took the precaution, however, of sending two of their number on ahead, as a kind of vanguard, for safety's sake.

By-and-by these men rode back, and reported lights ahead. It was evidently a village, and they must not pass through it, for if their pursuers rode back after going northwards some distance, it would certainly be at this village they would halt, to enquire if any mounted party had ridden through. To avoid the hamlet, therefore, was their very best chance of putting the mutineers off the scent.

Luckily the woods were open here, and they had no difficulty in making the detour, despite the fact that night had fallen.

On reaching the road once more they rode quite a long distance before they came to another village. And this they swept round just as they had the first.

They now felt comparatively safe, but as no one was very tired, and the moon had now arisen, they still continued to advance.

Soon they came to a branch road, which seemed to lead towards the river, and after some further conversation they determined to trust their fortunes to this.

About a mile along they halted, and resolved to rest for a time, for some of the horses were very fagged indeed, and more than one was lame.

They were really now in flight, however, and the rest could not be a very long one.

In about three hours' time a hand was laid on Jack's shoulder, and he sat up at once.

It would be now about three in the morning, and the moon shone very brightly indeed.

Somewhat to Jack's surprise he found his chief servant standing by his side, his horse's bridle thrown over his arm. The horse was wet in hide.

Jack jumped up.

"You have been riding then?"

"I have been reconnoitring. Have call at one house too. Suppose the sahib have gone he quickly be found out. But I—no."

"And have you got any information, my good fellow?"

"Much. Much. Cawnpore is in the hands of the Sepoy mutineers. Much murder. Much fire. No good go that way."

Jack found out afterwards that was not the truth, for it was not yet the end of May, and it was the first week in June before the Mutiny really broke out in Cawnpore. However in these days the very intentions of the mutineers were magnified into actions fought and won.

"Lucknow still safe," continued this faithful Sepoy. "We go there, Sahib?"

"Well, but there is the river to cross."

"Five miles from here that we can do in boat. One ford you call him."

"No, one ferry."

"One ferry so."

Jack now awoke Frank Wood, and after a hurried conversation it was determined to have some refreshment, then mount at once and make for the ford. They might meet those in their way who would be the reverse of friendly if they found out who they were, but there was less risk of the discovery of their identity if they travelled in the moonlight.

In an hour's time they had reached the ferry, and now they determined to carry matters with a bold and high hand.

Few were awake in the place, but it was a proof of the unsettledness of the times, that they were barely at the village before they were challenged by a sentry, and found themselves confronted by a gate.

"Ho, fellow!" cried Frank in Hindoostani, "open the gate quickly in the name of the King of Delhi!"

The sentry replied by turning out the guard. Frank flourished some papers.

"We are bearers of important dispatches," he cried, "for Oude. Do not detain us, but open the gate quickly."

The officer on guard was taken unawares. He seemed indeed to be but half awake, but he managed to ask some questions as to the state of Delhi.

"The raj of the infidel dogs of English is at an end" was Frank's reply. "Not one remains alive in the city, the king is reinstated on his throne. The dynasty is restored."

At these words the gate flew open as if by magic, and there was no further trouble.

In two hours' time the party were safe across the broad ferry, and cantering on towards Lucknow.

* * * * *

Although the actual conflagration of mutiny first broke out in Meerut, passing thence in one night's time to Delhi, the Sepoys had long before this exhibited a spirit of insubordination in Lucknow.

That fiend incarnate Nana Sahib had passed through the city early in spring. He and his emissaries were doubtless even then sowing the seeds of disaffection in the minds not only of the Sepoys themselves, but of the native princes.

The time had come, the very year of prophecy—the anniversary of Clive's battle of Plassey—and victory was sure and certain. That was the text of their sermons, which, it is needless to say, were not preached in public like the harangues of our anarchists on Tower Hill.

In ancient times, in Scotland, before a raid was to be made on the Lowlanders by the more warlike Highlanders, the fiery cross was carried from glen to glen to call the clans together. In India no actual fiery cross was carried, but Nana Sahib's very presence in the different towns he passed through had been enough to convince the natives that a change was soon to come, and that their deliverance from what they termed the tyranny of the infidel dogs of English was nigh at hand.

At the time that the Sepoys of Lucknow had first shown signs of insubordination, early in April of this year, Lawrence was doing his best to quieten the disaffected at Oude, and was in a great measure successful, though the Sepoys remained sullen.

At Umballah, far in the north, the excitement had been great even in March, and incendiarism rampant;

and it was reported to the Governor that the men of the native regiments had sworn to burn down every bungalow out of revenge for the greased cartridges, and it is said that within three months after the affair at Dum-Dum the Lascar's story had become an article of faith among nearly the whole of the Sepoys in Northern India.

But strangely enough even the Sepoys at this time respected, if they did not actually like, Henry Lawrence, and to the mass of the people he was looked upon as a friend.

HENRY LAWRENCE.

Let me tell you very briefly, reader, a little about this brave man's character. Although, then, he commenced his career as lieutenant in the Bengal Artillery, he was more ambitious to become a civil servant than to stick to the sword and cannon. His talents were recognised, and he soon found employment.

"The happiest years of his life," says Holmes, "were spent in the companionship of a wife whose character must be known and honoured by all who would know and honour his. With her to share his sympathies and his aspirations he laboured on year after year in different districts and at different occupations, but always with a single-minded desire to promote the welfare of the people, among whom his lot was cast, and to do his part towards realising his high ideal of the duties of the imperial race."

Nor, reader, were the people slow to find out that he had "in reality their welfare at heart, and no wish or desire to rule with a rod of iron."

Later on we find him writing thus to Lord Canning:

"I have struck up a friendship with two of the best and wealthiest of the chiefs, and am on good terms with all."

"In his labours," continues Holmes, "as well as in the formation of opinions regarding the problems of Anglo-Indian life, he allowed himself to be guided by sentiment as much as by reason, for his temperament was emotional, imaginative, and actively responsive to poetical influences. But that which gave special character to his benevolent toil was the passionate religious enthusiasm that inspired it. He was continually inflamed with a fervent desire to grow better every day. His religion was the religion of a plain Christian man, knowing nothing of doctrinal subtleties, but solving his simple doubts by a living faith in God. It was in the strength of this faith that he laboured to subdue his roughness of manner, his violent temper, his impatience to incompetent authority, his morbid sensitiveness to real or fancied slights, and trained and chastened almost to saintly perfection the many noble qualities with which his nature had been endowed.

"But no mere enumeration of his virtues would give a just idea of the strength and beauty of his character. To understand it aright the reader must follow him through the toils, the triumphs, and the disappointments of his life. He must picture him as a schoolboy, ever ready to acknowledge his faults, ever ready to stand up for the weak, and to do battle when called upon for the strong. He must accompany him on his surveying expeditions through the jungles, and note the thoroughness with which he does his work. He must watch him trying to bring the blessings of civilisation into the Punjaub, and labouring, not in vain, to inspire that little knot of disciples, who owed everything to him, with his lofty conceptions. He must listen to him pleading the cause of the fallen sirdars with his colleagues at Lahore. He must read his loving letters to his wife and children, and not shut his eyes to his querulous letters to Dalhousie. He must think of him as he knelt with his wife at his bedside, pouring his whole soul in prayer to God on behalf of the brother that had been preferred to him, and the people whose destinies had been removed from his control.

"He must think of him when, a few years later, he had lost the helpmeet of his life, and was nerving himself again by prayer to endure to the end of his pilgrimage. From that moment, although he could not wholly banish the bitterness of disappointed ambition, though he could never wholly banish the sense of desolation, the most glorious epoch of his life began. He was dead to the world now, though he never ceased to work for it. Thus, when we behold him in the last scene of his life, we feel that a Christian hero stands before us. He was only fifty years of age when he came to Lucknow, but he looked an old man, for his face bore the traces of many years of toil beneath an Indian sun, and the still deeper marks of a never-ending conflict with self. . . . Yet the raw Addiscombe cadet was easily recognisable in the matured soldier-statesman. He was still the fearless champion of the oppressed, the stern reprover of evil-doers; but as he got older he was more gentle and more forgiving than he had once been. His humility was such that he would have said of himself, 'O, that I had spent but one day in this world thoroughly well.'"

At a great Durbar given by Lawrence, at which were the native officers and about fifty privates of each regiment. Lawrence made one last appeal to the Sepoys, The officers sat in chairs, the men were grouped behind; and in addressing them, Lawrence, Chief Commissioner then of Oude, tried to speak to them as if from heart to heart.

But, alas! and alas! although they listened to him politely, and although the officers declared they were attached to our Government, it was afterwards found out that they believed that Lawrence had held this Durbar and addressed the Sepoys *because he feared them.*

Indeed, this Durbar, I sincerely believe, and all previous and subsequent appeals to the Sepoys, and all concessions made by us, were construed as evidences of our fear of the natives, and did more harm than good.

* * * * *

And now, while Jack Morrison and his little party are rapidly hurrying on towards Lucknow, afraid for their lives to go to Cawnpore, owing to the news they had heard—news that left them no alternative but to believe that that city was already in the hands of the mutineers, let us take a glance at Lucknow, and see what is going on there.

Martin Gubbins, you must know, was Financial Commissioner in Oude, and a somewhat bold or self-assertive man. But he was undoubtedly clever, and when news of the dreadful massacre and mutiny at Meerut came he foresaw at once that it would have a terrible effect upon Lucknow, and that sooner or later the Residency in that city would have to be defended. He therefore tried, but tried in vain, to get Lawrence to move on troops at once for the support of Lucknow. But Lawrence had to give way at last to a consensus of military opinion.

It was a few days after this that Gubbins telegraphed to the Governor-General, asking for full military power in Oude, and received it. He therefore immediately assumed the title of Brigadier-General and the command of all the troops in the province of Oude.

Now Lucknow was then one of the largest and most important cities in India. The place lay on the south side of the river Goomtee, and, like all very large Indian towns, it consisted of labyrinths of wretched, filthy, narrow streets; but here and there stood spacious, tree-surrounded mansions. The city in its most squalid aspects did not extend all the way to the river, however, but was separated therefrom by innumerable beautiful mosques and palaces. Among these we should remember the Secundra Bagh, the Shah Nujeef, the Chutter Munzil, &c. The names are hard ones, so I shall mention no more. Nor need I, because I give a skeleton map, which will show at a glance what sort of a place Lucknow was, how fortified, and how situated.

The Residency, however, requires a word or two of

description. It was a very noble three-storied structure, with balustrades around its roof. It looked all the more imposing from the fact that it stood on a brae-land that rose gently from the river's banks.

Close to the Residency was an iron bridge, and higher up the stream a stone one.

Kindly bear this in mind, reader, because we shall have fighting at Lucknow before long, and a strange tale to tell.

You will see the canal on the plan (page 316), and see that it joins the river, and is crossed by the Cawnpore road. Note also the military posts on the right side of the canal; the Alum Bagh, for instance, which was really a wall-surrounded garden about two miles from Lucknow on the road to Cawnpore; the Dilkoosha, a palatial building in an open space or park to the south, near the junction of the river and canal; the Charbagh, near the bridge over the canal, and at its junction with the Cawnpore road.

Well, the above is no doubt dry reading; but wait a little, or "bide a wee," as we say in Scotland, and Lucknow will

> "Show another sight,
> When drums beat at the dead of night,
> Commanding fires of death to light
> The darkness of the scenery."

But the great and surpassing beauty of Lucknow, Holmes tells us, was best seen from the roof of the Residency.

"Standing there on a clear summer evening one might have seen the distant chaos of the vast city gradually taking shape in narrow streets and twisting lanes, and nearer still in cupolas, columns, terraced roofs, gilded domes, and slender minarets, which, flooded in the yellow glow, rose in picturesque confusion above the rich foliage of the surrounding groves and gardens; while on the right stood the huge frowning pile of Muchee Bhowun, and behind the Goomtee river, recalling some tranquil English stream, meandered through the fertile plain, and past the bright cornfields, the mango-topés and the scattered hamlets of the Garden of India."

The Residency was badly placed, being surrounded by offices and bungalows instead of ramparts. Again, the only European regiment at first at Lucknow was the 32nd Foot, and that was stationed away to the east of the Residency, fully a mile and a half away, while the native regiments were in the city itself, or quartered on each side of the river. In case of mutiny the Sepoys therefore would have easier work than they had at Delhi.

I have said that Gubbins was clever and self-assertive. I hope this will not give you a wrong impression of his true character.

He was brave and daring, and full of the courage of his own convictions. Too much so, for he urged these to rashness; but he was, on the whole, a kind-hearted man.

Gubbins, seeing that the Mutiny in Lucknow was merely a matter of time, determined to make the Residency his great stronghold, and here he stored guns, ammunition, and all stores that would enable him to stand a siege.

Gubbins advised Lawrence to disarm the Sepoys. Lawrence refused, and in this I cannot help believing that he was wrong.

About the 28th of May our friend Jack Morrison rode safely into Lucknow, and very much surprised were the English to see both him and his disguised friends, Frank and Lily Wood.

CHAPTER IX.

A TRUE-BORN ENGLISHMAN—THE FATE OF CAWNPORE —A MARCH TO DEATH.

WHAT British boy lives who has not heard of that great hero Havelock? He was a man of whom we are all proud—a brave and generous soldier, an unselfish, but heroic commander, a true-born Englishman.

I wish I had space to tell you about his boyhood's days. For the simple reason that the boy is father of the man, I always like to trace my heroes from at least their teens, but here in this story of mine I have so many heroes that I cannot give the biographies of all even in brief.

Havelock, let me tell you, however, went to school at a very early age. He was born, as was also his brother William, at Bishopwearmouth, but his father afterwards migrated to Kent and bought a property there called Ingress Park, near to Dartford. And when only five years old he used to ride to Dartford every day, a distance of three miles, to attend school. From the age of ten till he was seventeen we find him at the Charterhouse, and this he has told many of his friends was the happiest time of his life.

Contemporary with Havelock were many remarkable men, such as the Dean of Durham (George Waddington), George Grote, the historian of Greece; Archdeacon Hale, who became master of the Charterhouse; Sir William Macnaughten, Lord Panmure, and Yates the famous actor.

The poor boy lost his mother when only fourteen, one of the bitterest griefs of his life. Yet had she not lived in vain, for she it had been who first taught the lad to pray, and religion ruled his whole life for good. It is not everyone who can say as Havelock said when dying in a dhooly under the shadow of the palms at Dakoosha Fort, "I have for forty years so ruled my life that when death came I might face it without fear."

All Havelock's three brothers were soldiers; his oldest, named William, was called the fair-haired boy of the Peninsula. He had joined the Light Division there before the terrible fight of the Coa, and distinguished himself afterwards at Waterloo, and he died at last sword in hand at the fierce fight of Ramnuggare.

I really feel at this moment half inclined to let this errant pen of mine follow Havelock through his military career, from his first seven peaceful years of home-life with the gallant 85th, throughout Afghanistan, Gwalior, and the Punjaub, and Persia, till, after the peace with the latter country, we find him most opportunely at Bombay. But this must not be. If, however, the reader desires to know all about Havelock which his memory can retain, let him read his life by my brave bright countryman, Archibald Forbes.

Even before the war with Persia was a thing of the past, ugly rumours were rife about the coming Mutiny.

Havelock then arrived in Bombay on the 29th of May, and there to his sorrow and astonishment got the news that the native regiments had mutinied, not only at Meerut and Delhi, but Ferozepore, and that disaffection was rapidly spreading over the Punjaub.

He started from Bombay on the first of June in the steamer *Erin*, two regiments of ours just back from Persia not even being allowed to land, but hurried on to Calcutta. The *Erin* however was wrecked at Caltura, and Havelock narrowly escaped with his life. He reached Madras safely, and went on soon after in the *Fire Queen* to Calcutta. He went there in company with Sir Patrick Grant, and was by him introduced to Lord Canning, the Governor of India. Grant knew Havelock well, and knew what he could do. Had they not fought together side by side at Maharajpore and Mudkee?

His Excellency at once commissioned Havelock to probably one of the hardest tasks it has ever fallen to the lot of man to undertake.

For by this time, June 17th, the Mutiny had extended with fearful rapidity. Nowhere 'twixt Allahabad and Agra, where our friends Mr. Mayne, his wife, and children were, was the authority of Great Britain recognised. At Lucknow Sir Henry Lawrence was surrounded by hordes of savage mutineers, while Cawnpore was in a far worse plight.

And it is to Cawnpore, while Havelock is making his speedy preparations to start up country, that we must now for a brief space direct the reader's attention.

THE FATE OF CAWNPORE.

No more sad or terrible story than that of Cawnpore was it ever the lot of historian to tell. Yet it cannot be avoided. All should know it. It is a blood-stain in the story of India under British rule that time can never efface. But all I *can* do to mitigate horrors in relating it I *shall* do. Indeed were there naught save horrors to speak of, I should dismiss the description with very few words; but there was heroism as well as horror, heroism not only displayed by men and soldiers, but by gentle ladies also, that makes us feel proud of our countrywomen, while we drop a tear for the fate that befell them.

A glance at the map, reader, will show you the position of Cawnpore, and you will have no difficulty in understanding that it was a place of very great importance from a military point of view. It was also the place near which Nana Sahib, the arch-fiend of the mutiny, had his estates and home.

Says Holmes, "In the spring of 1857 the British residents of Cawnpore were leading the ordinary life of an Anglo-Indian community. Morning rides, work in cutcherry" (the Courts of Justice), "or on parade, novel reading, racquets, dinners, and balls filled up the time.

"Pretty women laughed and flirted as they listened to the band in the cool of the evening, and talked perhaps of the delightful balls that the Nana had given at his palace up the river, before he had started on that inexplicable tour of his. Suddenly the news of the great disasters at Meerut and Delhi arrived, and the life of the little society was violently wrenched into a new channel."

Now Cawnpore was at this time the headquarters of a whole division of the army, namely, the 2nd Cavalry, Sepoys, and the 1st, 56th, and 53rd Sepoy Infantry.

No British troops? You may well ask that question. No, only about sixty artillerymen and a few invalids, but there was a very large number of civilian residents.

The native part of the town was not unlike that of Lucknow, and there was a sandy plain around it, then going south-east you came to the canal, beyond this were the lines or barracks of the infantry and cavalry, then farther on theatres, assembly rooms, and the church with its white tower raised above a grove of waving palms. Between the river and town were the cantonments. These were simply a long row of houses built of brick, with a compound around each, the whole surrounded by a very insecure-looking mound and a ditch. Near to one end of this stood the magazine, the treasury, and gaol.

When the dreadful news from Delhi reached Cawnpore Sir Hugh Wheeler, though probably not expecting a revolt of his troops, bestirred himself to furbish up a kind of defence-work within the cantonments. He chose the old Dragoon Barracks, from some inexplicable reason or other, and no more makeshift fortification was surely ever built. The walls of this single-storied house were hardly even bullet-proof, and it was *thatched with straw!*

Sir Hugh made no real batteries, merely surrounding the place with a mud wall about five feet high, in the gaps or embrasures of which his gunners would be exposed to an enemy's fire.

Had he been wise, surely it was the magazine itself

he ought to have chosen for a stronghold. It was strong and roomy, and protected on one side by the river.

The only excuse made, or that could have been made, for not taking possession of this place was that it was in the charge of Sepoys, whom to have turned out might have precipitated the Mutiny.

However, the makeshift entrenchment was ready at last, and even provisioned, but only after a fashion, for the duty had been left to natives, and flour and peas were about the only solids sent in.

Thither the women and children and the non-combatants were taken, and then commenced the agony of waiting and suspense. Sir Hugh had telegraphed to Lawrence before this, and he had sent him a few men—about fifty—as well as half a battery of guns. Knowing what we now know of the fiend and murderer Nana Sahib, we cannot help wondering that Sir Hugh Wheeler should have sent to him for assistance, asking him to take charge of the treasury. We cannot blame Wheeler altogether for this, however, when we remember that he and Nana had been on friendly terms so long. Had they not walked and talked together, smoked and had wine together, and spent evenings at the same billiard table? Had Nana not dined at his mess, and given balls and parties in honour of the ladies and gentlemen of the garrison? To suspect him seemed to Wheeler to be not only wrong, but decidedly cruel. In fact, he had thought at one time that it might be well to place the women and children under the protection of this Nana Sahib.

The Nana courteously came in with his Sepoys and took charge of the treasury. Very kind of him indeed.

The time wore on, and the anxiety was extreme. The men kept up their hearts, and those of the ladies and children as well as possible, and not one of the officers showed a symptom of fear. Yet each day, as they went off to do duty in the lines, their wives took farewell of them with a tearful affection that showed they hardly expected ever to see them more.

Then came the outbreak of the awful storm. The Government treasure which the Nana had so graciously and willingly taken charge of was at a suburb called Newabgunj, and thither on the eventful evening of the 4th of June galloped the mutinous Cavalry. The 1st Infantry went off next, and together they broke into and rifled the treasury, and, behaving like demons, smashed open the gaols and let loose the prisoners therefrom, destroyed public buildings, and took possession of the magazine.

Even yet Wheeler and his entrenched people hoped on. After satisfying themselves with plunder Sir Hugh felt sure, he said, that the mutineers would march on towards Delhi.

Alas! this hope was doomed to bitterest disappointment; for on the morning of the 6th Wheeler received a letter from the Nana, couched in punctilious terms, declaring his intention of attacking him speedily.

This letter had been received very early, and at sunrise this rebel army was within sight and sound.

We in our peaceful homes to-day; you, reader, sitting quietly with this book in your hand; can form no conception of the terror, the dread and agony, that now existed within those fragile defences.

The news ran throughout the cantonment with the speed of wildfire, and all were ordered to come at once into the entrenchment. What a dread awakening for those who still slept, for the mother with her baby at her breast, for the father who saw in the immediate future only death in its worst form for himself and family! There was no time even to cook or eat breakfast if indeed anyone could have desired it. All were ordered to their several posts, and the women, children, and sickly retired to the hospital, or crouched under the verandahs.

And of how many did this little band consist, think you, reader? Why, they numbered barely a thousand altogether, and of these about four hundred were women and children.

Prayers? Yes, they went to prayers, and probably never before did worship take place under such painful and agonising circumstances.

If these prayers were not eventually heard, if those weeping men and wailing women knelt in vain around their pastor, we must not question either the justice or the love of our Father. God moves in a mysterious way, and here in this world of sin and sorrow we see but dimly as in a glass.

Hardly had the clergyman ceased to pray ere the yelling of the advancing Sepoys could be heard, and looking up the frightened women and men beheld rolling clouds of smoke, through which tongues of fire leapt up, and showers of sparks. And yet the Sepoys came not.

It was indeed ten o'clock before the rattle of musketry

was heard, and round shot began to crash through the frail entrenchment amidst the shrieks of the women and children, the sound of the bugle, or rattle of the drum, and the quick, sharp words of command as the officers and men fell in.

The battle and the strife and terror had commenced, and by the afternoon of that day "the devilry," as Archibald Forbes puts it, "was in full swing," and from that time till the bitter end it never ceased either by day or by night.

No better description of this awful siege methinks was ever given than that by Holmes, and the authorities he in turn quotes in support of every sentence he writes are the best that can be appealed to. I quote a few lines here and there, and leave the reader himself, if gifted with imagination, to fill in the awful blanks, or read between the lines.

"Soldiers, civilians, and loyal Sepoys"—about twenty —"stood side by side replying as well as they could to the crushing fire of Nana's batteries, the infantry—each man with a pile of loaded muskets before him—astonishing the rebels by the swiftness and accuracy of their fire.

"Day and night all fought on alike. There was no rest for any except those to whom the sleep of death was vouchsafed, or if a man sank down exhausted under the heel of his gun, he was soon awakened from dreams of home, or coming relief, to a life-in-death within the entrenchment of Cawnpore."

In a week's time all the fifty-nine artillerymen were either killed or wounded.

Women as well as men fell victims to the enemy's fire.

A private was walking with his wife, when a single bullet killed both.

"Young Godfrey Wheeler, a son of the General, was lying wounded in one of the barracks, when a round shot crashed through the walls of the room and tore off his head in the presence of his mother and sisters.

"Little children straggling outside the wall were deliberately shot down.

"But the acutest sufferings were patiently and by some even cheerfully endured."

On June 11th a red-hot shot set fire to a barracks within which the women and children, the sick and the wounded were lying.

What a scene! Think of it, reader, just for a moment.

"The fire illuminating the darkness of the night; the helpless sufferers within the burning building mingling their shrieks for help with the ceaseless boom of the artillery and the swift, continuous roar of the flames; the soldiers running from their posts, and though girt about by two deadly perils—on one side the infernal fire from the enemy's batteries, on the other the downward crash of glowing masses of masonry and burning rafters—yet striving to extinguish the flames, and rescuing their friends from an agonizing death; while outside the unrelenting rebels, taking full advantage of the distraction of the garrison, worked their guns with feverish energy, as though they hoped, with the aid of the conflagration, at one stroke to complete the ruin of their victims.

"On the 12th an unsuccessful attempt was made by the mutineers to storm the position. The stern resistance, however, they received drove them back to their guns.

"The firing became as incessant as ever; and while round shot plunged and bounded over the open ground, hurled down masses of timber from the remaining barrack, and sent bricks flying in all directions, bullets pattered like hail against the walls, and broke the windows to atoms."

Starvation now was added to the other sufferings of the besieged. No wonder therefore that while the enemy was constantly being reinforced the numbers of the besieged were daily getting less and less, that some fell victims to sunstroke or died of thirst, and that some went mad.

There was but one well in the entrenchment; yet, though to reach it our noble fellows had to expose themselves to the fire of the enemy, they did not hesitate, urged on by the pitiful plight of the women and the wailing of sick and dying children.

The barracks being destroyed, there was no shelter now even for the women.

In this terribly trying time the behaviour of Captain Moore of the 32nd, one of the chief heroes of Cawnpore, deserves special mention. His cheerful demeanour and gallant example urged on the men to work, and his tender sympathy gave a ray of hope and comfort to the poor women, even in their direst and darkest hours of distress.

As to the women themselves, Forbes may well say that "a great lump rises in the throat as one bethinks him of their pathetic constancy and their awful sufferings; of British ladies going barefooted, after giving up their stockings to form cases for grape-shot, going unshod, unkempt, ragged and squalid, haggard and emaciated, parched with thirst and faint with hunger, sitting waiting to hear that they were widows."

Still more dreadful is it, dear reader, to think that at this terrible time babies were born!

There, I cannot go further! Let the end now come and speedily, terrible end though it be.

* * * * *

At sunset then, on the morning of June the 27th, after a false treaty had been signed by Nana Sahib, in which he promised the remains of the luckless garrison safe transport in boats down the river, the exodus from the wretched blood-stained entrenchment was commenced.

How sad they looked, for even the men had dire forebodings of what was to follow! How worn and wan, how wretched and ragged! So woe-begone a procession surely never before was seen. The wounded were borne along in palkees, the women on elephants or in waggons, the fighting men were on foot, many so weak that they but stumbied along leaning on the arms of sturdy mess-mates. Truly a mournful sight.

And whither were they going?

Would Nana Sahib fulfil his promise, and send these poor creatures down stream in safety?

Verily, no. It was but little over a mile they had to go from their entrenchment to the place where the boats were supposed to be waiting them. But their slow progress is really and truly

A MARCH TO DEATH.

CHAPTER X.

THE MASSACRE BY THE GHAUT—THE BOAT THAT DRIFTED AWAY—THE LAST SAD SCENE OF ALL.

I WOULD gladly draw a veil over the rest of the sad tale of Cawnpore, but the historian should not flinch from his duty, even if it be at times disagreeable and heartrending.

Wearily the poor people marched on and on till, coming to a bridge, they turned aside and threaded their way through a narrow glen, and presently came in sight of the Ganges.

Yes, there were the rude boats with their awnings of thatch that were to convey them down the river, and hope began now to beat in every heart.

Did it appear strange to any of them, we wonder, that there were over a thousand armed Sepoys by the Ganges to see them embark, or that squadrons of Cavalry were posted near the banks and under cover? Or that a host of unarmed natives, male and female, young and old, had come to witness the——tragedy?

Yes, horrible as it may appear, it was a wholesale

massacre of the little garrison that Nana Sahib had designed and ordered, and that his vile and fiendish general, Tantia Topee, had come to carry out. That mob of budmashes and gaol-birds were to see a scene such as they never before had beheld, and which, I trust, for the honour of poor humanity, turned many of them sick with horror.

The embarkation begins.

Now a bugle rings out in the morning air, and almost immediately after the Sepoys bring their arms to the shoulder and fire.

While a rain of bullets patters with dull, suggestive thuds in the midst of that helpless crowd, cannons add their deafening roar to the wild screaming of women and children, and grapeshot rakes the boats from stem to stern.

A few moments after this the thatched awnings of those boats take fire, falling in burning masses among the sick and the wounded, suffocating them to death or burning them alive.

Strong men leap overboard, only to be shot or cut down. Poor ladies, anxious only to save their children, crouch under the boats or flounder in the river—insane for the time being, hardly knowing what they are doing or whither they are rushing—while the Nana's fierce, relentless troops tear even the babies from their arms and rend them in pieces, and cut down the mothers with sabre or tulwar.

I let the curtain fall on the first part of this fearful massacre. It falls as word comes to cease for a time the slaughter.

And now the survivors, about one hundred and twenty-five in all—the large majority women and children, the remains of their tattered clothes in many instances torn almost completely from their backs, all bedraggled with mud and blood, many frightfully wounded—were driven like a flock of sheep back to prison in blood-stained Cawnpore.

The Boat that Floated Away.

The story of the boat that amidst the rain of bullets, the massacre and general confusion, pushed off into the stream and went floating down the Ganges, is to me as sad as any connected with the siege and massacre of Cawnpore.

These poor wretches became the target of Sepoys that ran along the banks, firing at them long after they had floated out and away beyond reach of the guns. They had neither oars nor sails nor rudder, and no food.

"The only thing that passed their lips," says Mowbray Thompson, "except prayers and shrieks and groans, was the water of the Ganges, for which, in their dying distress, the poor wounded and sick kept constantly crying."

What a day that was! Would it never, never come to an end? Would the sun never set, and the darkness afford them shelter and a little surcease from pain and danger? Again and again during the day and the night that followed they ran aground on sand banks. Day broke at last. It was the morning of the 28th of June. For a time there seemed no pursuit, but the boat grounded, and the Sepoys appeared in the after-

"The boat, that amidst the rain of bullets, went floating down the Ganges." *p.* 222.

noon. Five more were killed or wounded. Then, just before sunset, they saw a boat filled with armed Sepoys bearing down to attack them.

This boat also went aground, and now our poor war-worn men had one sweet morsel of revenge, for twenty of them left their own boat and attacked the Sepoys, killing them to a man. All this afternoon it had rained in torrents, and at night the wind increased to almost hurricane force, and the boat floated once more.

Then another day dawned, and to their horror the unhappy people on board of that boat found it was drifting in towards the bank, and that there quite a small army of natives were drawn up to receive them. What now should they do? Nothing but meet death as bravely as Britons ever do. There were still two officers, eleven men, and a sergeant unwounded. The officers were brave Delafosse and Mowbray Thompson, and all were burning for revenge.

> "When can men die better,
> Than in facing fearful odds."

Poor Major Vibart of the 2nd Cavalry was alive also, but too grievously wounded to lead this forlorn hope.

The gallant little party, to the astonishment of the natives, leapt with a wild cheer on shore, and, relieved of their weight, the boat drifted away. The soldiers and their officers fought their way right through the midst of the dastardly foe, dealing death and gaping wounds at every blow.

They were forced of course to fly at last, and found a

temporary shelter in a Hindoo temple. Around this the enemy swarmed and tried to fire the place, and finally to blow it up with gunpowder.

Nothing remained but to make a dash for the river. The thirteen sprang out therefore, swords and bayonets in hand, and fought their way once more through the murderers.

But six of their number fell before the rest reached the bank and plunged into the river, after throwing in their arms.

The yelling savages ran down the banks firing at them. The bullets struck and killed two, a third, unable to swim far landed and gave himself up, only to be clubbed to death at once; but the rest—four only, mind you—seemed to bear charmed lives, for although the shot splashed in the water ahead and astern and all about them they still kept on, and after a six miles' swim found shelter and safety in the house of a chief who was friendly to our Government. The saved, each of whom deserves a line to himself, were

Mowbray Thompson.

Delafosse.

Private Murphy.

Private Sullivan.

But what about the drifting boat? Ah, yes, that was indeed sad!

It was captured, and the whole of the eighty poor creatures in it, mostly women and children, were brought back to Cawnpore.

Surely they must have thought the bitterness of death was past. Alas! no. The men were torn from the shrieking wives and women who fain would have shared their fate, and shot.

Says a native who witnessed the return of these unhappy fugitives: "When they landed on the blood-stained ghaut I counted sixty sahibs, twenty-five mem-sahibs, and four children. The Nana said 'Take away the mem-sahibs from the sahibs, then kill the sahibs. Let the first Bengal Native Cavalry do the shooting.' Then cried one mem-sahib, 'Oh, I will not leave my husband, I will die with my husband! Shoot me too for pity's sake!'

"So she ran and sat down beside her husband, clasping him round the waist. Directly she said and did this the other mem-sahibs all screamed, 'We too will die with our husbands,' and they all sat down each by her husband. The husbands themselves cry 'Go back, go back!' but they would not. Whereupon the Nana gave orders to the soldiers, and they went up and tore them shrieking away by main force. Yes, it was terrible!"

So ends, dear reader, the tragical story of the boat that floated away.

* * * * *

The Last Sad Scene of All.

I shall not dwell long on this scene, reader, I can assure you. If it shocks you to read it, remember as you do so, that as I wrote it my eyes were wet with tears.

The twenty-five mem-sahibs then, and the four poor children, were confined along with the others at Savada House. And there they were left for a time.

Now you must know, reader, that while these awful tragedies were taking place at Cawnpore, others but little less terrible were happening elsewhere. For instance, the general mutiny at Lucknow, of which I have yet to speak, and which took place on the 30th day of May

But meanwhile both towards Cawnpore and Lucknow and Delhi relief armies were marching. Havelock was on the way. Indeed, as we shall presently see, this brave and excellent general was but one day distant when the last sad scene of the Cawnpore tragedy was being enacted.

After the massacre at the boats Nana Sahib returned to his estates and palace at Bithoor, and immediately caused himself to be proclaimed Peishwa. He looked upon himself indeed as a mighty conqueror, and upon the murder of the garrison as a great victory and a triumph for his arms.

This arch-fiend, the Nana Sahib, seated upon his throne, was installed as Peishwa with more than regal pomp and ceremony. The sacrament of marking the forehead was duly performed amidst the shouts and acclamations of his assembled warriors and people, and when darkness fell the whole city was *en gala.* Great bonfires blazed, dazzling fireworks filled the air, horns and trumpets brayed, and drums were beat, while all night long the yelling and eldritch screaming of the savages rent the air.

Ah! little cared the poor British prisoners now that guns should be fired, and hardly did they ask each other what the meaning of the firing might be. Their best and their dearest had been ruthlessly butchered before their eyes; all they longed for now was rest in death. Not rest in the grave, mind you. Nay, a grave even would be denied them, as it had been to their husbands. Their bodies might be left for the wild dogs to eat, or tossed into the river as food for eels and alligators.

They were to be made slaves of. Was that their doom? They believed so at first, for amidst the hooting, the laughing and jeering of brutal men, they were moved from the Savada House to the "Beebeeghur."

The Beebeeghur—it is an ugly name, and has an ugly meaning—was a small house, some say a hovel, down by the river, with scarcely room in it for a small family, and here they were penned like sheep awaiting the slaughter.

Major Gordon of the 61st Regiment describes the Beebeeghur as follows:

"It was a dismal kind of bungalow, in a small compound near what used to be the assembly rooms. There was a narrow verandah running along nearly the whole of the front. At the two ends of it were bathing-rooms, opening both into the verandah and into the side-rooms. Then came an inner entrance room, and then one about sixteen by sixteen, and then another open verandah as in front. It was, in fact, two small houses built on exactly the same plan facing each other, and having a space enclosed between them."

This place was under the very shadow of Nana Sahib's palace, the place at which every night he now held revels, rejoicings, and debaucheries.

And out from this crampy, crowded bungalow every day a few of those tender English ladies, who but a few weeks before were walking happy and free in their own gardens or around the cantonments, were dragged to grind corn for the Nana's household.

This is considered in Eastern countries the crowning degradation of the conquered, and has been so considered for thousands of years. (*Vide* Isaiah xlvii.)

Of these wretched, starved, and terror-stricken women and children, suffering the agonies of thirst and heat and semi-suffocation, Gordon tells us that from the 7th of July till the fatal and horrible morning of the 15th twenty-eight died. Some, it is said, put an end to their existence in fits of frenzy. Nor can we wonder. Nine of these succumbed to cholera, three to dysentery and diarrhœa, three sunk from their unattended wounds, the others—somehow. But one was a baby only two days old. Think of it, reader!

How long the accursed Nana might have kept the poor prisoners alive, or what he might have done with them eventually, may never be known. For news came of the advance of Havelock, and the Peishwa gave orders for the massacre. Nana might have given the fatal order in a paroxysm of rage and hatred of the whole Christian race, or because he feared the revenge that Havelock would seek for the murders he had already committed, and thought he would best consult his interest by leaving none alive who could tell the tale.

It matters not. The fiat went forth. The awful deed was done.

There were among the prisoners five or six men. These were first dragged forth and butchered in the presence of the Nana himself.

After this terrible commencement parties of Sepoys

were told off to fire through the doorways and windows, of the rooms, upon the women and children.

But it seemed as if such a task was even too sickening for Sepoys to commit; most of whom we are told fired at the ceilings, so the dreadful work proceeded far too slowly to please the Nana.

He was angry and worried that morning at the news he had heard, and would not feel happy till his prisoners were all dead. Besides there were the fearful cries proceeding from the Beebeeghur Bungalow, the shrieking of the infants, the prayers, the entreaties, and pleadings for mercy of the ladies, and all these annoyed his highness.

So—O horrible!—several great gaunt and strong butchers were sent for from the bazaars. The firing ceased now, and to some extent the cries. Then the butchers threw off their garments, and strode into the rooms armed with long knives and swords. . . . .

Long after the shrieking ceased and the butchers, dripping now with gore, came forth from the accomplishment of their awful task, groans were heard issuing from the Bungalow.

I shall not enter into further details. To describe a deed like this in graphic language seems almost a sin.

All night long the bodies lay in the awful rooms unburied, to be dragged forth next day—some young children still alive—and cast into a well.

An Indian well, reader, is a mere reservoir about say twenty feet in diameter and fifteen deep.

Into this cemetery, there were thrown the hacked and

maimed corpses of over two hundred British women and children.

Did not such a crime as this cry aloud for vengenace?

Can we wonder that the very name of Cawnpore became afterwards a battle-cry among our brave soldiers, and spurred them on to deeds of what might be called the very fury of heroism.

Or can we wonder that the Indian Mutiny now became a very war to the death, or that scant mercy was dealt out to prisoners, or even to the wounded in the field after a battle?

Even in this hour of his ghastly triumph Nana's black heart seemed to turn faint, and if he succeeded in deceiving others he could not himself believe what he preached, that the British rule in India was crushed for ever, that the British sun had set by the blood-stained walls of Beebeeghur.

BOOK III.

Gentle Peace Returning.

"When wild war's deadly blast was blawn,
And gentle peace returning,
Wi' mony a sweet babe fatherless,
And mony a widow mourning."

BURNS.

Book III.

CHAPTER I.

THE ANNIVERSARY OF ALMA.

AUTUMN had spread her crimson mantle over the hills and braes around Glen Tulloch. The heather had been in bloom for weeks, but at early morning and all day long the sound of the sportsman's gun was still to be heard on the hills, though the grouse were now getting wild, the glorious twelfth being long since past.

Colonel Lindsay, albeit he was "slightly lame in one leg"—it was in this way he himself would sometimes allude to his sad loss, and laugh as he did so—was most enthusiastic where gunning was concerned. He was never tired of tramping over the moors or over the mountains, the two lairds, Morrison and Saunders, being sometimes his companions. Sometimes only, however; they had less leisure than the good old soldier, and had led less of a life in the wilds.

But one day the trio were coming homewards over the hills, and had just reached a spot whence far beneath them the bonnie glen spread out in all its sylvan beauty, the stream winding down through the green maze of meadows in its midst like a curling silver thread.

They had made good bags to-day, and in the good old fashion they carried them too. Never a ghillie nor keeper had they. They loaded their own guns and followed their dogs. For such an innovation as beating would have been considered something akin to sacrilege among these grand old hills.

"Well, Lindsay," said Morrison, sitting down on a green bank, a kind of oasis in the midst of the blooming heather, "I don't know what you may be, but I'm tired. Getting old, I suppose."

"Nonsense," said Laird Saunders, "neither of us is very old yet, and it seems to me that Lindsay here will never get old. Why how he does walk, to be sure!"

Colonel Lindsay laughed, and threw himself on the grass beside his bulky bag.

"Well, friends, I have been tired in my time. This is the 20th of September you know. And it was on the 20th of September the glorious battle of Alma was fought. That was the finest day's shooting ever I can remember."

"You were tired that day?" said Saunders.

"I was tired after the fun was all over. There were a good many more men there who were more tired than I, and there were some headaches next morning, I can assure you, especially on the Russian side. Ah! war is a fearful thing. We talk of honour and glory. Well, when a younger man, I believed in such things. Neither honour nor glory, however, is very tangible. I don't think, on looking back to my career in the army, that I would exchange such a day as we have just spent for even the glorious 20th itself. Look at that sunset, men, is it not beautiful beyond compare?"

It was indeed beautiful, though only one-half the setting sun was visible; but this was glaring red through a rift in a bank of grey-blue clouds, that lay along the western horizon like a most fantastic pile of rock-work. This bank of cloud was fringed, as to its upper edge, with gold. Above it, in a sea-green sky, inclining to saffron, floated little streaks of crimson cirrhus. Then higher still another rolling cloud-bank all purple and bronze; and above all, the clear pale-blue sky, in which by-and-by the stars would shine.

"Yes," said Saunders, speaking slowly and thoughtfully, "it is a bonnie, bonnie sky, but ——"

"Now let me finish the sentence for you," said Lindsay, interrupting him. "'But,' you were going to say, 'I should like to know what my poor boy is doing at this present moment.'"

"And I was thinking of my dear lad too," said Morrison. "Surely it is time I was hearing from him once again. His last letter was such a delightful one. He was journeying on to Delhi, borne along by faithful Lascars, as he called them, with faithful Sepoys riding by his side; the scenery all around him, more beautiful, he says, than any dream. But, oh, Lindsay, Lindsay, since then Delhi has been drenched with British blood —— and ——"

"And you fear your boy is among the slain. That's it, isn't it?"

"You read me like a book."

"Well, let me tell you, Morrison, and you too, Saunders, that I am not going to listen to any Jeremiads—not on the anniversary of Alma, anyhow! All is well that ends well."

"Heigho!" sighed Morrison, "but the end hasn't come yet."

"No, the end hasn't come yet; but the end will come soon and sudden to thousands of those murdering mutineers. I'm no seer, like your friend Fey Fraser; but I feel confident that both your boys are safe, and I think I can almost tell what they are doing at this moment."

"Tell us, Lindsay! tell us!"

Colonel Lindsay lay back on the grass and shut his eyes. He was silent for a short time, then spoke.

"Your boy, Saunders, is marching up country with his regiment. There is nothing can stand against those brave kilted warriors. I can see your Willie charging the Sepoys in line, with stern, set face and flashing eye. More than one fall before him. But the battle is won, and he is waving his Highland bonnet above a great gun he has just helped to capture. Willie is safe and sound."

"And what about my lad Jack?"

"Why, Laird Morrison, from a civilian your Jack has changed to a soldier. He is in command of a company, and right bravely do they fight wherever mutineers dare show face."

The Colonel half rose now.

"You think I'm talking nonsense, don't you? Well, call it so if you like, but I believe my words will come true. There is nothing we can do to help our boys—for they are mine, my friends, as well as yours; that is how I feel—but I was going to say there is nothing we can do to help our boys but pray for them. Men, I have never yet prayed earnestly for anything in this world without receiving an answer in peace."

"You give us hope and comfort," said Saunders.

"I'm glad I do. We three are all as one, you know, though, my dear Saunders, I greatly rue the sad misunderstanding that sent your poor boy a-soldiering."

"What was to be would be," said Saunders sadly.

"But we," said Lindsay, "must not question it. It doubtless is all for the best; and if poor Annie, my daughter, but lives all may yet be well."

The Colonel's words bore reference to an illness that Annie Lindsay had gone though, if indeed she could be considered even yet out of danger. The doctor had recommended foreign travel, and she and her father had spent the winter, the spring, and a considerable portion of the summer, in wandering from place to place on the Continent.

Then she had expressed a wish to come home. Annie said she was coming home to die, but, contrary to all expections, the girl had greatly improved in health since she returned to the glen.

I may mention here that there was the most perfect understanding between Annie and her father, and she kept no secrets from him any more than she did from her mother.

Did a long letter she had received from Jack Morrison, I wonder, have anything to do with her partial restoration to "health"?

I think it did, for in this letter Jack had told Annie all he had told Willie in his letter to him, and a good deal more too. If Annie had read that letter over once she had read it over a dozen times.

But she was now in daily expectation of receiving a letter from Willie himself.

It had almost broken the girl's heart to think she had driven him from home, and that he had gone away with hard and unkindly thoughts of her.

And now hope had arisen in Annie's heart.

Well, hope tells many a flattering tale, but, nevertheless, in a case like Annie Lindsay's, hope is a far more effective medicine than any that a doctor can prescribe or administer.

In cases like poor Annie's then Shakespeare was quite right to say:

> "Throw physic to the dogs; I'll none of it."

Of course the dogs would have none of it either, so it would have to lie there.

But when Macbeth says to the doctor:

> "Can'st thou not minister to a mind diseased,
> Pluck from the memory a rooted sorrow,
> Raze out the written troubles of the brain?"

and so on, and so forth, and the doctor replies:

> "Therein the patient
> Must minister to himself,"

he makes a far wiser reply than if he had said, "Oh, yes, certainly I can; a little cod liver oil and a seidlitz powder will just meet the requirements of the case."

* * * * *

There was what the Colonel called a quiet little dinner-party at the Lodge that evening, to celebrate the anniversary of that ever-to-be-remembered battle of the Gael—Alma.

The Colonel himself was in the best of spirits, and talked so hopefully, and was apparently so full of happiness, that everyone around the table, including the mothers of Jack and Willie, were constrained to be happy also; and Annie herself was almost gay.

"As we are all by ourselves to-night," he said, "quite *entre nous*, I insist upon you ladies staying to talk with us over the walnuts and the wine, in the good old fashion."

"I am willing," said Mrs. Saunders, with a pleasant smile.

"And I too," said Mrs. Morrison.

"Well," continued the Colonel, laughing, "I'll see that my wife and Annie don't get away. Consider yourselves all under martial law to-night, ladies.

"And now I have a toast to propose, which even my little girl will not refuse to respond to, if it should only be in water. On this day of days I propose the health and happiness of the hero who led the clans to victory on the heights of Alma—the brave old Colin Campbell.

"Yes, Mrs. Saunders, I am glad to see that bright

sparkle in your eye. We all love Colin. He was my general. He is by this time your son's."

"Poor, brave fellow," said Mrs. Saunders, and I think that the sparkle in her eye was the sparkle of a tear; "but don't you think, General Lindsay——"

"Oh, bravo!" cried Lindsay, interrupting her, "I've got promotion. General Lindsay sounds delightful."

"I meant to say 'Colonel,' I assure you, sir; but I was thinking so much about Sir Colin. Don't you think, my dear Colonel, that he is a little too old for the terrible work he will have out in India?"

"Oh, bless you, no, madam! The brave are never old. Don't judge by me, you know, because I have already got one foot in the grave."

"Ah, true," said Morrison, "but judging from your exploits to-day in the hills, Lindsay, you know how to hold on with the other one."

"Dear old Sir Colin," Saunders put in. "Farewell to his hopes of settling down as a country gentleman, planting kail and keeping pigeons. I wonder if it be true that when the Queen herself asked him to go out to India he burst into tears, and said, 'I'd carry a musket for a lady like you'?"

"I daresay it is true. Sir Colin was nothing if not gallant. But, like that of every real Scotsman, his love and loyalty for Queen Victoria are sincere. Well, as you say, Saunders, it will be a year or two yet before the hero of the Alma can settle down, and plant kail and keep pigeons. But he's coming back safe and sound, and, Saunders, he is going to bring our poor soldier-boy with him."

Though very cheerful, Annie Lindsay had spoken little, but this last sentence of her father's appeared to get straight away to her heart. She gave one appealing glance to her mother, and hurriedly left the table. Annie had gone no farther than the drawing-room, and Mrs. Lindsay found her on the sofa in a paroxysm of tears.

"Hush! darling; hush!" said her mother, patting and soothing her as if she had been a baby. "Don't cry, Annie; don't cry."

"Just a little, mother; just a little," the girl sobbed "because they are tears of hope and joy."

But when, some time after this, the gentlemen joined the ladies in the drawing-room they found Annie seated at the piano as if she never had been crying at all.

And a very pleasant and happy evening was spent.

When Annie knelt beside her bed that night, with hands clasped and tearful eyes upturned to heaven, very sincere, very heartfelt, was her prayer that God, who rules on earth and sea, would send Sir Colin safely home, and quickly give our arms the victory.

Did she pray for anyone else? Not by name, but Heaven can read hearts, and in thoughts we can pray quite as earnestly as in words.

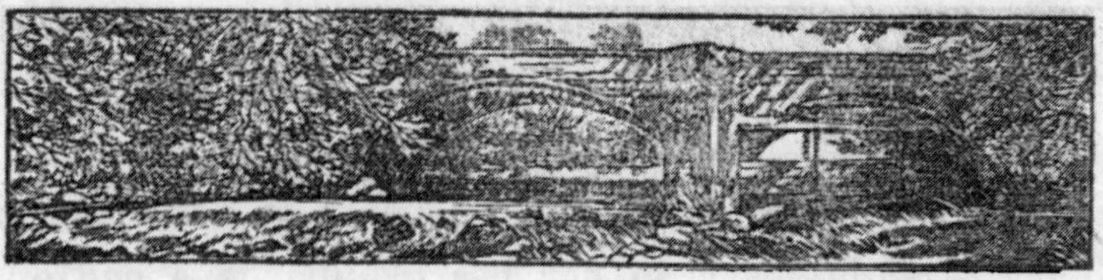

CHAPTER II.

HAVELOCK AND NEILL.

IT was the 30th of June before Havelock reached Allahabad, though he certainly had made no delay on the road. A glance at the map, reader mine, will show you the position of this important town. It stood on the Doab and near to the junction of the Jumna with the Ganges. Its great fort was a strong one, and one well-stored with the munitions of war, but nevertheless at the commencement of the Mutiny, like many other important places in India, it was not garrisoned by a single European soldier, and as it contained a large number of English residents, it is little wonder that they felt uneasy, not knowing what a day or an hour might bring forth.

There was one regiment of Sepoys here, however, that was much beloved by its officers and greatly trusted by all, namely the 6th Native Infantry. And indeed so demonstrative in their loyalty were they that they had volunteered to be led against Delhi.

There was no trust however to be put in Sepoys by civilians, and nothing that the officers of the 6th could do was sufficient to allay the fears of the English, or rather British, residents at Allahabad.

But the festival of the Eed had passed over and still there was no mutiny.

The time flew by and it was now the 4th of June. On that day came news of the insurrection at Benares and of the immortal Neill's doings there, and this news, it was reported to the officers of the 6th, had greatly excited the men. Their loyalty was apparently at an end; their obedience seemed merging into mutiny.

Not only were the civilians, men and women, beginning to get afraid, but those in authority as well. The magistrate himself appeared to think it highly probable that the mutineers driven from Benares by the brave and dashing Scotsman Neill, would make a rush for Allahabad —he had begged Colonel Simpson of the 6th to send a detachment of men and guns to defend the bridge, by which the rebels would have to cross the Ganges if they marched upon the town.

Simpson not only did so, but sent cavalry also to defend the cantonments.

Now listen and judge for yourself whether these Sepoys, who desired but a short time before to be led to Delhi were greatly to be trusted.

It was considered that the guns would be of more service if taken to the fort, and Lieutenant Harward had received an order to convey them there, and proceeded to do his duty. To his astonishment the men of the 6th refused to obey orders. They would take them to the cantonments, but not a gun, they swore, should enter the fort. Harward acted as promptly as any soldier could, and immediately sent orders to Lieutenant Alexander to dash on from the cantonments with his cavalry, intercept the mutineers and seize the guns.

Alexander drew his sword the moment he heard the news, and dashing in front of his company called to them to follow him. *Three* did so, three only, and the rest at once joined the enemy!

A few minutes after this brave officer fell from his horse — shot by the very men he had so recently commanded!

The work of the mutineers had commenced in earnest. On they rushed now, both cavalry and infantry, towards the lines. The officers had gone to mess, but quickly turned out when they heard the yelling and the shouts. They believed even now that they could trust their men, and could quickly bring them back to reason.

Their voices could not be heard. Their gestures were in vain, and as they rushed towards the men they were received by a volley, and five went down.

Having slain their officers, the murderers, fired with a desire for further slaughter, swarmed off towards the city, and there the work of death was re-commenced.

It was now night, and such a night! The darkness was everywhere lit up by the plundered and burning houses of the Christian population; cries and screams of agony rent the air as the Europeans were dragged into the streets, to be foully murdered in a more brutal way than a mob slays mad dogs at home in London. Even women and helpless children were murdered or tossed half dead back again into the flaming ruins of what had been but a few hours before their happy homes. Only the few white men and women who had found refuge in the fort were saved. But here even in the fort itself was danger, for not only were Sepoys of the 6th regiment in charge of the guns, but Sikhs as well.

It was a critical moment; one angry word, a frown even from a British officer, would have caused these men to turn, and then not a European would have been left alive in the fort.

Luckily there was a hero here who took in the situation at a glance. This was the gallant Captain Brayser, of the Sikhs. He called to his men to follow him, and luckily they obeyed. He caused the English artillerymen, a mere handful, to stand to their guns, which were levelled at the Sepoys, and to fire at once if the Sepoys did not pile arms at the word of command.

A few minutes after this these Sepoys, leaving their muskets behind them, were marched out of the fort, and safety was, for the time being, secured.

But there was no sleep for anyone during all this terrible night—the yelling of the budmashes and Sepoys as they plundered the town effectually prevented that—and no one knew what might happen next, or what the dawning of day might not have in store for this beleaguered garrison.

Would Neill come to the relief? That was the question—Neill, or the mutineers from Benares?

Benares was a city of Hindoos or Brahmins, a Holy City indeed. Holy from their point of view; very beautiful from that of anyone who has ever visited it.

Trace it out on the map, reader, and you will see it lies farther down the Ganges than Allahabad, and on the other bank of the river.

In coming up stream, Holmes tells us "the steamer after shooting past a little promontory, entered a broad, crescent-shaped reach, which, sparkling in the sunshine, washed the curved shore like a miniature bay. For two miles along the left bank a succession of broad flights of steps descended into the water, and upon them swarmed multitudes of preachers, pilgrims, worshippers, loungers, and bathers, clad in dresses of many colours, while the mellow music of a hundred bells resounded above the hum of human voices.

"From the steps rose tier above tier, pagodas, mosques, round towers, and arches, covered with fantastic decorations; long-pillared arcades; balustraded terraces; noble mansions with carved balconies and gardens, rich with the dark green foliage of tamarinth and banian trees; and high above the highest roofs soared the two stately minarets of the Mosque of Aurungzebé."

It is strange, but true, that religion, true religion and trust in God, seem ever to exalt the bravery of heroes. The career of Havelock is one proof of this fact, and crowds of others might easily be adduced.

Colonel Neill, of the 1st Madras Fusiliers, was probably as brave a man as ever faced a foe. At the time of the outbreak of the great mutiny he had seen about thirty years' service, and had proved, in many a well-fought field, that he was not only a man in the truest sense of the word, but a leader of men.

He was also, Holmes tells us, "tender and loving to

those dear to him, merciful to the weak, and ever ready to sacrifice his own comfort for the well-being of his soldiers; a staunch friend but a terrible enemy. No responsibility could awe him. No obstacle could stop him."

But above all, reader, he was a Christian in the truest sense of the word. Some might say that there was something of the superstition of the old Covenanters in Neill's character. Men like Neill believe that God Himself calls them to do special work. When therefore this brave Scot was summoned to Calcutta with his splendid regiment, he believed he was commissioned by heaven itself.

We have a proof of the straightforwardness and daring of Neill in an incident that occurred at the railway station at Calcutta. He had arrived before the main body of his men, and the station master hurrying up told him that he must make haste and get aboard, as the train was already late.

"But," said Neill, "this is impossible, my men have not yet arrived."

"That is nothing to me," said this Jack-in-office, "I must send on the train."

"This to me, fellow!" cried Neill.

Then turning quickly round to a sergeant, "Put that man immediately under arrest," he said, "and not only he but the stoker and engineer as well."

Then Neill coolly and quietly waited, and not until every man had arrived, and was safely on board, did he permit the train to start.

It was the 3rd of June when Neill arrived at Benares. He soon showed here also what manner of man he was.

Brigadier Ponsonby consulted him as to the expediency of disarming the 37th regiment of Sepoys.

"Certainly," was Neill's reply.

"Well," said the Brigadier, "I'll have it done tomorrow."

"Ah! Brigadier," replied Neill, "in such a matter as this there is nothing like taking time by the forelock. It must be done at once!"

Spottiswoode, of the 37th, then called out his men, and ordered them to pile arms.

They proceeded to obey; but just at that moment our European troops were seen filing on to the parade ground, and a panic seized the Sepoys. They were to be shot in cold blood, they thought, or even a worse fate might befall them.

In a few minutes, nay, in less time, a furious battle was raging, and even the Sikhs, by some mistake or another, joined against the Europeans. Ponsonby lost his head—he nearly lost his life; but Neill marched up to him, and saluting, said boldly, "General, I assume command!"

Only the quick action of Neill on that day secured the victory to the Europeans, quelled the rising, and secured Benares even from the revenge of the now irritated Sikhs.

On this anxious and terrible night the Christians had been taken for safety to the roof of the Mint, and there at last they fell asleep,

Next day batch after batch of mutineers were hanged.

But the Mutiny had spread to Jaunpore, and to country districts all around.

Meanwhile that little force in the fort of Allahabad was in sore distress; while all around them in the city anarchy reigned supreme, and rapine and murder were installed as her handmaidens.

But the hero came at last. With the first detachment of his troops, a mere handful of fifty determined fellows, Neill marched into Allahabad on the 11th.

He had rough work before him, however; for, sad to say, not only the Sikhs at the fort, but the volunteers as well, had given themselves up to drink, and the whole place was a pandemonium.

By the 18th Neill had subdued not only the town, but all the country adjoining, though some terrible acts of cruelty and injustice were doubtless committed by volunteers and Sikhs by way of retribution. It is even said that these men sallied out of the fort into the streets, slaughtering every native that they came across.

The valour and energy of Neill at this trying time can hardly be overestimated. We can understand a man being courageous when in good health, but poor Neill had been struck down with sickness or physical infirmity. He felt almost at death's door through sheer exhaustion; but still he kept up his heart, and even, when unable to walk, had himself carried on to the ramparts of the fort, so that he might personally superintend every operation that was carried on.

Cholera, however, unfortunately broke out on the 18th, and "there was no means," says Holmes, "of mitigating its horrors. Punkahs and medicines were almost entirely wanting. Eight men were buried before midnight. Twenty more were buried next day."

It must have been cholera in its most awful form too, for we learn from one authority that so fearful and appalling were the shrieks of the sufferers, that two ladies in a room over the hospital died of fright.

So far Neill had done noble work.

But Lucknow was now in the hands of the mutineers, and this brave soldier considered that his work was only just begun. Moreover, he determined to try to succour Cawnpore.

On the 25th of June Havelock left Calcutta, and in five days' time he reached Allahabad, to find that, notwithstanding the terrible fact that Neill's troops were more than decimated by the ravages of the cholera, he was preparing to send on a force to succour Cawnpore.

Neill had to work against fearful odds therefore, but when Havelock reached Allahabad he found that Major Renaud was just under arms with a column, and that evening he marched forth.

On July 3rd a further force of one hundred men of the Fusiliers were sent up the river in a steamer to co-operate with Renaud, and to cover his flank.

This contingent was under the command of Captain Spurgin.

Meanwhile Havelock was getting ready for his campaign with all haste, and personally superintending even the most minute details, so that nothing might be wanting to secure victory.

This brave and clever general had even inaugurated a well-paid intelligence department. In other words, reader, a corps of native spies. With such a squad as this there is only one way of dealing. You must hold out towards them both hands. The right hand is filled with gold, the left grasps a greasy rope that may already have choked the life out of more than one foe. The gold is to be the reward of faithfulness, the rope the guerdon of treachery or deceit.

Havelock marched from Allahabad at last with his whole force.

Not a large one certainly, but, nevertheless, it was indeed a band of heroes.

CHAPTER III.

THE FOE FOUGHT LIKE FIENDS.

A BAND of heroes? Yes, undoubtedly. What was the strength, think you, reader, of the little army with which Havelock marched from Allahabad through the mud, the slush, and the drenching rain? Why barely over a thousand British troops, composed of men of the 78th Highlanders, the 84th and 64th, about 140 Sikhs, under Brasyer, and some volunteer cavalry with six guns.

This does not reckon Renaud's column, which had gone on before. But with this small force Havelock was going on to Cawnpore, on against fearful odds, on to encounter dangers unknown, on to victory or to death.

Gloomy indeed were the first few days of their march, and

> "Toilsome was the road to trace,
> The guide abating oft his pace."

But in their heavy coats—for Havelock had been unable to procure any light or summer outfit for his men—the men struggled forward. In front and all around them, we are told, they saw but "a vast and dreary waste of country, dotted here and there with the charred ruins of forsaken villages."

No living beings in those villages, but proof enough that Renaud had been here, for the dead swung by the neck to almost every available post, and swine and dogs ran hither and thither in the deserted streets, feeding off the half-putrid corpses.

After a few days of tiresome marching they neared the village of Futtehpore, and Colonel Tytler was sent forward with the cavalry to find the enemy. He did find them, and that too in great force. And as the men sat cooking the morning meal Tytler's dragoons dashed rapidly in, pursued by the white-coated horsemen of the foe.

Merrily sounds the bugle. The men pitch pots and pans to one side, and fly to their arms. Warm indeed was the welcome the mutineers received. They had made sure of victory, thinking they had only Renaud's little band to deal with, and before they had recovered from their surprise Havelock's Enfield rifles and his guns were playing havoc in their ranks.

The position occupied by the rebels was a strong one, but it was gallantly, nay I might almost say gaily, captured by the British, the lads in trousers emulating and rivalling the lads in kilts in deeds of valour. The enemy was chased into and through the town, their guns captured, and their rout completed with much slaughter.

Our fellows were permitted to loot and plunder Futtehpore as an act of just retribution.

On the 15th day of July, that terrible day of the massacre at Beebeeghur in Cawnpore, was fought and won the battle of Aong, a strongly entrenched village.

But our victory cost us dear, for while boldly leading on his men poor Renaud, the gallant and true, was slain.

Then came the fight of Pandoonuddee. This was a remarkable one in several ways. Beaten back from Aong after a hard fight of five hours, on the morning of the 15th the enemy made a stand six miles off. Here they were greatly enforced by troops from Cawnpore.

Havelock's men were worn out with their morning's fight with thirst and heat, but the brave general knew he could trust them to fight that day again, and so after a few kindly words he gave the order "Fall in." The men had scarcely commenced breakfast, but there was not a moment's hesitation.

Haste indeed was imperative, for the enemy was making preparations to blow up the bridge across the Ganges, and if they succeeded in this they might not only delay the general's advance, but spoil all his plans.

After a two hours' march through groves of mango trees they sighted the bridge, and were received by cannon shots that tore through their midst, wounding many men. This hot reception however but served to stimulate our brave fellows. On dashed Maude with his artillery, and unlimbering near the river directed his fire towards the enemy's guns, while the Enfields in skirmishing order made short work of the gunners.

Some time after this with a wild shout, bayonets to the front, our Highlanders charged over the bridge. The enemy reeled and fled before them, their guns were captured, and victory merged into a rout. But our poor fellows were now utterly worn out, and threw themselves on the ground to sleep or to die, they seemed to care not which. Food but few of them could have eaten, had it been ever so appetising. Nor can we wonder at their seemingly hopeless conditions. Two battles in one day under the broiling heat of an Indian sun. Think of it you may, reader, though to realise it is impossible!

But next day harder fighting still was before them, and fiercer heat to bear.

To make matters worse they had passed but a weary, restless night, and there was little to eat, the meat having gone bad.

Fain would Havelock have permitted his men to entrench themselves, and remain though but for a day, to recover from the toils of the battle and the march. But Cawnpore was now only twenty miles distant. On they must push therefore, in the hopes they might yet be in time to save British lives, for they knew nothing then of the sad and fearful massacres.

Sixteen miles under a broiling sun, heavily clothed and armed and with little food, is it any wonder that man after man dropped fainting out of the ranks or went down with sunstroke? Then spies came in with the intelligence that the Nana Sahib with five thousand men had left Cawnpore, and was drawn up in battle array some miles ahead.

This time the Nana seemed determined to do or die. Well his force was certainly a strong one compared to ours—five to one. He had disposed them skilfully too.

For calculating that Havelock would deliver a front attack, his army was drawn up like a crescent, with its wings resting on fortified villages.

Havelock however was not to be fooled in this fashion. Supposing that he had advanced straight on, he would have found himself opposed by the bulk of the Nana's army, including his artillery, and while striking hard at this the enemy's right and left wings would have outflanked him, and attacked him in the rear. The whole British force might thus have been annihilated.

Our Havelock sent forward a body of cavalry, under pretence of attacking the Nana in front, while he and the bulk of his little army advanced under cover, and threw themselves upon his left flank. It was a bold measure, and prettily executed; but the enemy endeavoured now to change front, and his artillery was making sad gaps in Havelock's forces. Something must be done to silence these, for our little guns were powerless to do so.

"Bring on the tartan." That was the command, if not the exact words. "Bring up the Highlanders!"

The tartan did come, and that too with a will and a vengeance. There were hundreds of the mutineers who had never heard such a wild, ringing slogan as that before. There were scores who would never hear it again.

The Highlanders charged with fixed bayonets, and after a brief and bloody struggle the gunners were slaughtered at their guns, the village was in our hands, and the left wing of the foe a disorganised rabble fleeing for their lives.

Some of the fugitives rallied on the centre, but again rose the Highlanders' slogan, again Havelock led them on. The 64th were now side by side with the lads in the kilts, and by their united efforts the Nana's centre was reduced to disorder and chaos. The little band of volunteer cavalry completed the rout and discomfiture, and the battle seemed already gained.

A village in which the enemy's right lay was pluckily seized by the Highlanders and the 64th, who vied with each other which should enter first and which should do the greatest deeds of valour.

But the worst was yet to come.

The Nana and his army, though apparently routed, and racing for dear life's sake back towards that blood-stained city, for some reason resolved to make another stand, and even to assume the offensive. In this they were all but successful, for our fellows had gone on too far, leaving the artillery behind, and were lying on the ground to rest, when Nana, with a reserve gun, turned at bay.

Havelock saw that the crisis had now come. Now it must be death or victory. Never perhaps—not even at Alma itself—was a bolder charge made by British men. The foe fought like fiends. But our men would not be denied, and although the ground was littered with dead and dying men they kept steadily on, and finally, with deafening "hurrahs!" captured the gun and drove the enemy in one confused, disorderly mass back into the city.

The Nana did not stop here, but rode on to Bithoor, and the natives too, dreading, as well they might, the vengeance of our troops, fled into the country and hid themselves in every thicket and jungle.

No wonder that after this great battle Havelock gathered his little army around him, and congratulated and thanked them heartily.

"Soldiers," Marshman makes him say, "your General is satisfied, and more than satisfied with you. He has never seen steadier or more devoted troops, but your labours are only beginning. Nevertheless between the 7th and 16th you have, under the Indian sun of July, marched a hundred and twenty-six miles and fought four actions. But your comrades in Lucknow are in peril, Agra is besieged, Delhi is still the focus of mutiny and rebellion. Three cities have to be saved and two strong places to be de-blockaded. Your General is confident he can effect all these things, and restore this part of India to tranquillity, if you will only second him with your efforts, and if your discipline is equal to your valour."

On the 17th of July, just as Havelock and his brave fellows were about to march into the city, news of the last of the massacres reached him.

There may be men still alive who can remember that sad and melancholy march into Cawnpore.

Can we wonder that when they came to the Beebee-ghur, and silently and fearfully entered the rooms in little groups of twos and threes; when they saw the blood lying ankle deep in clots upon the matted floor; the shreds of clothing, the long locks of hair, the pillars and walls all scored with sword-cuts, the children's blood-stained broken toys, and that awful well with its mass of human remains, they lifted up their voices and wept aloud.

Nothing but sadness and gloom prevailed that day and night; the men hardly spoke save in hushed and awesome voices, and nothing was heard but the wailing of the bagpipes playing laments for the dead that were being buried.

Even Havelock himself was oppressed by the general gloom. His heart was sad indeed, but his heart must not fail in this hour of need, and he even tried to smile as, turning to his son at table, he said, "If the worst comes to the worst, Henry, we shall die like men, with our swords in our hands."

Meanwhile how fared it at Lucknow?

CHAPTER IV.

OUR DEFEAT AT CHINHUT—JACK'S BRAVE DEED—DEATH OF LAWRENCE.

IT was on the 30th day of May that the Mutiny broke out at Lucknow.

Lawrence had not been without warning that it would take place that night after the firing of the nine o'clock gun. He was dining in the evening at the Cantonment Residency of Mariaon,* and hardly had the boom of the gun shaken the jalousies ere the sound of musketry firing was heard coming from the lines.

But brave Lawrence had all his wits about him. With the utmost coolness he rose from the table, and with all his guests went out. At the door was drawn up the native guard, whom at the first sound of firing their native captain had turned out.

This officer asked Wilson if the men should load.

This was a supreme moment; but both officers were

---

* *Vide* plan of Lucknow, p. 316.

equal to the occasion. Had they shown the slightest symptoms, even by a quaver of the voice of nervousness or fear, both would have been dead men next moment.

Wilson coolly referred the question to Lawrence.

"Certainly!" was the bold reply.

And then, while the rifles of this Sepoy guard were pointed directly at him, and the men were putting on the caps, he boldly addressed them as follows:

"I am going," he cried, "to drive those blackguards out of the cantonments; take care, during my absence, that you all remain at your posts. Permit no one to do any damage here or to enter my house. If you fail in your duty, then on my return I will hang you!"

And the men obeyed, and this Residency was, we are told, the only house in cantonments that was not burned or plundered during this night of terror and destruction.

Lawrence now directed his efforts to preventing anything like collusion betwixt the mutineers and the citizens, and for this purpose he sent a party to guard the road that led into the city.

In this he was successful. The mutineers, it is true, shot their Brigadier as he was endeavouring to restore order. They burned the mess place, but were disappointed in their hopes of finding their officers within.

The mutineers belonged entirely to the 71st Infantry, and early next morning they retired towards the racecourse. Thither went Lawrence to punish them, and over sixty prisoners were captured, but as the mutineers were now joined by the 7th Cavalry it was deemed injudicious to pursue them farther.

Inside the city on that same day, however, a rising was attempted, the standard of the prophet was raised, and for a time matters looked very serious indeed.

Thus was the second mutiny at Lucknow quelled.

Meanwhile other country districts of Oude, that had till now remained quiet, rose in rebellion.

The Sepoys, at Seetapore, murdered their Commissioner, civilians and officers, women and children.

Sad indeed was the story of one of the parties who escaped. "This consisted," says Holmes, "of Sir Mountstuart Jackson, his sister Madeline, Lieutenant Burnes, Surgeon-Major Morton, and Sophy Christian, a dear little child only three years of age."

These poor fugitives made their way to a fort belonging to a rajah, Lonee Singh, and begged him to take pity on them. They were worn out with fatigue, their clothes were in rags, and their bare feet lacerated with the thorns of the jungle through which they had passed.

Well, this Rajah's pity was certainly of a questionable sort. He kept them all night in a cowshed, and next day started them off to a small unfurnished house in another quarter of his estate.

Here they found a Captain Orr with his wife and child, who had made their escape from the mutineers at Aurungabad. But next day the rajah drove the Orrs into the jungle. Here they had to burn fires at night to scare away the wolves. But wolves even were better companions than the roving bands of mutineers, who were scouring the country in search of all fugitives. On the 12th of July they were allowed to creep back, wretched and forlorn, to join the others, and here they lay and suffered miseries untold until the 6th of August, when the whole party was once more driven into the jungle, and this deceitful rajah now put a party of mutineers on their track, but though they hunted for them for hours they failed to find them.

"But," says our informant, "the fugitives had little cause to rejoice over their escape. The rays of the sun beat fiercely on their heads, and the thorny brushwood of the jungle was so low that they could find no shade. Torrents of rain poured down upon them at times. Wild beasts howled around them. Then intermittent fever attacked them, and deprived them of the power to bear up against their other sorrows."

On August 26th Orr somehow got a letter which he read to his companions, and once more hope revived in their hearts, for it promised early deliverance. But that deliverance never came.

Lonee Singh, the wretched rajah, would have delivered them up to the British, had he thought they would be successful, but when he believed that their rule in India was at an end, then on October the 20th he sent a band of his fellows to capture the poor hounded fugitives, and their sufferings were now increased tenfold.

They were hunted down, ruthlessly seized and packed together in a cart which went jolting on to a village where the rajah's vakeel—a man who it is said owed his advancement in life to Captain Orr—placed iron fetters upon the legs of the male prisoners, and when Mrs. Orr fell on her knees and beseeched him to spare them this indignity his only answer was a fiendish laugh.

Was it any wonder that at the sight of the fetters

poor Dr. Morton fell into a convulsive fit, or that Lieutenant Burnes went raving mad.

Then came the awful journey to Lucknow, during which they received but once a day a scanty dole of the coarsest food and hardly a drop of water. Arrived at Lucknow, which was now in possession of the rebels, they were jeered and laughed at by mobs of savage roughs, then thrown into prison—only one room. The poor women were crazed for water, and shrieked aloud for it. It was brought at last, but in a vessel so foul that they could not touch it. How did all this end? I hardly like to tell you, so saddening and awful is it. Week after week of horror went past.

Then, one day in November, brutal Sepoys entered the room, and barely granting the men time to say farewell to the ladies, pinioned them and dragged them away. Probably none of the four could have endured their terrible sufferings much longer, so weak, worn, and emaciated were they. And the rattle of musketry that followed told the weeping women the sad tale of their relief.

Poor Sophy was gone long before this, and it was not till March 19th that the two ladies and the unhappy child were restored to their friends.

Such a fearful experience as this it happily falls to the lot of few in this world to undergo.

* * * * *

After the Mutiny of the 30th of May, Gubbins tried hard to get Lawrence to disband the Sepoys, one and all.

Lawrence refused; he still had faith in them; besides, there were 600 Sepoys who could be trusted. A compromise was therefore made, and instead of being disbanded, all the native troops save these few hundreds were granted leave of absence until November.

The fortifying and provisioning of the Residency (*vide* plan) now went on apace; Lawrence, who had been ill, wanted to strengthen and defend the fort of Muchee Bhowun, but Gubbins would not hear of this, and Lawrence, a man of less strength of will, had to give in.

He gave in to Gubbins on another point also, and this it was that caused the real siege of Lucknow.

The Sepoys had been collecting in large numbers in the neighbourhood, and Gubbins strongly urged that the British force, instead of lying idle in Lucknow, should be led out against them.

A force numbering about 700 men, one half British, was therefore got ready for action, and marched out next day to the village of Chinhut.

Among the officers were Jack Morrison and Frank Wood. Frank was already a soldier by profession, but Jack had in a manner drifted into the army. He had shown himself exceedingly active in every way since his appearance at Lucknow, and showed too that he had many of the sterling qualities that help to make the perfect soldier. Jack had courage and activity. He knew also the meaning of the words "duty" and "obedience."

He was proud indeed therefore to find himself in command of a company of cavalry that he had raised and broken in from very indifferent material indeed. Jack's soldiers were little else than a drove at first, but they were in fairly good form on the morning of the 30th of June, when the little army marched forth to fight the rebels.

Chinhut was ten miles to the north and east of Lucknow, but when the troops reached a rivulet called Kokrail, a march of four miles, and no enemy was in sight, Lawrence determined to return, for his troops were already tired and war-worn and hungry.

All might have been well had not an officer brought word to Lawrence that the enemy was not far off. The orders to return were accordingly countermanded, and the little army went wearily on once more.

It was a pity indeed for Jack Morrison that in this his first real fight the British should have been defeated. Indeed, it was worse than a defeat, this affair of Chinhut. It really ended in a rout; while the enemy's horse artillery, riding along the flanks of the British, poured in a constant discharge of grape-shot.

Some of the 32nd were so tired before the bridge over the Korkail was again reached, that they threw themselves upon the ground to die. What had made matters worse was the fact that many of Lawrence's native cavalry had deserted.

But now here was the bridge. Could they cross it? This seemed impossible, and would have been, but for the courage and determination of Jack's little squadron of volunteers, for the enemy's cavalry disputed possession of the bridge,

Jack on horseback was at his best. Now he waved his

"On they dashed, Jack and his brave little troop."

p. 265.

sword and pointed to the bridge. On they dashed, he and his brave little troop; and so fierce and determined was their onslaught, that the enemy's cavalry went down before it, were hurled back, and thrown into confusion. In this bright little *mêlée* Jack himself took a very active part indeed. As his sabre flashed right and left in the sunlight, the great steed on which he rode seemed actually to ride over his foes. They went down before him man and horse, and soon the bridge was gained.

But danger was not over. The bheestie-wallahs, or water-carriers, had fled, and many of our poor fellows would have sunk to rise no more had not some native women taken pity on them, and given them "wherewithal to slake their thirst."

Lawrence and some of his staff had ridden on before to warn our people at the Residency. But from the windows of the stronghold they had seen, even before the arrival of the Chief Commissioner, that the day was lost.

And soon commenced a scene of agony and confusion that it is impossible to describe. Hurled along in front of overwhelming numbers of the rebels, our poor fellows came swaying and staggering up to the verandah, and were quickly admitted. The women too, shrieking in terror, ran for their lives to hide themselves and children in the rooms.

The siege had begun.

The whole force of Sepoys had by nightfall surrounded the place, and all night long their watch-fires could be seen and their wild shouts heard, while ever and anon their artillery belched forth fire and shot that came crashing through the windows or even the walls of the Residency.

A word here about the Muchee Bhowun. Lawrence had troops there, a large quantity of ammunition and stores of every sort, and it was, like the Residency itself, exposed to the fire of the enemy. It must be relieved at all hazards; so on July 1st, the second day of the investment, a kind of rude semaphore was invented, and by this means Lawrence managed to communicate with the fort.

While, then, that night the enemy were busy looting and plundering the town, Colonel Palmer of the fort, after spiking his guns and laying a train, silently left the place with his men, and succeeded in getting safely inside the Residency. Almost immediately after a terrific explosion shook the city to its foundation, and the magazine was no more.

Everything was now confusion inside the fort, for the siege had commenced ere Lawrence was quite prepared for it. Even the bastions were unfinished, and it was found almost impossible to get natives to work at them under fire of the enemies' guns.

A sad picture is given by one authority of the desertion of native servants after the wounding of the Commissariat-General. We can hardly marvel at this, for the men knew not where to apply for rations. Then the artillery bullocks, having no one to attend to them, wandered about helplessly moaning for food or water, and in many cases tumbled into the wells. The horses, too, for the same reason went mad with thirst, and tore and kicked each other in their agony.

The end of my present chapter must be saddened with a brief account of the death of poor Lawrence himself.

He was in bed, tired and weary, and almost ill, when a shell burst into his room, a huge mass of masonry fell, and after that for a time all was still.

Wilson and the doctor were soon on the spot, and bore the wounded Commissioner to another room, but a glance told the surgeon that the wound was mortal.

Lawrence lingered until the morning of the 4th, when he passed away. For many hours before this he was insensible. This was merciful, for a far from peaceful death-bed was his, the roar of the guns going on all day and all night long, and shot and shell thudding and bursting against the walls.

But Lawrence had obtained peace nevertheless—the peace that passeth all understanding. He died a soldier's death; he filled a soldier's grave; for they laid him side by side with some of his own brave privates who, like himself, had fallen in their country's cause, and the thunder of the enemy's guns was the only salute that was paid them.

CHAPTER V.

THE AWFUL SIEGE—WHAT LILY TOLD THE AUTHOR.

JACK MORRISON began now to realise something of the horrors of war.

He had never laid himself out to be a soldier, but, nevertheless, he could not help, while leading that brilliant charge at the bridge of Kokrail, experiencing something of

> "The stern joy that warriors feel
> In foemen worthy of their steel."

Now, however, he was to see warfare under quite a different aspect, deprived of all its pomp and its panoply, with nothing around him except scenes of hopelessness, death in its ugliest forms, misery, want, and woe.

Brigadier Inglis had succeeded poor Lawrence in the command of the Residency. He is described as "a plain and honourable Christian gentleman . . . a staunch friend, a lover of all that was high and noble, a soldier of unsurpassable gallantry, and just the man to defend a weak position obstinately to the very last, and thus to obey the dying commands of Lawrence—'*Never surrender!*'"

And weak indeed was the position he had now to defend, against most fearful odds. Just think of this, reader, the assailants of that frail palace fort were over 6000, and were being constantly reinforced, while those inside the walls numbered but 1690 men, many of them natives, many of them infirm and old.

Never surrender! No, there was little chance of that. They had heard of Cawnpore, and they knew the fearful fate that awaited them as soon as they fell into the hands of the ferocious and fiendish foe.

Never surrender! No; the walls of the Residency might tumble down and bury those heroes, but in defence of their helpless women and hapless children they would fight to the bitter end.

So weak, however, was the Residency, that it is said not a room in it was safe. The wounded were often killed in their beds, and women sometimes found that during the night even their pillows had been pierced with bullets.

The fire of the besiegers was terrible and incessant.

The 20th of July was a day that will never be forgotten by those who are still alive as I write, and can remember their personal experience thereof. For tired at last of bombardment the enemy ceased firing.

The dread silence that followed was for a time more fearful to those—especially the women—inside the Residency than even the thunder of cannon and rattle of musketry, for well they know that the enemy was about to attempt carrying the place by storm.

The besieged garrison was not held long in ignorance as regards the plans and intentions of the enemy.

Early in the forenoon a mine was sprung, and scarcely had the dust and *débris* fallen to the ground and the smoke cleared away before the cannonade was renewed with increased activity, and under cover of this the rebels rushed on to the assault.

Great credit has been given to them by many writers for the vigour and the valour displayed in this attack. Again and again they essayed to cross the ditch, they even made daring efforts to place their scaling-ladders against the walls, but so terrible was the fire of our troops, both British and native, and so well-planted was every shot that the enemy, failing to face so deadly a hail, fell back at last defeated and disheartened.

Their loss was enormous, while ours was in comparison only very small.

The bombardment was now renewed with greater activity than ever. New batteries were being built, and it was only too evident that the enemy was resorting to mining as a last expedient.

Mining, however, is a game that two can play at, and Captain Fulton of the engineers, one of the chief heroes of Lucknow, knew his work, and did it well. There were in the 32nd several old Cornish miners, and these he chose as his assistants.

Eeriesome and dangerous work this at the dead of night, listening with ears on the ground between the intervals of gun-firing for the muffled sound of miners pickaxes and spades underground, and sinking counter-mines right down in front of them.

Fulton, we are told, would sometimes descend these shafts himself with revolver and lantern, and waiting until the enemy's miners got through shoot them dead as they came crouching along.

But again and again during this sad and terrible siege mines were sprung and efforts made to carry the Residency by storm. Yet they all failed, although once a breach was made ten yards long, and on another occasion the besiegers were all but successful, for the explosion of a mine not only blew up a part of the wall, but a small house also, hurling several of our officers and men into the air. Strangely enough, however, these soldiers fell inside, and were almost unhurt. Even with this success the Sepoys hesitated to storm, though their officers leapt into the breach and endeavoured to get them to follow. It goes without saying that these officers paid with their lives the penalty of their daring.

The deed of Inglis in recapturing this house and expelling the enemy at the point of the bayonet was one of very great daring. Though Captain Fulton himself told him that to retake the house was impossible he thought he would try. He erected a barricade of planks and boxes, and from this a gun enfiladed the breach. Before sundown he made his grand charge, and cleared out the enemy at the point of the bayonet.

By the courage and cleverness of a man called Ungud, who succeeded in reaching Havelock's camp, the besiegers received a letter from that brave general. This was near the end of August. The letter gave them hopes of rescue in about a month's time, no sooner. "For twice," said Havelock, "in trying to reach you have I been obliged to fall back upon Cawnpore before the foe. Rather, however, perish sword in hand than even dream of negotiating with the wily foe."

Jack Morrison was not only a most resolute and daring young fellow, and just the sort of man one would have chosen to lead a forlorn hope, but he held the opinion that nothing was either menial or derogatory that bore the impress of duty. Hence we find him on many occasions during the siege fighting like a private soldier at the batteries, Enfield in hand, for he was a splendid shot; we find him among the foremost men in that brave little bayonet charge with Inglis when the house was retaken from the enemy; but we find him also doing work right cheerfully at many parts of the Residency that, on ordinary occasions, is expected only of the lowest order of Indian servants.

Jack Morrison was never ashamed to cast off his jacket, roll up his sleeves, and go right heartily to work at anything his hands might find to do if it was for the good of the beleaguered garrison.

Above all he was pleasant and cheerful. He was therefore a great favourite with the ladies and with the poor children, and many a kind office he performed for both.

But his good services ended not even here. It must be remembered that sickness was very rife during the siege, and wounds of the most terrible kinds of every day's occurrence. Jack thought, therefore, that in his spare moments he might help the doctors.

"I'll make a capital nurse," he said, laughing. "My mother taught me, you know."

And his services were most gratefully accepted.

Well, Jack was himself an assistant, and Jack also had an assistant.

Who was it? Why Lily Wood, Frank's sister.

Poor girl, she was here, there, and everywhere, often exposing herself almost recklessly on behalf of those she was trying to aid and succour.

I am not at all sure, mind you, reader, that Jack was not in love with Lily. He did not *make* love to her. How could he in such a place? Besides, it would have been taking an unmanly advantage of her. But I must say that he was never better pleased than when near her, and doing something to make life a little easier for her.

Lily Wood, it will do you no harm to know, reader, is still alive, and what follows in this chapter and in the next was taken down from her own lips one day, not many weeks before I began to write this ower-true tale.

WHAT LILY TOLD THE AUTHOR.

"I think," said Lily, "that I soon made myself a favourite with most of the women and children in the Residency. You see, I had nothing to do, and only my dear brother Frank to think about. And Jack did you say? Well, yes, and Jack. But I knew that both of them were well able to take care of themselves, and somehow I never lost faith in God. I prayed constantly, not only night and morning. Indeed, during all the time I was working—and most of us ladies *did* work too—I seemed to be holding communion with God and with Jesus. He seemed always near to me, and I knew that eventually we should be saved, or rather what remained of us.

"One of my chief and best friends was the buxy's wife. A buxy, you must know, is just a pet name for a paymaster. She was the first friend that I had at cantonments too, for when Jack and Frank and I arrived at Lucknow, and I told her that I wasn't a boy at all, but only a poor girl in disguise, and in a terrible plight, with my hair all cut off, and feeling dirty and dreadful all over, she laughed, and said she would soon make that all right, with the exception of the hair. I sighed, because, woman-like, I really had felt parting with my hair very much.

"'Is your brother, the jemadar, a girl too?' she said, glancing at Frank.

"'Oh no,' I said, 'he is a real boy, and so is Jack.'

"She smiled, because Jack was more than six feet high, and didn't look a bit like a girl—not one little bit.

"When I reached Lucknow the ladies had already been sent to the Residency for safety, but were allowed to spend the day in cantonments with their husbands.

"They had heard the dreadful news from Delhi and from Meerut, and even before the outbreak of the Mutiny at Lucknow they had all lived a very anxious life. Mrs. Buxy told me that the way the Sepoys used to look and scowl at her terrified her so much that she used to start from her sleep at night in wild terror, and be glad to find it was only a dream.

"We had had a sad time of it during our flight to Lucknow, though of course if Providence had not so ordained, it might have been much worse. The Sepoys that came with us, I am glad to tell you at once, remained faithful to the British flag all throughout the siege, but, alas! only five of them lived through it, the others fell by the guns of the besiegers or by cholera.

"Mrs. Buxy, as I may call her, had a very beautiful house in the cantonments, and treated me with such kindness as I never could forget. I shall ever remember that delightful bath and my first meal afterwards. It was only a small chop and sweet potatoes. I only hope I did not eat like a savage.

"Well I went on to the Residency, and then came the night of the terrible 30th of May. Although we all felt sure enough that mutiny was to come, somehow nobody had expected it so soon, and even Sir Henry Lawrence himself was not prepared.

"So you may judge of our anxiety as we stood that sad night on the roof of the Residency watching the smoke and flames of the burning houses, and listening to the firing.

"Mrs. Buxy's husband was absent at Futtehpore with eight officers and a detachment, so he was safe from the danger of this night. But the wives of the officers passed a terrible time; some almost went mad with anxiety.

"At one o'clock in the morning an orderly arrived at the Residency with the comforting assurance that this mutiny had been quelled, but with the news also of the sad death of Brigadier H——, who was murdered almost as soon as he had reached the parade ground. The brigadier was a great friend of the Buxies, and poor Mrs. Buxy was now in great grief.

"Next day brought her further sorrow, namely, the news that her beautiful bungalow, where she had spent so many happy days, and which was endeared to her by so many tender memories, was a heap of smouldering ruins. Some of her property was brought into the Residency, and she wept womanly tears over its charred remains, and especially over the plate, which was just recognisable, but so knocked and battered about as to be quite useless.

"After the 15th of June it was considered unsafe for anyone to remain longer at cantonments, so everybody was ordered into the Residency.

"Things continued quiet until the 30th of June, and although we had to endure the discomfort of overcrowding, and were deprived of the pleasures of exercise, still we had our servants, we had food, we had fruit, and, greatest luxury of all, we had ice.

"Almost every other day fugitives from Oude came in, and the sad news they brought us of towns and villages that had been burned and plundered by the enemy, kept us in a continual state of anxiety regarding our own ultimate fate.

"Then came news of another massacre. Poor Mrs. W——'s mother and sister and brother were among the victims, though how they died or what cruelties they suffered before death we never knew.

"We had not told Mrs. H—— of her poor husband's death on the parade ground. She had left him at Lahore and believed he was safe, and nobody had the heart to undeceive her.

"It was as well we did not, as things turned out, for,

oh! dear me, she was attacked by cholera on the 29th of June. I shall never forget that deathbed nor the agonies she endured.

"But in the intervals of pain she managed to ask me to take charge of her child, dear wee innocent Katie, then she breathed her last. Yes, it was a happy release, and her sufferings had been soon over. But it was heart-breaking to hear her leaving loving messages for her husband, not knowing that he had gone on before.

"It was next morning that I fetched Katie to my room. That was a never-to-be-forgotten day. Lawrence with his little army was just starting forth to march to Chinhut to fight the rebels. I was told that through some mismanagement the troops had been made to fall in without having a chance to finish breakfast, and very woebegone and tired they all looked.

"No, not all, Jack Morrison on his tall black charger looked to me like some ancient warrior king. Perhaps I should have told you before that Jack had become a volunteer-soldier, and that by his own exertions he had raised and drilled a troop. I heard the general himself say that but for his prowess and bravery the whole of the little army would have been annihilated at the bridge of Kokrail, while they were in full retreat back towards the city.

"Never while I live shall I forget the terror, the confusion, and the dismay that reigned as our poor soldiers came pouring in, many of them dangerously wounded, all of them weary, exhausted, and faint.

"Happily our supply of ice had come in that day, and

with Jack by my side—for the great fellow was as good a nurse and surgeon as he was a soldier—I administered drops of iced water to many a stricken man, and only those who have felt the effects of a scorching summer's sun in India can really appreciate the luxury and relief afforded by a morsel of ice. How fervently, though faintly, many a poor fellow blessed me and Jack for our services on that sad day!

"But soon the firing of guns and musketry grew terrific and alarming. The round shot taking effect on those parts of the walls of the Residency that had been considered most safe, struck terror to the hearts of every one.

"Even as I was stooping down at my box a round shot came in through the window and dashed another box containing a bonnet Mrs. Buxy had given me all to pieces. It buried itself in the opposite wall, and filled the room with dust and *débris.*

"On the very day that the troops marched forth to the fatal field of Chinhut poor Mrs. W——'s only child was seized with cholera. In a very few hours it was dead. The husband was then at his post in the city.

"But think of her bereavement—mother, sister, and brother cruelly murdered, and now her only child lying there a sadly-distorted corpse. No wonder that the poor mother was frantic with grief.

"Sir Henry now found that it would be impossible to garrison Muchee Bowhun. The fort occupied a position in the very heart of the city, and from its appearance and commanding site was called by the natives the Nose of Lucknow.

"It was therefore evacuated at midnight, and its gallant defenders came in without losing a man.

"Mrs. Buxy and her five children, with dear little Katie and myself, were now in one small room by ourselves, the Residency proper being found so unsafe that nearly all the ladies had left it.

"The blowing up of Muchee Bowhun caused us very great alarm, it shook every building, smothered us all with dust, and extinguished every light. I could not tell what was up. The world seemed coming to an end. I seized Katie in my arms, and rushed to the staircase. There stood Sir Henry shaking hands with those who had just come from the fort, and he assured me that there was no cause for alarm.

"Poor Mr. W—— was there, and heard now for the first time the sad news of the death of his child, whom he had left but the day before the picture of health and beauty.

"Next morning many married ladies were sent to a low building called the Brigade Mess, and formerly the King's Hospital. It was a large and lofty room, pillared down the centre, and loop-holed. But there was but little room for each bed. The husbands when off duty slept on the floor.

"The firing was now fearful.

"Poor Sir Henry Lawrence was himself dangerously wounded in his own room by the bursting of an 8-inch shell. He was gently lifted, carried out, and laid tenderly on a bed in Dr. F——'s own house.

"No sadder scene, they told me, than that around his death-bed could be conceived, as, knowing that he soon must depart, he gave his dying orders to his staff. He preached a little sermon that none could ever forget. But even on his death-bed, with weeping friends around him, he could not forget his duty. He particularly warned them to be careful in the expenditure of ammunition, and over and over again said, 'Save the ladies!' How this was to be done none could tell, but perhaps poor Sir Henry was raving. Up till now we had owed our safety to his forethought and judgment, and we should never look upon his like again.

"I never before or since met a man who so commanded esteem and respect, and when at prayers in the Residency I could with difficulty withdraw my gaze from him, for a kind of heavenly radiance seemed to settle upon his calm but careworn face that it would be impossible to describe in words.

"Poor Sir Henry!"

CHAPTER VI.

LILY CONTINUES HER NARRATIVE — THE HIGHLANDER'S SLOGAN.

"THE married ladies," said Lily, "had indeed but little comfort or privacy in their large barrack-like room. For apart from the fact that it was loop-holed, their husbands being with them, they could make but little change in their attire night or day. Besides, General Inglis and his staff used to come into the apartment at all hours of the night if any alarm had been given, or the muffled sounds of mining were heard.

"But some of these ladies managed to screen off a portion of the room, and thus enjoy the greatest luxury imaginable in a hot climate; namely, a bath.

"We passed a weary, anxious time at the best. Perhaps the best was when we were engaged making jackets or skirts for ourselves, or doing some sewing and mending for the officers. My best time, if there was any best in it, was when I was attending to the sick and wounded in company with Jack. I think I see his honest red face even now as he bent kindly over some poor sick soul, or gently raised his head and shoulders that he might partake of a little nourishment or his medicine.

"Lights were all extinguished soon after dusk, at which time we retired to bed, but on moonlight nights we sat up to talk of home. It was now the end of July. Should we ever, ever be rescued?

"Then glorious news reached us. Havelock had been communicated with, and was hastening to our aid. But as day went by, and no Havelock appeared, our hearts grew sick with the hope that was deferred, and sometimes we were silent and dumb with despair.

"It was terribly hot now. Our room was sometimes so stifling at night that sleep was impossible, and oh, it was weary, weary for us to lie and think of the homes in England, and the friends we never more might see. Besides, there was the constant roar of the great guns, and the sharp rattling of musketry; and there were the thoughts too, that at any time a mine might be sprung right under the very room where we lived.

"Many mines were exploded close to the outer walls, and after this—immediately after indeed—we could hear the raging of a terrible battle. Nor did we know who might be conquerors, or how soon the dark and vengeful faces of the foe might be seen as they rushed into our rooms to drag us out to death.

"A terrible sufferer was a poor little boy, Charlie M——, but God took him at last. He had been a great favourite of mine; for though often in grievous bodily pain, he had borne it like a little hero. The tears fell from my eyes thick and fast as I helped to wrap up his poor attenuated little frame for burial.

"The enemy had erected fresh batteries, and when one day a round shot came roaring and crashing in through the Brigade Mess it was deemed no longer safe, and the married ladies were moved, and distributed among the other houses.

"I had many dear friends among the garrison. We all suffered together, but I think by death the children suffered most. I have known as many as five of these to be buried in one night.

"There were times during the siege when flies became a terrible plague, and one could not help thinking of the Egyptians, when we saw our food and even the very spoons we were conveying to our mouths darkened with these terrible pests.

"Then there were mosquitoes, but these were not so numerous, and we were acclimatised to their venom.

"The heat was at times hard to bear, and used to make us languid, weary, and sick, and there was not enough water to quench our thirst.

"I spent much of my time with Jack in the hospital, or helping my lady friends who had young children, or working or sewing for the men.

"Officers as well as men did what they called 'sentry go,' and that too calmly and heroically if not cheerfully.

"No one can wonder if the men sometimes seemed to have lost all heart and hope, and even exhibited fits of bad temper towards those in authority over them.

Or they would expose themselves recklessly to the fire of the enemy, replying when cautioned that it mattered but little, the relief would never come, and the sooner they were stretched dead the better.

"I sometimes wonder now how we were able to bear all our fearful sufferings so well as we did. But God tempers the wind to the shorn lamb, and I believe our troubles had created a kind of apathy in our minds, that helped the weary, hopeless time to pass more quickly by.

"Oh, the deathbeds that kind-hearted Jack and I witnessed during those long and terrible months of siege! I would not harrow anyone's feelings by describing them.

"Poor Mrs. B——'s husband died of fever, and so terrible was his delirium for some hours before he became exhausted that his wife was not allowed to see him.

"Mrs. B—— received the news afterwards with the calmness of a grief that knew not tears.

"My dear friend Mrs. Mary M—— soon after lost her sole remaining boy, Henry. His sufferings were so acute before he wore away that I for one was glad when his eyes were at last closed in death.

"And now my dear wee Katie fell ill from the confinement and the want of pure air, for the whole atmosphere was by this time tainted with fearful odours, which added greatly to the sufferings of every one of us.

"Food too grew scarce now, and rations were reduced to about half.

"Pounds would sometimes be paid for a single ham,

fourteen pence for a pound of coarse flour, while fifteen shillings was frequently given for a bottle of beer.

"The last time a mine was exploded was, I think, on the 5th of September, and immediately afterwards the enemy made a most determined attempt to storm. They were repulsed, however, with but little loss to our side, though theirs must have suffered severely, for at eventide Jack told me cart-loads of the wounded and the dead were seen crossing the bridge towards cantonments.

"Dear though every kind of food was, I managed to secure just one bottle of wine for my darling Katie. Would she live, I wondered?

"I wondered; but at times so hopeless was I that I seemed almost to think 't were best if the end should come. Ah! better surely she should lie sleeping in her little grave than fall into the hands of the savages, to meet the fate we all might meet, the same fearful sufferings as those that our friends at Cawnpore had gone through.

"The 24th of September was a sad day to me. My Katie died in my arms. She seemed to fall asleep at last. Better, I thought as I kissed her brow, that she should be cradled in our loving Saviour's arms, than live to endure the trials and temptations of this world without a mother's care.

"Mrs. R——, the wife of one of the soldiers, made her a little shroud, and poor Jack Morrison brought her a makeshift coffin. How sweet and lovely she looked!

"Jack talked gently to me, and laid his hand upon

my shoulder. But somehow this only made me cry the more.

"Then they took my Katie away.

"I got another little pet after this, but none like Katie. For one night, when the firing was wilder and more terrible than ever, dear Mrs. H. W——'s baby was born.

"Our native troops began now to desert, and it has been rightly said that those who remained were becoming so despondent, that it needed all the arguments and soothing assurances of the British officers to strengthen their loyalty. And no wonder, for more than a third of the European soldiers had perished during this long and terrible siege, and the survivors were fearfully depressed and hopeless. Since the beginning hardly ever a day passed that there was not a funeral. The Brigadier himself had not slept with his clothes off since the middle of May, and so worn was he with anxiety and toil, that many of us feared he would soon break down entirely.

"And, despite all our care, the wounded were in a sad plight. Their sores festered dreadfully, and the blue-bottle flies could be scooped up from off a wounded limb in handfuls. Jack, who assisted the doctors, told me that in every case where a leg or arm had to be amputated, death from exhaustion was almost sure to take place.

"The odour from the makeshift hospitals was so fearful, that we wondered anyone could live therein.

"Then, while many were down with low fever, some died with cholera, and some with small-pox, while several patients in their delirium escaped from the hospitals, and went wandering round, till taken and led, or even forced, back to their wards and their beds.

"Oh, it was a terrible, terrible time!

"Could we hold out till reinforcements should arrive? This was a question that soon came to be freely discussed among the men as well as the officers, and the general opinion was that it was exceedingly doubtful.

"I read somewhere afterwards, and I quite believe it is true, that 'many of our men had been heard to declare that they would shoot their wives with their own hands, sooner than suffer them to fall into the power of the enemy.'

"My new pet, the baby, was rather a wakeful and restless young lady. Well, about 12 o'clock one night I was trying to rock her to sleep in my arms, and singing low to her, when I thought I could discern an unusual commotion in the next room, which was occupied by General Inglis and his staff.

"To listen at or to look through chinks in that doorway was surely excusable to ladies in a plight like ours, so my conscience did not check me for what I now did. I laid baby gently down upon the bed, then I went and peeped and listened also.

"The spy Ungud had just returned, and the news he was telling the general and his officers was wildly exciting.

"Havelock was coming! Havelock would soon be here! He was within but a few days' march; a battle would be fought, and then, oh, joy! we should be relieved.

"I rushed from bed to bed to awaken the others and

tell them the glad tidings. But I was weeping almost hysterically, and for a time they must have thought the tidings were far other than joyful. But they understood me at last, then with small compunction every one of them by turns went to peep or to listen.

* * * * *

"Need I tell you what a day of gladness that 25th of September was, when from the roof of the ramparts we could hear the shouts of our advancing friends, hear the wild skirl of the bagpipes, and the Highlanders' slogan?

"Then that meeting, when our hero Havelock, looking sadly war-worn and weary, stood at last in the midst of us with his brave fellows clustering round him.

"No; I will not attempt to describe the state of our feelings, the handshakings with dusty, thirsty warriors, the half-spoken enquiries after husbands, brothers, mothers, or friends, that were answered almost before they were uttered, the embracing as brother met sister, or husband wife, the loud laughing, the weeping for joy, and the glad exclamations and ringing cheers in which even the sick crept out of their beds to join.

"Teddy C——, who came in with the relief, told us of the escape of Mrs. Mary M——'s sister, with her husband and family from Futtehpore, and he gave us a graphic account too of the advance upon the city, and their march through it under a tremendous fire—a fire that none but heroes could have faced or stood under; for even Havelock himself said, that during all his career, and in the thirty-seven battles in which during his lifetime he had taken part, he had never before been under so awful a hail of shot and bullets.

"But it was do or die; it was death or victory.

"This was the first relief of Lucknow.

"But Sir Colin Campbell had yet to come, and the forts had to be taken before we could be finally relieved and taken south, and away from all these dreadful scenes.

"All sadness was not yet gone, however, and Jack and I during the next two months had still to soothe many a dying pillow, and to close many an eye that ne'er should open more.

"One death-bed I shall ever remember. It was that of poor T——. Somewhat self-opinionated I had always considered him, and somewhat hasty in temper, but I knew him to be warm-hearted, good, and kind and brave even to a fault.

"He it was then who volunteered to bring the 'doolies' containing the sick and wounded by a safe pass into the Residency.

"Through some mistake, however, he took a wrong turning, and soon found himself in a square in the city, that placed his party directly under a heavy fire from the enemy.

"And the gallant fellow, in trying to rectify his error, was shot through the arm, and soon after severely wounded in the temple.

"The doctors amputated the arm, but they told Jack that from the very first they had entertained no hopes of his case.

"He and I had not always been the best of friends, but nevertheless in his last moments he sent for me.

He himself had not given up all hopes of living, even if the surgeons had.

"I went at once.

"Jack Morrison was sitting on a box by his bedside facing the dying man. There were more in that room wounded to the death, and low moans of pain came from many a bed, while here and there I noticed the scanty coverlet drawn up over a soldier's head, and knew that all his griefs and pains were over. That hospital had once been the banqueting-room of the Residency, and barely six months before this, it had been the scene of a very different assembly from that which filled it now. For then, I was told, a bright and gay throng had been assembled to do honour to General Anson. Many who that evening had sparkled with smiles and laughter had suffered and passed away.

"The saddest thing, to my mind, connected with poor T——'s death was his evident anxiety to live. He put his one hand, and drew me closer to him as he whispered, 'Pray for me. O pray for me, that I may recover!'

"I could only press his hand in reply.

"Had I attempted to speak the tears would have choked my utterance."

CHAPTER VII.

YOUNG HODSON'S RIDE—BRAVE DEEDS AT DELHI.

GENERAL ANSON, whose name was mentioned in last chapter, was Commander-in-Chief of the British forces in India before Sir Colin Campbell. He had laboured hard at Umballah to disabuse the mind of his native troops of the impression that the British Government had determined to break their caste by the issue of cartridges greased with the fat of pigs or cows. They listened respectfully enough to all he had to say, but the native officers told him plainly, that although personally they themselves harboured no such belief, the general fears of the army continued the same. We know now that they only spoke the truth.

But even at this time, authorities tell us, Anson was so little impressed with the symptons of mutiny, that he did not think it worth while to make a single representation to the home authorities about them.

It was no wonder then that the Governor-General, who knew little of India, should have failed to perceive that the great Mutiny was at hand. But Anson afterwards ordered the trial by court-martial of the mutineers of Meerut. After the capture of Delhi by the rebels, although difficulties of all kinds surrounded him, it is clear he did not do all he might have done, and there is a probability that some of the terrible miseries and massacres that followed were due in some measure to the dilatoriness of General Anson and his subordinates.

Canning had ordered Anson to take Delhi with a part of his force, and to detach another portion of it to overawe the districts 'twixt Delhi and Cawnpore.

YOUNG HODSON'S RIDE.

Ever hear of this plucky and fearless ride, reader? It was one of the most brilliant things ever accomplished in the North-West of India in these troublous times and only shows what a bold and fearless Englishman can do in the hour of need.

Anson then, although tortured by anxiety and worn out by sickness, was making preparations to obey Lord Canning's orders, and to march upon Delhi, although in his own mind he doubted his ability. Before, however, he could start it was necessary that he should open up communications with General Hewitt at Meerut; but this seemed a sheer impossibility. It did so seem until brave young William Hodson, a lieutenant of the Company's 1st Fusiliers, volunteered for the task. And fraught with danger and difficulty it was.

I give you here a mere outline of this daring ride, if, reader, you are possessed of any imagination you may fill in the details for yourself. The distance then from

Kurnaul, whence he rode, to Meerut, is one hundred and fifty miles, and all this was through an enemy's country, every bush in which might have been supposed to conceal a foe. He accomplished the feat in seventy-two hours, delivered his message, and rode back to Kurnaul, and in four hours more, hurrying on in the mail-cart, he presented himself before his chief.

That chief now began to think in earnest of his march on Delhi.

It was well for India, perhaps, that a few days after this poor Anson was lying dead of cholera at Kurnaul.

* * * * *

"Well, then," said Lord Panmure to Sir Colin Campbell, when that brave general accepted the chief command in India, *vice* Anson dead, "Well, then, when will you be ready to start?"

"Oh, to-morrow, I suppose," was the little-expected reply.

And on the morrow—July 12th, 1857—he duly started.

When asked about his outfit his reply was quite characteristic of the gallant Scot.

"Oh, bother the outfit," he said. "I can easily get all I want in Calcutta."

* * * * *

When Willie Saunders, corporal of the dashing 93rd, and his stalwart companions listened to what all considered Sir Colin's last farewell at Portsmouth, little did they think that he would meet them once again in India, and once again wave his sword at the head of his kilted warriors, and lead them on to victory. But such was to be the case.

Sir Colin arrived in India in August, and at once took command of the army.

And what a terrible state the country was then in the reader already partly knows. The regular native troops of Bengal were all mutineers. And those in Bhopal, Indore, and Gwalior had joined the terrible movement.

That Gwalior contingent was probably the strongest anywhere, and was supposed to be invincible. It amounted to no less than seven regiments of infantry, two regiments of cavalry, five companies of artillery, besides a magazine and siege train. And it numbered among its generals such men as the accursed Nana Sahib and Tantia Topee.

The army investing Lucknow was supposed to be then from one to two hundred thousand strong. Lower Bengal, Bombay, and Madras were quiet, but we had lost Bundelakand, which Burns describes as "a roadless country of forts and fastnesses filled with a turbulent population, the name Bundela having to the Lowland Hindoo much the same significance as a cateran in Scotland, or a moss trooper on the border." Oude was at this time in the clutches of the mutineers, and the whole of the country lying between the Ganges and the Doab was a seething mass of disorder and insurrection.

At this time Sir James Outram, just returned from the Persian Wars, was appointed to the chief command of Cawnpore and Dinapore. He had gone to the front with Colonel Napier (Lord Napier), then of the Bengal Engineers, and, as we have seen, brave Havelock was pushing on towards Lucknow, while Brigadier Neill lay in his rear.

Sir Colin Campbell's task was therefore a gigantic and even Herculean one.

But he was not the man to fear it. In a war like this not only the general in command, and every officer and man under him, must count his own life as nothing—he must do his best, his whole best, and nothing but his best.

Day after day now fresh troops were arriving at Calcutta, and sailors too, and as they came Campbell sent them on to the front. On the 20th of August, for instance, Captain Peel of the *Shannon* came in. Five hundred of his brave blue-jackets with ten eight-inch guns were at once started for Allahabad.

The little army that was besieging Delhi under General Wilson, was about this time reinforced by the brave Brigadier Nicholson with 2500 troops, both native and European, from the Punjaub.

Then the siege of Delhi was begun in earnest, batteries were thrown up and completed with all haste, and the ground was cleared for breaching. Supplies of men and guns too kept pouring in, and at daybreak on the 14th of September the assault commenced.

In a former chapter I gave an account of the fall of this important city, and the terrible massacres that followed. But an attempt was now to be made to reconquer the town and re-establish British authority therein. If this should fail, then indeed our rule in

India might be considered all but lost. But in the soldier's lexicon there is no such word as fail.

We have seen how in their attempts to storm the Residency the Sepoys feared to face our Englishmen, but fell back in disorderly flight, stumbling over the heaps of their own dead and wounded. We must now briefly glance at the storming of Delhi, and see how our men can fight in a breach. I take my account from various authorities, but chiefly from Burne's *Clyde and Strathnairn.*

After the completion of the British batteries, then, the cannonade commenced. This was on the 11th of September, and from that day until the assault we poured an incessant storm of shot and shell upon the city walls, until near the Kashmir and Water Bastions two practicable breaches had been effected.

Then came the awful tug of war.

"The attack," says Burne, "was made by four columns with a fifth in reserve. The first, commanded by Nicholson, consisted of H.M.'s 75th, the first Bengal Fusileers, and 2nd Punjaub Infantry. The second included H.M.'s 8th and 61st regiments and the 4th Sikh Infantry. The third consisted of H.M.'s 52nd, the 2nd Bengal Fusileers, and 1st Punjaub Infantry. The fourth was made up of detachments of European regiments, the Sirmoor battalion of Gurkhas, the Guides Infantry, and the Kashmirian levies. The reserve was composed of the 60th Rifles, the Kumaon battalion of Gurkhas, and the 4th Punjaub Infantry.

"The fourth column advanced first, and was intended as a diversion in favour of the real attacks. It was not very successful. But the other three columns, under cover of the guns of our batteries, made a most determined charge on the Kashmir Bastion, the Water Bastion, and Kashmir Gate.

"With a fierce and exultant shout the first and second dashed onwards and scrambled into the ditch, applied their ladders to the scarp of the wall and swarmed up into the breach under a murderous fire of musketry.

"The blowing open of the Kashmir Gate was the most perilous exploit of the day."

Lieutenants Home and Salkeld commanded the explosion party, which really was a forlorn hope, and consisted of two sergeants, Smith and Carmichael, Corporal Burgess, Bugler Hamthorne, and twenty-four Native Engineers.

In spite of a terrible fire of musketry, the bags were attached to the gates, and Sergeant Carmichael proceeded to lay the train. He was shot dead. Salkeld rushed up to complete the work. He was shot likewise, and fell into the ditch, but he handed the match to Burgess. Burgess fired the train, and then fell, mortally wounded.

And now the bugle rings out the charge, and with a ringing British cheer on and on comes the column. Nothing can withstand them. They dash in, leaping over the bodies of the slain Sepoys. They have barely time to see evidence of fearful sacrifices of Europeans that have taken place but recently, nor a poor English lady, naked, covered with wounds, chained to a stake by the bastion, and jabbering—mad!

If they do see these things, it but nerves their heart for the slaughter, and turns their wrists into triple steel.

That night St. George's banner, broad and gay, waves over the Kashmir Gate.

Poor Nicholson was shot!

In a few days after this gallant assault the whole city was in possession of the British. The king's grey head was respected, but his sons were shot.

So fell Delhi!

* * * * *

On the 16th of September General Outram reached Cawnpore, but he generously left the actual relief of Lucknow Residency to Havelock. "I shall accompany you," he wrote, "only in my civil capacity of Commissioner. To you belongs the glory of relieving the city, for which you have already struggled so much; but my military service is at your command, and I shall serve under you as a volunteer."

No wonder Sir Colin admired this great statesman-soldier, or that he told his friends that he considered Outram's behaviour most chivalrous and handsome.

* * * * *

Outram and Havelock, when they entered Lucknow and relieved the Residency, had intended to remove the garrison, with its women and children, to a place of safety. But this was found impossible in the face of such fearful odds.

They *must* remain therefore until Sir Colin Campbell could come to their relief, and, as Burne says, share with the original garrison all the perils and hardships of an investment.

CHAPTER VIII.

IN FRONT OF LUCKNOW—WHAT BOLD KAVANAGH DID.

THE gallant 93rd regiment, in which our hero Willie Saunders was already acting-sergeant in the Grenadier Company, was pushed up country but a few days after its arrival.

Willie was delighted at the prospect of seeing active service. He was delighted also at his promotion, which his friend Mc Kinnon assured him would soon be confirmed. Besides it gave him the right to mess with the other sergeants, and this in itself was a step in the right direction.

Very cheery was then the letter he wrote home to his mother.

"But," he continued in this epistle after giving her all the news of the voyage, and telling her all his adventures as well as sending her a copy of Jack's letter, "I am not sorry that all this has happened, I am not sorry that I have become a soldier, for these, dear mother, are stirring times, and if I live who knows but that I may yet win a commission. I know I have your prayers and dear father's for my success, and though I am going with my regiment to fight against terrible odds, those prayers will ever comfort me in the darkest hour that may come. And it is something within me that speaks, mother, when I say that living I will never disgrace my country nor my colours, and if I am killed I shall not be found with my back to the foe.

"All our fellows are terribly excited over the massacre of Cawnpore, and are determined to have revenge. And God knows, mother, we may have much more than this to avenge before we reach Lucknow, for I am told that the garrison there and the poor women and children are in dire straits, that Havelock has been beaten back, and that everything is in hopeless confusion.

"I shall know more soon. We are not going to let the grass grow over our boots I can assure you, mother, before we reach Lucknow.

"We are all very cheery and hopeful too. Sergeant McKinnon has been *such* a dear good friend to me. I am sure that but for him I should not now be acting-sergeant.

"Peter McKay says *he* doesn't want any promotion, nor any responsibility. He can fire a gun, and he can wave a claymore, or drive a dirk through a 3-inch deal board, but he wouldn't be a sergeant for all the world.

"You remember, mother, how he and I used to work away at sword exercise. Well Peter was always better than I with the sticks, and now he has developed into the best swordsman in the Grenadier Company, if not in the whole regiment.

"Poor Jack Morrison! I have already told you of the dream I had about him. I cannot help believing, mother, that he is in a terrible position. Oh, how I misjudged him! If I do not see him again alive and well, the sorrow will darken my whole life.

"As to Annie Lindsay—well, you may remember me kindly to her. I must tell you, mother, that I fear I love her just as much as ever; but I am going to try harder and harder than ever to forget her. I have plenty of pride, that will help me—and I have my sword, that is going to be my bride."

* * * * *

On November the tenth we find that the gallant 93rd was encamped along with the rest of the force intended for the final relief of Lucknow about five miles from the Alum Bagh. (*Vide* plan of Lucknow, p. 316.) It was indeed a brave and splendid regiment, and the only really complete one there, numbering, it is said, over one thousand men in the very prime of manhood, seven hundred of whom had the Crimean medals on their breasts.

Next the army was divided into brigades.

"Then the whole force was formed up into a line of columns," says Forbes Mitchell, "to be inspected by Sir Colin Campbell himself.

"The 93rd formed the extreme left of the line in quarter distance column, in full Highland costume, with feather bonnets and dark waving plumes, a solid mass of brawny-limbed men.

"The old chief," says the same writer, "rode along the

line, commencing from the right, halting and addressing a short speech to each corps as he came along.

"The eyes of the 93rd were eagerly turned towards Sir Colin and his staff as he advanced, the men remarking among themselves that none of the other corps had given him a single cheer, but had taken whatever he had said to them in solemn silence.

"We were now formed into close column, so that every man might hear what was said. When Sir Colin rode up he appeared to have a worn and haggard expression on his face; but he was received with a cheer, or rather shout of welcome, that made the echoes ring from the Alum Bagh and surrounding woods.

"His wrinkled brow at once became smooth, and his wearied-looking features broke into a smile.

"'Ninety-third,' he cried, 'when I took leave of you at Portsmouth I never thought I should see you again. I expected the bugle, or maybe the bagpipes, to sound a call for me to go somewhere else long before you would be likely to return to our dearly-loved home. But another commander has decreed it otherwise, and here I am prepared to lead you through another campaign. And I must tell you, my lads, there is work of difficulty and danger before us—harder work and greater dangers than any we encountered together in the Crimea. But the eyes of the people at home—I may say the eyes of Europe and of the whole of Christendom—are upon us, and we *must* relieve our countrymen, women, and children now shut up in the Residency of Lucknow. Soldiers might cut themselves out, or die sword in hand. We have to rescue helpless women and children from a fate far worse than death. When you meet the enemy you must remember that he is well armed, and that he can play at long bowls as well as you can, especially from behind loopholed walls. So when we make an attack you must come to close quarters as quickly as possible. Keep well together in threes, and use the bayonet. Remember that the cowardly Sepoys, who are so eager to murder women and children, cannot look a European in the face, when that look is accompanied by a touch of the cold steel.

"'Ninety-third, you are my own lads. I rely on you to do the work!'

"'That ye may, Sir Colin,' shouted Peter McKay, unable to restrain himself. 'We'll bring the women and bairns out, or we'll die wi' you in the attempt.'

"And now another ringing cheer arose, and this was taken up all along the lines."

The route finally determined upon by Sir Colin was through Dilkoosha Park and along the Goomtee river, attacking the Dilkoosha palace and Park, the fort of the 32nd mess-house, the Secundra Bagh, the Shah Nujeef, and the Moti Munzil.

Hard words to remember, reader, I grant you.

After the mud fort of Jellalabad had been gallantly taken and destroyed on the 13th of November, the force returned and camped all night under arms before the Alum Bagh.

Next day fighting begun in earnest.

That day for the first time in his life Willie Saunders knew what an engagement meant. But right bravely did he do his duty. Men fell dead or wounded around him, he had no time for pity or for thought. He must dash on with his company, for a masked battery had opened upon the attacking force from behind the palace of Dilkoosha.

Lieutenant Roberts—now Major-General Roberts—went down with his horse almost at the first volley and it was thought he was killed. His horse never rose again, but he did, and was soon as active as ever. The artillery now came up, and very soon had taken that masked battery in flank, and the Sepoys were running for their lives to the Martiniere fort.

But on the 15th Peel's brave bluejackets came up in the afternoon, and with the 93rd gallantly carried the Martiniere, and this was held by the Highlanders during that night.

Next day three days' rations were served out, and Sir Colin Campbell once more briefly addressed the lads of the 93rd.

"He loves us best of all, you see," said Willie Saunders, his youthful enthusiasm getting the better of him for once.

"Ah, Willie," replied Sergeant McKinnon, "Sir Colin loves every man that can fight, whether they wear breeks or the kilt. But I must allow his heart warms to the pipes and tartan."

The Story of Kavanagh.

Some days before the attack on the Secundra Bagh, that I shall presently describe, a kind of forlorn hope was undertaken and carried out by one of the imprisoned garrison of Lucknow, which for coolness and daring is probably unexampled in the history of the Indian Mutiny.

Although from the date of the entrance into the

Residency of Outram and Havelock, communication between them and Sir Colin Campbell was constantly kept up by means of well-paid native spies, who really carried their lives in their hands as soon as they started on their dangerous missions, still, in order that the success of the commander-in-chief's enterprise might be secured, it was almost necessary that he should be made acquainted with the topography of the city and its surroundings by someone who had lived therein, and who could act as guide—that man to be if possible —an European.

Sir Colin had maps it is true, and Outram had given him, by means of his spies, his own ideas of the route that should be followed.

Yet the risk was extreme. The little army was about to march against such terrible odds as probably had never before been faced. Even should they be victorious at the outset, how would it end if they had a long march to make through narrow and tortuous streets, in which perhaps barricades would be thrown up every here and there, while every house on each side was loopholed for musketry? In such a case indeed a wrong turning might mean the total annihilation of the whole force.

When Outram and Havelock received Sir Colin's message they were for a time completely nonplussed. How could they possibly ask any man to undertake a task fraught with such terrible danger? For if caught, it did not mean death only to the unhappy man, but death with cruelties and torture so refined that one shudders even to think of them.

But the right man came forward in the nick of time.

He came too all unbidden. He was an Englishman, or at least a Briton, and his name was Kavanagh. He is known till this day as Lucknow Kavanagh. No, not a soldier, but simply a Government clerk, but a man that knew Lucknow well, and every street and lane in it.

There were many in the garrison that heartily wished it had been someone else, for, *entre nous*, reader, Kavanagh was no great favourite with anybody. Holmes, who by the way does not mention the fact that he was not well liked, tells us that Kavanagh was "a man of great physical strength and of iron nerve," and that "the prominent features of his character were a vanity and self-importance so preposterous as almost to amount to insanity."

This seems ungenerous, even if it be not unjust. However Kavanagh felt, or something appeared to tell him, that he alone was cut out to lead this forlorn hope. So after persuading a native spy, whose name was Kanonjee Lall, to be his companion, he went direct to Outram, and told him that he and Lall were prepared to make the hazardous attempt. Outram and Havelock at first could hardly believe, that the brave fellow realised the fearful danger of failure in the enterprise and its awful consequences. But being at last persuaded that he did, their hearts went out to him, and they gladly accepted his offer.

It was not till now that Kavanagh began to reflect on what he had undertaken. To his credit be it said, however, it was not for himself he cared, but for "the ruin that should befall his wife and children if he should fail."

"I vainly struggled," he himself writes, "to convince

myself that it *must* be done, till the convulsions of my heart were relieved by tears."

But he never had a single thought of retreating from the undertaking.

By half-past eight that same night he was ready. He had disguised himself as a budmash, for he could talk the language like a native.

In his belt, but concealed by his clothes, he had placed a revolver, and with this, should he be discovered, he determined to commit suicide rather than to fall into the hands of the Sepoys, to be tortured to death by knives, by hooks, and fire.

Though disliked by many, there was not a person in the garrison whose heart did not warm to him for undertaking what was considered something akin to self-immolation. And many a kindly wish and hearty "God protect you, Kavanagh," went with him as he and his companion said "good night" and passed out through the British lines into the night and the darkness.

They crossed the river by a ford silently, fearfully.

Onwards now they journeyed up the left bank of the river until they came to a bridge of stone, and by this they boldly re-crossed the river and found themselves in one of the principal streets of Lucknow. And now indeed they required all their courage and *nonchalance*. But it did not desert them. They even kept talking and laughing, that they might not excite suspicion. One or more natives addressed them.

Some eyed them so narrowly that Kavanagh thought his time had come, and his hand wandered mechanically to his belt.

But they got clear through the city, and soon found themselves in the open country.

Their real danger was only now commencing, for here they were in Dilkoosha Park, and this was still in the possession of the enemy.

And now they lost their way.

Fearfully, and with beating hearts, they wandered about for what seemed hours, now stopping to listen to sounds in the distant city, or sounds near at hand, and sometimes hiding under the bushes, but dreading capture every moment.

They came at last to a hut, and then Kavanagh did a bold thing. It is but death anyhow, he thought, and coolly he entered the hut and awoke the occupants, and told them he was going with a friend to visit some relations in a distant village, and that he had lost his way. He chatted for a little time quite pleasantly with the people in the hut, who kindly—ah! little did they know what they were doing—told him how to regain his way.

But once more into the darkness they went.

But they now pursued their way with somewhat better heart.

It was by this time just three o'clock in the morning, and presently they could hear right ahead of them the tramp of soldiers coming towards them.

What should they do?

Flight would only precipitate matters; but so frightened was Kanonjee Lall that he threw away a dispatch he was carrying to Sir Colin.

Kavanagh's coolness did not desert him. Instead of seeming in the slightest degree uneasy he marched boldly up to the Sepoys.

"Glad to meet friends," he said. Then he told them the same story he had told the occupants of the hut, and asked these Sepoys the best and safest way to the distant village.

Completely taken off their guard they directed him, and unsuspected Kavanagh continued his perilous journey.

For two long hours they wandered on. It would soon be morning; but Kavanagh by this time felt so exhausted and weary that he recklessly insisted on lying down to sleep.

They could see nothing, but the slight noise they made alarmed a native sentry.

"Who goes there?" was the challenge that rang out.

Once more Kavanagh fingered his pistol.

Was the challenger a friend or a foe?

He started up and went boldly forward, and, lo! he was in the British camp. A few minutes after this he found himself in the presence of Sir Colin Campbell himself.

No man appreciated bravery and deeds of derring-do more than the Commander-in-Chief, so it goes without saying that Kavanagh and Kanonjee Lall received their due meed of praise and a right heartfelt hand-shake.

Probably Kavanagh never slept sounder than he did for an hour or two after this.

He had won the Victoria Cross, and certainly no man ever won it better.

When daylight came the signal that was to announce Kavanagh's safe arrival was hoisted on the Alum Bagh, and great was the rejoicing in the beleaguered garrison.

CHAPTER IX.

CAWNPORE IS AVENGED.

IT was the evening before the battle, and our little army was encamped near the fort of Martiniere. No tents to-night; they must sleep on the bare ground, arms by their sides, knapsacks for pillows. Nor did the Commander-in-Chief himself fare one whit better. For Sir Colin was a true soldier, and when on the war-path would drink his tea from a private's canteen, and be content with the humblest fare.

The night before the battle! Yes, and who could tell, who could even guess, what the morrow had in store for him or for his brave companions? No one could say further than that he meant to do his best, that he meant to do or to die. Figuratively speaking, from the humblest private to the generalissimo himself, they would come back *with* or *on* their shields. But there must be no back about it. Their way led onwards. Onwards to the cannon's mouth; onwards against a hail of musketry; onwards through breach and battlement; onwards until they could reach through fire and smoke to relieve the women and children and soldiers, who were starving behind the ruined Residency walls. To fail in their enterprise meant annihilation for every man in this little army, and every man knew it; and it meant also destruction to every living creature within the beleaguered garrison. But even success itself would be dearly bought, and many a brave Englishman and stalwart Scot, now so full of hope, now so light of limb, would be lying stark and stiff before another sun should set.

* * * * *

By nine o'clock to-night silence reigned throughout the Highlanders' camp, though it was broken, ever and anon, by the thunderous booming of the guns still plying their deadly rain upon the Residency. Among the trees and bushes the fire-flies danced, and great bats went wheeling hither and thither in the starlight. Many of the men were already asleep, others lay with their heads resting on their palms, thinking of their far-off British homes.

But one little group deserves special notice. Five in all they were, and Willie Saunders was the central figure. Peter McKay was there, it is almost needless to say. The others were two corporals and another private.

Willie had been reciting to them, quietly it is true, but most effectively. He had gone over the whole of that wonderful production of Burns's genius, "Tam O' Shanter," and an encore had been demanded and acceded to.

When a tall Herculean figure in tartan kilt and plumes glided silently up to the little group, Willie was just repeating some portions of Campbell's spirited lines to the memory of Burns—

> "And see the Scottish exile, tann'd
> By many a far and foreign clime,
> Bend o'er his home-born verse, and weep
> In memory of his native land,
> With love that scorns the lapse of time,
> And ties that stretch beyond the deep.
>
> "Encamp'd by Indian rivers wild
> The soldier resting on his arms,
> In Burns's carol sweet recalls
> The scenes that bless'd him when a child,
> And glows and gladdens at the charms
> Of Scotia's woods and waterfalls.
>
> "And thou, young hero, when thy pall
> Is cross'd with mournful sword and plume"—

It was at this very moment that McKinnon himself, bending down, placed his hand on Willie's shoulder.

"Tam o' Shanter, if you like," said McKinnon, sitting down on the ground; "but let us have nothing about coffins and palls."

"I'm glad to see ye, sairgent," said Peter McKay, "or raither to hear ye speak, for I canna weel see your face."

"Are you there, Peter?"

"Ay, sairgent, and far (where) else would I be but wi' my foster-brither on a nicht like this?"

"True, true," said the sergeant. "We may not be all together this time to-morrow night!"

"Ha!" cried Peter almost fiercely, "there'll be sore heads among the Sepoys lang ere nine o'clock the morn's nicht. Man! sairgent, though, a lump comes to my throat when I think o' the murdered bairnies and their lady mithers a' flung higgledy-piggledy into the awfu' well o' Cawnpore! My bluid rises to the boilin' point, and seems to sing aloud for revenge. Sairgent, I'm goin' to fight wi' a will the morn!"

"And I!"

"And I!"

"And I!"

The words seemed spoken by everyone in the group.

"Bravo, boys!" said McKinnon. "We'll fight; we all shall fight. And to-morrow when we rush on to the breach, while slogan rings, while bagpipes skirl, one word will be our battle-cry."

"Cawnpore!"

It was a muffled shout, and a simultaneous one, that even those not far away who were asleep heard, and repeated it in their dreams.

There was a momentary silence. Then Willie's voice rose in bold and steady monotone.

> "Tho' our perishing ranks should be strew'd in their gore,
> Like ocean weeds heap'd on the surf-beaten shore,
> Each soldier, untainted by flight or by chains
> While the kindling of life in his bosom remains,
> Shall victor exult or in death be laid low,
> With his back to the field and his feet to the foe;
> And, leaving in battle no blot on his name,
> Look proudly to heaven from the death-bed of fame."

The conversation changed now from the heroic to the homely. It was commenced by Peter McKay himself.

"I'm nae sure," he said, "that I winna fall mysel' the morn in the tulzie. If I dae, Willie, you'll no forget to tell my auld mither, when ye gang hame to the glen, that her laddie was killed crackin' croons (breaking heads) to avenge Cawnpore!"

"Hush, lad, hush!" said McKinnon in a half whisper. "We mustn't forbode. But, Willie," he continued, "if I had my wish now, can you guess where I'd be?"

"I think I can," said Willie. "You wouldn't be far from Dover, nor far from the Albyn Inn and bonnie Ellen Grey."

"You're right. Dear girl! I'll never forget that day in the little inn. Willie, I hardly knew the lassie loved me till then."

"Well, Fergus, she is, maybe, thinking of you even now."

"She is, maybe, praying for us all," said Sergeant McKinnon; "for I'm sure she isn't the girl to pray for one of us and not the other."

"Well," said Peter, "I've a bit lassie that is mebbe prayin' too. I'd like to be back for an 'oor or twa the nicht in the dear auld glen; but, sairgent, dye ken fat (what)?"

"Well?" said the sergeant.

"I wadna want to gang hame, even to see Jeannie, unless I was sure o' gettin' back to crack croons in the mornin.'"

* * * * *

Follow the line (in the plan of Lucknow), reader, from the Alum Bagh to Dilkoosha park and house, thence leftwards to the Martiniere, and so on to the city, and it will give you an idea of the route taken by Sir Colin in his advance.

By means of semaphores on the Martiniere and Residency the army of relief and the beleaguered garrison could communicate, so that Outram and Havelock were perfectly aware of what Sir Colin's movements would be.

The route from the Martiniere took them across the canal.

It was still night, and the stars shining, when the forces under the guidance of brave Kavanagh and the spy Kanonjee Lall arrived at a small village on the east side of the Secundra Bagh. Here a halt was made that the heavy guns might come up.

But at daybreak the enemy was driven through the village in fine style.

Indeed, the defenders had evidently been deceived as to Sir Colin's route, for he had made a reconnaisance, and they had gone to meet him in another direction.

When half-way through this village, Forbes Mitchell tells us something transpired that did not tend to mitigate the feelings of hatred our fellows bore to the Sepoys. "Here," says that author, "we saw a naked wretch of a strong muscular build, with his head closely shaven except for a tuft on his crown, and his face all streaked in a hideous manner with white and red paint, his body smeared with ashes.

"One of the Highlanders wanted to drive a dirk through him, saying he looked like a murderer, when Captain A. O. Mayne—not Jack Morrison's Mr. Mayne—interceded for him, saying he was harmless.

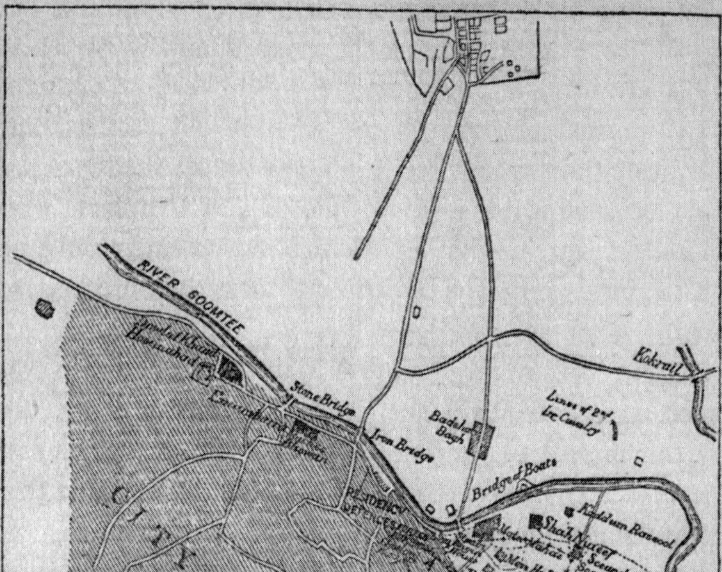

PLAN OF LUCKNOW.

+ + + + Route of Generals Havelock and Outram, September 25th, 1857.

• • • • Route of 78th Highlanders, September 25th, 1857.

-------- Route of Sir Colin Campbell's army, November 14th to 17th, 1859.

"Hardly had the young officer finished speaking ere the painted scoundrel pulled out a blunderbuss and shot him dead. It goes without saying that the murderer was bayoneted next minute."

Shortly after this the Highlanders, with whom we have most to do, came right in front of the loopholed fort, Secundra Bagh.

It was a two-storied building in the centre of a garden, which had a wall around it. Major Blunt's artillery, and Travers with his eighteen pounders, did glorious service. The gallant bluejackets helped to man the guns as coolly as if they had been on board their ship. The thunder of war had begun in earnest, the Highlanders meanwhile being ordered to lie down for shelter under a mud wall.

The fire from the fort was of a murderous and terrible character, and had the weapons been well aimed, it would have been impossible for our force to have stood against it.

As it was, our artillerymen were falling fast, and the 93rd, in their burning anxiety, could scarcely be kept quiet behind their shelter, albeit Sir Colin cried, more than once, "Lie down, 93rd, lie down. Your lives are not your own to-day, and every man is worth his weight in gold to his country."

But at every loophole the 93rd kept firing, and every protruding musket drew a shot. The only fault of the men was that their eagerness to fight caused them to expose their heads and shoulders too often.

At long last—and what an interminable time it had seemed—a kind of breach was made. It was a mere hole indeed, but the 4th Punjaubees went manfully and gallantly at it, shouting as they did so their shrill battle cry.

Colonel Ewart was in command of the seven companies of the 93rd who were supporting Peel's guns, Colonel Andrew Leith Hay having been detached with the other three companies to clear the old 32nd Barracks.

The 93rd were burning to follow the Punjaubees.

They soon had a chance.

For the two European officers who led them fell, and seeing this they wavered and halted. It was a moment of extreme anxiety for Sir Colin, but he quickly turned to Ewart.

"Colonel Ewart," he shouted, "bring on the tartan. Let my own lads at them. Forward, men, forward!"

"Before," says Mitchell, "the command could be repeated by the colonel, or the buglers had time to sound the advance, the whole seven companies like one man leapt over the wall with such a yell of pent-up rage as I had never heard before.

"It was not a cheer, but a concentrated yell of rage and ferocity that made the echoes ring again, and it must have struck terror into the defenders' hearts, for they actually ceased firing, and we could see them through the breach rushing from the outside wall to take shelter in the two-storied building in the centre of the garden, the gate and doors of which they firmly barred."

Of this glorious fight I cannot give many details. Is it not historical?

But let me mention that high above the charging cheer rose the wild skirl of the great Highland bagpipe, the pipe-major and his seven pipers playing the brave old tune the "Haughs o' Cromdale." It is said that when after the fight Sir Colin complimented him for the manner in which he and his men had played, John McLeod, the pipe-major, answered naively—

"Weel, sir, I just thocht the boys would fecht a' the better wi' a bit Scots lilt to help them on."

I have said that the breach was but a hole. This is true, and so small was it that hardly could three get in abreast, though pushed by those behind.

A Sikh officer was the first through, but killed of course, so says Holmes. But gallant Forbes Mitchell tells us that "it has always been a disputed point who got through the hole first. I believe the first man inside was Lance-Corporal Donelly of the 93rd, who was killed inside, then Subadar Gokul Sing, followed by Sergeant-Major Murray of the 93rd, also killed, and fourth Captain Burroughs, severely wounded. It was about this time," says this author modestly enough, "that I got through myself, pushed up by Colonel Ewart, who immediately followed."

Colonel Ewart was almost immediately after engaged in a fierce fight with five or six Sepoys, and he shot them down right and left.

The Sepoys fought that day as devils may be supposed to fight.

Sergeant McKinnon, Willie Saunders, and Peter McKay found themselves fighting side by side, the sergeant in the centre. Peter's bayonet did fearful execution, so too did the claymores of his companions.

Soon after getting in, however, Peter somehow found himself possessed of a claymore also. I have already said that he was a splendid swordsman. But Peter had an adventure on this same day, that I shall presently tell you of, and in which he all but met his match.

Meanwhile the fighting inside the Secundra Bagh was of a fearful description. No quarter was given. How could the enemy expect it after all their massacres and inhuman acts of cruelty?

"The air," says Holmes, "was rent by the screams of the rebels for help, the loud commands of the officers to go in among them and destroy them with the bayonet, and the wild yells and curses of the British soldiers as, in answer to despairing appeals for mercy, they bade their victims remember Cawnpore.

"In the midst of this awful scene a fire suddenly burst forth, and many of the rebels, who sought an easier death by flinging themselves on the bayonets of their opponents, were remorselessly hurled back into the flames. Those who had not yet perished retreated into the towers at the angles of the building. One of these was so obstinately defended that it was found necessary to bring up artillery, and for a time the fierce shouts of the victors and the sullen utterances of the vanquished were drowned in the deep thunder of the guns, and the crash of masses of stone falling from the wrecked tower.

"Still from the topmost rooms there poured an incessant musketry fire, but the stormers forced their way up the stairs with fixed bayonets, and though the caged rebels smote them wildly from above with their tulwars they could not escape, they could not repel the rising tide.

"The corpses of the slain, pitched down from the windows above, fell with a dull thud on the ground, and when towards sunset the horrid din was hushed, two thousand dead, but not one living rebel, remained in the Secundra Bagh."

Some authorities give the number as nearer to three thousand, counting not only the fighting men, but the budmashes, for none were spared.

It seems horrible, but it is none the less true, that in their agony of terror many of the poor wretches tried to hide themselves under the heaps of slain.

But night was coming on, and before darkness fell Sir Colin determined to capture a mosque called the Shah Nujeef, which had been turned into a fort.

The place was in a garden about one hundred and fifty yards from the Secundra Bagh, and was surrounded by a strong high wall, with bush or jungle and mud cottages outside.

It was near to the bush where Peter McKay met the turbaned old Hindoo who was so nearly doing him to death. Peter carried his gun and bayonet, but he had managed to keep the claymore also. The man who attacked him was tall and powerfully built, though his beard was white as the snow on Ben Rinnes. He seemed to have been running amuck, and while his eyes glared in fury he waved aloft a blood-dripping tulwar.

Peter was not afraid, yet as the fanatic attacked him he dropped his gun and bayonet, and though with his sword he kept defending himself against blows that fell like wintry rain, he kept retreating hastily till he had enticed his enemy into a comparatively quiet place.

It was then that Peter drew himself up to his full height, and forthwith assumed the offensive, while some of his comrades, Willie Saunders among the rest, stood by astonished.

"Noo, my birkie," Peter cried, "here we have it a' to our twa bonnie selves, and I'll just gie ye a taste o' the good claymore. Hooch! here's at ye!"

The old man fought well and skilfully, and he fought in silence.

But Peter's Aberdeen tongue never ceased to wag any more than did his sword.

Clash, clash, whish, whish, went the claymore, with sparks at every stroke. No two men could have been better matched.

"Man!" cried Peter, "ye play richt weel. Wheet! Losh! ye nearly drove my harns (brains) out that time." Clash, clash, "Missed again, Borlam Dick. Now what do ye say to this? This is Lonach fashion, hooray!" And Peter grasping his claymore with two hands made so sudden an onslaught on his antagonist as to break down his guard, slice a piece off his turban, and roll him on his back.

A less practised swordsman would now have ended the combat at a single blow.

Not so Peter. As he afterwards told Willie this duel was the only bit of real recreation he had enjoyed that day. So he merely leaned on his sword for a moment, and looked quietly down at his prostrate enemy.

"Tak' your breath, Borlam," he said. "Faith! ye'll need it a' before Peter is done wi' ye. Oh, ye needna gnash your teeth and glower like a cock eatin' leeks, I never struck a man yet when he was doon, so you 're safe eneuch."

A moment after, the combat was renewed with treble ferocity on the part of Peter's enemy.

"Noo," said Peter, "wi' a due respect"—clish, clash—"to your"—whish, whash—"capital swordmanship, I maun even"—cling, clang—"bring this scrimmage to a"—whing, whang—"conclusion"—clish, clash. "Did ever ye hear tell o' the auld seventh cut"—whing whang—"Far are ye noo, Borlam Dick?"

Where, indeed? Borlam Dick, as Peter called him, was stretched lifeless on the ground.

"Cawnpore," said Peter, and went back to pick up his gun and bayonet.

CHAPTER X.

"THE EYES OF BOTH WERE DIMMED WITH TEARS."

BUT harder fighting still was in store for the brave little army of relief that evening, before they could think of rest. Alas! the rest which many of them would obtain would be the sleep that knows not breaking. For a long time in vain did Peel's heavy guns thunder against the walls of the Shah Nujeef. The walls of the fort replied with a force and fury there was no subduing.

And night was coming on.

Sir Colin's men too were falling in dozens around him. The crisis of battle had indeed come at last.

The time had come for such decisive action as can only be taken by a hero, that hero himself a genius. The time had come, and the man was there. That man was the white-haired general on his white horse, he with the grim, war-worn, but kindly face, whose every glance gave hope and confidence to the men who knew and so dearly loved him. They were his own lads, as he loved to call them, the men who had fought by his side on the red fields of Balaklava and Alma. He gathered these around him now, and once more proceeded to address them, though the words he spoke were few and simple.

But by this time, Mitchell tells us, "the sun was getting very low, a heavy cloud of smoke hung over the field, and every flash of the guns and rifles could be clearly seen. The enemy in hundreds were visible on the ramparts, yelling like demons, brandishing their swords in one hand and burning torches in the other, while they shouted to us to come on. But little impression had been made on the solid walls of masonry. Brigadier Hope and his *aide-de-camp* were rolling on the ground together, the horses of both shot dead, and the same shell that had done this mischief had exploded one of our ammunition waggons, killing and wounding several men.

"Altogether the position looked black and critical, when Major Barnston and his battalion of detachments were ordered to storm. This, although a made-up battalion, advanced bravely to the breach, and, I think, their leader, Major Barnston, was killed, and the command devolved on Captain Wolseley. He made a most determined attempt to get into the place, but there were no scaling ladders, and the wall was still almost twenty feet high.

"During the heavy cannonade the masonry had fallen down in flakes, but still leaving an inner wall standing almost perpendicular, and in attempting to climb up this, the men were raked with a perfect hell of missiles—

grenades and round shot . . . arrows and brickbats, burning torches of rags and cotton saturated with oil, and even boiling water was dashed upon them. In the midst of the smoke the breach would have made a very good representation of Pandemonium."

The stormers were therefore driven back, and it was then that Sir Colin called upon the gallant 93rd to make one last, one desperate attempt to capture the place.

"My brave fellows!" he shouted, his voice having a touch of almost pleading agony in it, "it was not my intention to have called upon you to-day for further great effort, or to storm positions; that building in front must be carried, and the 93rd must do it. Remember, lads, the lives at stake inside the Residency are those of women and children, and they must be saved! I myself will lead you!"

"No, no!" cried a hoarse Scotch voice; "your life is far too precious to risk, Sir Colin! Stay behind, General; we will lead ourselves!"

It is a question, however, whether even the Highlanders could have been successful against the breach from which the battalion of detachments had been beaten back, had not Sergeant Paton of the 93rd discovered a breach in the north-east corner of the rampart adjoining the river Goomtee.

To reach this the Highlanders had to rush down a ravine.

This they quickly did, Paton himself leading the way to show them where he had discovered the breach, which indeed was little more than a cleft.

Meanwhile a feint was made at the former breach, but

when the enemy saw that the other gap was discovered, and that the furious 93rd were storming there, they gave up heart, and part fled in terror through the back gate and away towards the river, and the rest made for the Motee Munzil or Pearl Mosque.

Scores of the enemy, however, were slaughtered before they could escape.

Poor Sir Colin! It had been an anxious time for him, but now as he listened he heard the wild shout of the Highlanders rising and swelling high over the din of the battle, and he knew the day was ours.

* * * * *

* * * * *

It was but a war-worn kind of sleep our heroes had that night; for in their dreams, even the men seemed to be fighting their battles over again, and once more slaying the slain.

That night some of the soldiers, who were not dead beaten, had to remove about five thousand pounds of loose gunpowder from the tomb of the Shah Nujeef, which gave this extemporised fort its name; and hardly had they finished ere from across the Goomtee came the roar of guns and shells, and red-hot shot fell thick and fast upon the place.

Men so war-worn and weary, however, as were the 93rd can sleep under any circumstances, and so, though often muttering aloud, and even shouting, "Cawnpore! Cawnpore!" in their dreams, the gallant fellows slumbered on.

* * * * *

LITTLE DRUMMER ROSS.

The story of the Shah Nujeef would scarcely be complete did I not tell you of this boy's exploit. Little drummer-boys if brave are usually great favourites in a regiment, and sometimes they are possessed of a splendid audacity which one might almost call "cheek."

Without doubt this little drummer Ross had complete possession of all his faculties, and was quite as agile as any powder monkey that ever trode the decks of a man-o'-war in the days of Drake or Nelson.

At daybreak, then, an order was given to communicate with the beleaguered garrison the results of yesterday's fighting, or at least to let them know by signals that we were in possession of the place. A rough but strong rope ladder was therefore got together and fixed to the roof of the dome, and up this a lieutenant and sergeant with the little boy Ross swarmed to make the necessary signals. These were the waving of the regimental colours and a feather bonnet; while at the same time boy Ross was to sound the regimental call on the bugle.

It was a bold adventure, and one of very great danger, for soon they were noticed by the enemy, and round shot came hurtling towards and over them.

After they had descended it suddenly occurred to that irrepressible young monkey Ross that he for one hadn't had enough of it. So up he went again, hand over hand, waved his Highland bonnet, and once more sounded the call. What cared he that he drew more shot from the foe. He crowed like a cock at them in insolent defiance, and when his officer ordered him below at once he still lingered, says Forbes-Mitchell, "until he had tootled forth two verses of Yankee Doodle."

When he did come down, and was called to account by Lieutenant McBean for gross disobedience of orders, he looked up in the officer's face with a comical smile, and begged forgiveness. "But ye maun ken, sir," he said, "that I was born when the regiment was in Canada, and when my mither was on a visit to an aunt in the States, and as sure as death, sir, I couldna come doon till I had sang Yankee Doodle just to mak' my American cousins envious when they hear o' a' the braw things done by the 93rd, and that their littlest and wee-est drummer laddie sang Yankee Doodle under fire on the highest mosque in Lucknow."

This lad was in reality only a child, being but twelve years old, and small for his years.

What could Lieutenant McBean do, therefore, but bite his lip to hide a smile, and order the little rascal about his business.

Well, I never heard that little drummer-boy Ross received the Victoria Cross, but there are probably men to-day wearing it who are not half so brave as he.

* * * * *

There was much to be done yet before the Residency could be relieved, more daring engagements, more taking of forts, and much more hard fighting. But on the 17th of November—the very day after the wild tulzie at Secundra Bagh and the Shah Najeef—amidst a storm of bullets, the generals, Havelock and Outram, with Napier, Eyre, and young Henry Havelock, rushed across a piece of vacant ground and entered the fort of Motee Mainzil safely. Here the first to meet them was Hope Grant. With him Havelock shook hands, and then advanced towards the men, who were cheering wildly.

Havelock was moved to tears, and could say but little. The little speech he did make, however, was received with a burst of enthusiasm, and soon after this he and General Outram joined Sir Colin Campbell himself.

I need hardly say that as soon as the soldiers in the garrison had seen that Sir Colin Campbell had silenced the Secundra Bagh, they did all they could to lessen the distance he would have to traverse before he reached the Residency. They stormed two buildings after mining them, and drove the enemy pell-mell to other parts of the city.

The withdrawal of the garrison in safety, with all the women and children, was an enterprise of very great difficulty, but it was successfully accomplished at last. Then Sir Colin retired to the Dilkoosha Park once more.

He had effected his object, but though he was earnestly entreated to take complete possession of the city he stedfastly refused. He had all along, he said, regarded the Residency as a false position, and one not worthy any longer to be held. And he added he would need all his little army to completely re-conquer India.

I may add here that although the British garrison at Lucknow, that had undergone such terrible sufferings, was thus relieved, the city now fell into the hands of the mutineers, who restored its forts and rendered it what they considered impregnable. But in the following March Sir Colin laid siege to it once more in right good

"The officer rapidly advanced, his two brown hands outstretched."

p. 331.

earnest, and I need hardly add that he captured it. For an account of this memorable siege I cannot do better than refer you to Kaye, Gubbins, or Holmes.

* * * * *

It was not until the evening of the 22nd that after their long estrangement Willie Saunders and his dear friend, honest Jack Morrison, met upon the heights of Dilkoosha.

Willie, indeed, had no idea that Jack was in Lucknow He often thought of him, often prayed for him, and he never forgot that dream, though as often as not he thought of him as one who was dead and gone.

But on this particular evening, while Willie sat beneath a tree, quietly talking to his friend, stalwart McKinnon, who, with the exception of a shin-wound from a tulwar, had gone through the fighting without a scratch, and while both were watching the sun sinking red and low over the city, a private came up.

"A gentleman wants to see you, Sergeant Saunders."

Willie sprang up in a moment.

A tall figure in officer's uniform, but somewhat ragged and worn, was approaching. His back being to the rosy sunset for a few seconds Willie did not know him.

The officer rapidly advanced, his two brown hands outstretched.

"Willie!"

"Jack!"

Not another word could either say for fully half a minute. Their hearts were far too full. And will it be believed—the eyes of both were dimmed with tears.

CHAPTER XI.

DEATH OF HAVELOCK—EN-ROUTE FOR CAWNPORE.

WHAT a deal they had to say, however! What a deal they had to talk about and tell each other, when at last they could speak!

The sun went down; the stars came out; bats flew about, and fire-flies danced round every bush, and still they sat and talked.

At last Willie jumped up.

"You will not go yet, Jack," he said. "I will be back in a few minutes. I must see poor Peter McKay."

"Oh, I'll come with you, Willie. I had forgotten to ask about him. Is he ——."

"Yes, I fear he is fatally wounded. His left hand was shattered with a shot, and has been removed, but Dr. Munro gives me but small hopes of him."

They met one of the surgeons and eagerly enquired about Peter.

"Doing well, sergeant," was the reply, "and was asking about you."

"Peter McKay," said Willie, quietly approaching the place where his foster-brother lay. "Peter, I am glad you are a little better. See. Who do you think I have brought to see you?"

Willie let the light of a lantern shine on Jack's honest, good-natured, but somewhat worn face as he spoke.

"What," cried Peter, half raising himself from his pallet of grass, "is it possible? Oh, this is a joyful nicht!"

He extended his one hand as he spoke.

"Man!" he added, "I was preparin' to tak' leave o' this sublunary sphere, but not a hair o' me will dee [die] yet. Sit doon, sir, sit. Mr. Jack, sit doon."

It was twelve o'clock before Willie and Jack parted that night, and they might have sat together for hours longer, and still not told each other all they had to say.

"Good-night, Willie."

"Good-night, dear Jack. Isn't it just like old times?"

"Just like old times."

"Good-night."

"Good-night."

* * * * *

THE DEATH OF HAVELOCK.

Poor Havelock!

The brave, the good, the true!

He lay dying in his tent. Dying on a doolie, his son Harry, the boy soldier, although wounded in one arm, seated on the ground beside him, attending with his other hand to his father's wants. It was known even on the

23rd that it could be but a question of time, known by his doctors, known by the great hero himself. Nor did he repine. "I die happy and contented," he said. "For forty years I have so ruled my life, that when death came I might face it without fear."

On the very evening before his death Outram himself had a most touching interview with him. "His tenderness," writes this general, "was that of a brother. He told me he was dying, and spoke from the fulness of his heart of the feelings which he bore towards me, and of the satisfaction with which he looked back to our past intercourse and service together, which had never been on a single occasion marred by a disagreement of any kind, nor embittered by one angry word."

Next day the hero quietly, painlessly, breathed his last.

They carried him to the Alum Bagh in the very doolie in which he had died, and there they buried him under the shade of a mango tree.

A simple monument enough. And they tell me that the letter H which some kindly hand carved in the bark is still faintly visible.

"On the low plain by the Alum Bagh," writes one of Sir Colin's officers, "they made his humble grave, and Campbell and Outram and Inglis, and many a stout soldier who had followed him in all his headlong march, and through the long and fatal street, were gathered there to perform the last rites to one of England's noblest dead.

"But," he adds, "as long as the memory of great deeds and high courage and spotless self-devotion is cherished among his countrymen, so long will Havelock's lonely tomb in the grove beneath the scorching Eastern sky, hard by the vast city—the scene alike of his toil, his triumph, and his death—be regarded as one of the most holy spots where her patriot soldiers lie."

The requiem for the dead was the volleys they fired over his grave, and the tears shed by even strong, stalwart men of the Ross-shire Buffs, told how dearly he had been beloved.

So they left him alone in his glory.

"'T is a soldier lies there—but his voice now is gone,
And lowly the hero is lying;
No sound meets the ear save the crocodile's moan,
And the breeze 'mid the palm trees sighing.
But lone though he rests where the camel is seen
Through the wilderness heavily pacing,
His grave in our bosoms shall ever be green,
And his monument ne'er know defacing."

* * * * *

* * * * *

On the morning of the 27th of November all was bustle and stir, for Campbell was leaving with his great and precious convoy, and an army of about three thousand men.

"Good-bye," he said to Outram. "Nay," he added, "I will not say good-bye, but *au revoir*. You will be able to hold your own for a month or two here at the Alum Bagh. Then—— I will return and wipe those rascally Sepoys out of Lucknow."

This was a morning of sad partings, as well as of bustle and stir; for Willie and Jack had to say good-bye once again. The former was going with McKinnon and his company. And Frank Wood was going with his sister home to England *viâ* Calcutta, if ever they should reach it alive.

Poor Peter McKay was among those who were borne along in doolies. He would never fight again.

"But when I go home," he told Jack and Willie, "I'll tell them all about you, and I'm sure they will a' be richt glaid to see me. I'll get a wooden left han'; and losh! I'll be able to dae a bit o' work among the kye and cattle, just as in the dear auld times."

There were tears in Lily's eyes as honest, brown-faced Jack bade her good-bye.

There was moisture in Jack's too, and a tremor in his voice that told the tale of how dear this sister of Frank's had become to him.

Before going any further let Lily herself say a few words about the march from Lucknow, because this gives us the story, with a few of its details, from a woman's or girl's point of view.

LILY SPEAKS AGAIN.

"Never while I live shall I forget that day of our deliverance from Lucknow, with all its danger and its din and its anxiety! It was about four o'clock on the 19th of November when I with three other ladies, after packing our few belongings into as small a compass as possible, were ready to leave the Residency.

"Our carriage had once been a very comfortable kind of buggy, no doubt; but now it was a mere skeleton—no cushions, and it had been riddled with shot. Our two horses were so miserably ill and starved, that but for the assistance of big, sturdy Jack and my brother Frank I do not think they could have dragged it along at all. Many parts of the road were still exposed to the fire of the enemy, and exceedingly dangerous. One more particularly so; and here we had to leave our rattle-trap conveyance, and crawl along a trench dug for us by the Highlanders.

"The whole town seemed a wilderness or desert of ruins, and the fearful din and uproar and terror were distracting in the extreme.

"It was a terrible experience, altogether. One of my friends, however, recognised the ruins of her old home, and she was homeless now indeed, without husband, brother, or children.

"We reached the Secundra Bagh at last, and the brave soldiers came crowding round us—our deliverers they were—to shake our hands, many of them offering us tea out of their own canteens.

"The air all around the Secundra Bagh was still tainted with the blood of the slain. It seemed like a huge charnel-house or butcher's *abattoir*, though the dead had already been buried.

"The Dilkoosha had been one of the king's palaces, and was situated in beautiful gardens, or rather gardens that had been beautiful. And these gardens had been the scene of many a pleasant party and merry picnic in the days for ever gone. We left the Secundra Bagh after a few hours' halt, and were borne along to the Dilkoosha in doolies, with all the children and also the wounded.

"Arrived at the Dilkoosha we found that the officers

were all ready to receive us, had thrown open their mess tents, and spread a cold collation for us. And, oh, how sweet it tasted after all the privations we had so long undergone! We slept on the ground that night in make-shift beds, but we had the sweet satisfaction of feeling that we were safe. Indeed, when I awoke next morning, for a time I could scarcely believe it was not all a happy dream.

"Soon after poor Havelock breathed his last I and my friends were all packed into a kind of hackery, but it was hours of weary waiting before we started. I fear, from an incident that occurred, that we ladies grumbled a little, for an elderly gentleman walked up to us, and, raising his cap, said—

"'May I ask you, ladies, if there is anything wrong, or any cause for complaint? I have some little authority at headquarters, and might possibly be able to assist you.'

"You may easily guess how ashamed we all were. But little did we know at that moment who the gentleman was.

"It was late that evening before we reached the Alum Bagh, and terribly tired and almost ill we were with the heat and the dust and the jolting.

"I have thought of that jolting journey in the hackery many times since, and thought at the same time of the far more terrible journey our poor doomed and wretched countrywomen had to make, back to Cawnpore from the blood-stained ghaut of massacre to the fearful prison which they would never leave alive. What a contrast! And yet we were peevish, and cried and grumbled like sick children.

"Once more, then, we were on the road *en route* for Cawnpore.

"Our moving camp in column was nine miles in length, and all day long we were pushed on—not rapidly, that would have been a treat; but slowly, *so* slowly—and only permitted the briefest of halts now and then. It was late and dark before we reached our bivouac, and but for my brother Frank would not have found out the place appropriated to us. It took him an hour to find it, so great was the bustle and confusion. Meanwhile we had been moved some distance, so that when the poor fellow came back he found us gone, and had quite a long and weary hunt for us.

"For two hours more we waited in a ploughed field, till our tent came and was pitched; but no camels had yet come up with our baggage, so we had to do the best we could. Our lodging was on the cold, cold ground as the song says, only luckily we had canvas above us to shield us from the dew.

"About daybreak the messman came to say we could have coffee and tea and food. What a treat! We called to him to hurry, and we were just comfortably settled down on some boxes the camels had brought up, and having a nice warm breakfast, when in the grey dawn we noticed a figure approaching, and heard a voice exclaim—

"'Why, whose nice tent is this? Ladies? Oh, certainly *they* must be seen to, and have their tea and their coffee *They* must be attended to first. My poor wounded soldiers lying out in the open, are of not the slightest consequence.'"

"And away he went grumbling.

"It is needless to say that we abused the old man most heartily among ourselves, and even called him a bear and worse. It was the same gentleman who had come to our hackery at Dilkoosha. It was Sir Colin himself. But when some one told him the opinion we entertained of him he laughed right pleasantly nevertheless.

"We were soon *en route* for Cawnpore once again; but this was to be our last day's journey. We had to halt, however, on the banks of the river, and then heavy firing was heard, and to our dismay we were told that the city had once more fallen into the hands of the rebel foe."

CHAPTER XII.

THE SHIP SAILED SOUTHWARDS AND AWAY.

SIR Colin Campbell's reasons for leaving Lucknow so hastily and hurrying on to Cawnpore were, that he had heard no word for days from Windham, who was holding the city, and was naturally anxious to get to his assistance.

And as it turned out greatly indeed was that assistance needed; for with his small force it would be impossible to render the place defensible for any length of time.

Tantia Topee, too, had taken the opportunity afforded him by the absence of the Commander-in-Chief to gather a huge army together in order to march against it. These included the forces that had been under Nana Sahib, and altogether made up a force of about twenty-five thousand men.

Feeling certain of victory Tantia Topee crossed the river Jumna on the 10th of November, after detaching a strong force to keep a grip on Calpee, and commenced his march upon Cawnpore.

Windham waited, but waited in vain, for the appearance of Sir Colin's vanguard, nor could he get any news of him, and he naturally concluded that he had been unsuccessful at Lucknow, and was probably besieged there in some of the forts. Although a very brave man, Windham lacked the capabilities of a great general. He could not remain inactive, however, and therefore he marched forth to meet Tantia, and defeated him. He did not follow up his victory, but fell back on Cawnpore.

Now Tantia was as long-headed a general as any in the rebel army, if not indeed *the* cleverest. He naturally asked himself the question, Why had Windham fallen back on the city instead of pursuing his conquest? The answer came quickly enough — Cawnpore was not defensible. He at once resolved therefore to attack it, and of his intentions Windham, from lack of spies, was kept for a time in ignorance.

Not long though, for while reconnoitring about twelve o'clock he heard the roar of Tantia's artillery, and hastily proceeded to do his best to repel the attack.

This was on the 27th of November, and on that day began the second battle of Cawnpore. Things went badly from the first. His dispositions were far from wise, and one of Windham's officers actually retreated without even a show of resistance, from a village he ought to have held at all hazards. Then the drivers deserted, and ammunition failed, till at last he was obliged to fall back upon a position on some brick-kilns.

Luckily just as the enemy was commencing to attack the entrenchments in full force, reinforcements came up from Futtehpore. By means of these he managed to repel the foe.

Carthew, the Brigadier who had received orders to fall back, had now contra orders to return. But on the whole the day ended sadly, and knowing well that next morning the enemy would again attack him with all his force and all his fury, Windham spent an anxious and harassed night.

Next day's fighting was terrible, and on the whole Colonel Carthew was the hero. But Sir Colin had arrived and taken charge, though his forces had not yet come up.

"The night," says Holmes, "passed quietly. But looking out at daybreak, Tantia saw that the plain beyond the farther bank of the Ganges was white with the tents of another British army. Knowing that that army would soon be upon him unless he could prevent it from crossing the river, he caused his artillery to open fire upon the bridge. Peel's heavy guns and all the British field batteries swiftly replied, and for some time the banks of the river were over-clouded with smoke, but the rebels were gradually overpowered and obliged to abandon their attempt. Then the advanced guard of Sir Colin's army moved on to the bridge, and followed by the women and children, the sick and wounded, the long train of baggage carts and the rear guard crossed the canal, and encamped on the plain hard by the entrenchment, from which, five months before, another procession had issued forth to die."

The position of the rebels, however, was still a very strong one, and there was no chance of dislodging and punishing them, until he could despatch his convoy of women and children with the sick and wounded to Allahabad.

Lily Wood tells me that though before reaching the bridge terrible firing was heard, the real truth that a great battle was raging, being carefully concealed from them.

They got settled at last in the artillery barracks, while the moon shone brilliant down on a sad scene of desolation everywhere around them.

Lily and one of her friends left Cawnpore travelling in a palkee. This was comfortable enough, but still there were no tents for the convoy except what they managed to erect with boxes and shawls, thus securing enough privacy to enable them to enjoy the luxury of ablution and even a bath.

At long, long last, however, the refugees from the sad siege of Lucknow were safe in Allahabad, from which in due time they were despatched to Calcutta.

A few weeks after this Frank and his sister were safely on board ship and setting sail for England. There were also very many invalids and wounded men, and among these was our honest friend Peter McKay.

Lily offered her services as nurse, and these were gladly accepted by the surgeons, so that she and Peter became great friends.

"If ever there was an angel on earth," Peter McKay told the junior surgeon, "or if ever an angel stepped in shoe leather, Miss Lily Wood is one."

The doctor laughed a little, for the idea of angels wearing shoes was somewhat new to him.

But what perfect peace now reigns on board that ship, as she goes sailing south and away towards the Cape, the glad sunshine sparkling in every rippling wave, the breeze that fills each sail fanning the cheeks of those that lounge languidly on chairs on deck, bringing back the glad glow of health to their cheeks, and to their hearts the hope and joy to which they had so long been strangers!

Is it any wonder that they look back with horror to the days they spent in the murder-tainted air of Lucknow, or that they converse in whispers of the dread and awful massacres of Delhi and Cawnpore? Not a soul there surely that morn, noon, and night, does not rise in thankfulness to the God who saw fit to shield them from danger and death, and restore them to peace and to safety.

And yet amidst all their joy many a tear is shed, when they think of those dear friends they never, never can see again.

CHAPTER XIII.

FATE OF THE ARCH-REBEL TANTIA—FINAL BATTLE OF LUCKNOW.

I DID not make my last chapter a long one, because I was unwilling to darken its close by the relation of further fighting. Let that ship sail southwards and away with her precious freight of rescued women and children, and the uncomplaining sick and wounded, to their peaceful homes in England, but we have still to linger a little while longer on India's burning plains.

It is but right the reader should know something of the fate of the fiend Tantia Topee. His master, the Nana Sahib, was never captured. All that we can say of him is that he fell into the hands of God.

I have said then that the rebels held a strong position at Cawnpore.

But Sir Colin was now free to act, and though his army was but a small one—consisting of only 5000 infantry, in four brigades, six hundred cavalry, and thirty-five guns—every heart therein was brave and true, and every man longed to strike a blow at the monster Tantia, and once more avenge the foul massacres of Cawnpore.

Sir Colin determined to attack with all his strength the camp of the vaunted and so-called invincible Gwalior Contingent. If he secured the Calpee Road he could cut off their retreat.

The third battle of Cawnpore, therefore, was commenced on the morning of the 6th December, by Windham, who, with guns and mortars, poured a terrible fire into the centre and left of the enemy.

The fire was so hot and incessant, and so many of Tantia's men fell before it, that, considering this was the main attack, he drew forces from his right which stretched down behind the canal towards the Calpee road, in order to repel it.

Greathead's men next closed quickly on to the line of the canal, and engaged the centre with musketry fire; and farther to the left Walpole's brigade crossed the canal, and sweeping past the town, kept back by sheer pluck and determination the Sepoys that tried to come out. From the extreme left onwards next dashed the cavalry and horse artillery, while other two brigades of infantry—those of Hope and Inglis—rapidly crossed the plain in two lines. The fire of the enemy, who were massed behind the brick-kilns, though hot and well directed, could not repel them; but they quickly fell back upon the bridge that spanned the canal. This was *the* point that, seeing its importance, they determined to keep, and for a moment it seemed as if they would succeed. So terrible was their fire, that for a time the attacking brigades were staggered and faltered. This was the critical moment.

But hark! There is the deep rumbling of heavy guns heard and the shouts of Peel's sailors. Up and on they dash, those brave bluejackets. It is a deed well worthy of being recorded, for they dash not only at the bridge but on to it, and there they plant a gun. Hurrah! How those guns roar out. And, hurrah! how the previously disconcerted brigades of Hope and Inglis shout and rush onwards. The bridge is theirs. They are on it, they are over it, many dashing through the canal itself. Nothing can withstand that wild charge. The enemy is scattered like chaff before the wind, and our brave fellows race on to the camp of the Gwalior contingent. The surprise of the enemy is complete, and their rout also. Sir Colin himself presses on in pursuit, and soon he is joined by his artillery. What a scene it is! Says Holmes, "Passing cartloads of ammunition strewn along the road, spiking numbers of abandoned guns, and, dealing death without remorse, they urged on their panting horses mile after mile, and never paused until the hunted rebels, throwing away their arms in despair, fled from the roar to hide themselves in the, jungle, or disperse over the country in every direction."

It was midnight before the victorious cavalry returned.

Tantia's army was smashed, and but for the dilatoriness of Mansfield, Tantia himself might have been a prisoner in our hands.

But he escaped.

Only for a time, however. His doom was impending, and I must now tell you briefly how this fiend in human form managed to elude us for a time, and what happened to him eventually.

* * * * *

For want of transport, then, Sir Colin Campbell was obliged to lie for a time inactive at Cawnpore, and was therefore unable to follow up his victory. Well, he had smashed this army of Tantia, but he had not yet smashed the power of the rebel general himself.

Accordingly we find Tantia, in the middle of the following March, laying siege to the fort of Chirkaree, and the dominions of a loyal chief of that name.

We find him fighting bravely at the battle of Betwa, and bravely too at Koonch. We find him at Gwalior in conjunction with the Ranée of Jhansi, which city —a bold stroke indeed—they seize. The Sindia had marched out to meet them, but his whole army was captured, or rather went over bodily to our enemy Tantia, the Sindia himself fleeing to Gwalior.

Tantia and the Jhansi had Sir Hugh Ross to deal with, however, and after desperate fighting that brave general with his handful of an army retook the city, which had been called the Gibraltar of India, and Tantia Topee, leaving guns and everything else behind, now fled.

The whole story of the flight and pursuit of this fiend is too long to tell. It is a matter of history, but a history that when well told reads like a romance.

At long last we find Tantia Topee hiding in a dismal

jungle, hemmed in on every side, hunted like the wild beast he really was.

This jungle belonged by rights to Maun Singh, though he had been deprived of his estates for participation in the rebellion. One day Tantia met Maun Singh himself in hiding in the forest, and it really was by establishing communication with the latter and offering him a heavy bribe that Tantia was eventually captured. This ending certainly dispels a portion of the romance of the strange story, but in no way else could Tantia have been taken.

They seized him in his lair at the dark hour of midnight, and bore him in triumph, if there was any triumph about it, away to the fort of Sepree.

He was tried by court-martial, and although he made some show of defence he was condemned to death.

And no man deserved hanging more richly.

For three days Tantia lay in his cell fettered and pinioned, impatiently waiting his doom. That came at last, for on the 18th of March, at five o'clock in the afternoon, he was led forth to die. It was a grim spectacle that execution!

The troops of the station were all drawn up in the form of a hollow square, in the centre of which stood the scaffold.

Then, with head erected, but looking a ghastly image of despair, his manacles still upon him, Tantia was marched forth from the fort, surrounded by a company of British soldiers.

Every place whence a peep could be obtained of the notorious rebel was crowded with sightseers, and they had a good opportunity of gratifying their curiosity, for delay of twenty minutes occurred before Major Meade was ready to read the charge, the finding of the court, and the dread sentence.

As he waited thus for death did Tantia think, I cannot help wondering, of any of the terrible deeds of his life, or of that awful scene of massacre that he superintended at the ghaut on the Ganges by Cawnpore, where men were shot, women sabred, and their helpless babies torn limb from limb by his brutal and infuriated soldiery?

But here comes Meade, and now the end will soon follow. He calmly, even sternly reads the sentence, and no sooner has he concluded than the fetters are taken off the condemned man. Had he exhibited any fear? None, I think, but the twitchings of his face showed both nervousness and impatience, while the reading had proceeded. Now, however, as if anxious that all should be speedily over, he mounts the steps firmly and quickly, and stands beneath the rope. When pinioned, of his own accord he puts his head into the noose, and next moment the bolt is drawn, and he is ushered into eternity to appear before a greater tribunal than man's.

So died Tantia Topee.

And this was really the last act of much import in the tragedy of the great rebellion.

* * * * *

* * * * *

But in following the fortunes and misfortunes of this arch rebel, we have for a time lost sight of our heroes, Willie and Jack.

They parted then at Lucknow, Jack Morrison remaining behind at the Alum Bagh, Willie Saunders and his friend Sergeant McKinnon going on to Cawnpore with Sir Colin Campbell.

Force of circumstances had caused Jack to become a soldier, and, as we have already seen, a right good one he proved to be. But, nevertheless, he had not forgotten that he was still the civil servant and secretary to Mr. Mayne, the magistrate at Agra.

Whether, however, the Maynes were alive or dead, for the present time Jack had no means at all of knowing. All he could do was to mention them in his prayers, and often and often he thought of poor little Teddie and his innocent wee sister Jessie.

Would he ever see them again, he wondered. Would gentle peace ever return, and enable him to go back to Agra and take up his duties under that kindest of masters, Mr. Mayne. More than once he had dreamt of that beautiful bungalow, and that he was riding Teddie and the mongoose, cockertiecoosie,* with Jessie running by their side laughing and shrieking with delight.

But from such dreams he awoke to the stern realities of warfare.

Jack Morrison proved himself as useful under General Outram in the camp and fort of Alum Bagh, as he had done at the Residency during the first terrible siege of that place by the rebels, and the general had given him command of a company.

* Cockertiecoose, Scottish "On his shoulders."

Even before Sir Colin Campbell had left for Cawnpore, Alum Bagh was much strengthened by earthworks. On the whole the position—which was by no means a small one—was well fortified, and capable of great resistance, having trenches, batteries, and abattis, besides a fort that protected its right flank. But seeing that the Alum Bagh itself and this fort had to be well garrisoned, Outram had not much more than two thousand men to spare for action in the field.

Now just think of the mighty force of rebels that was opposed to this little European army. They were said to be more than thirty to one, and to number altogether about one hundred thousand men.

It was some time, however, before they managed to pluck up courage enough to attack Outram, for Sir Colin Campbell had given them a lesson they were not likely to forget in a hurry.

Outram, I wish you to remember, reader, had managed to keep up communications with Cawnpore, and these communications the enemy determined to sever. At all events they tried to do so; but Outram was ready for them, and defeated them with such fearful slaughter that for three whole weeks they did not resume the offensive. But on the 12th and again on the 16th of January they renewed their attack, and were once more discomfited and obliged to retreat.

Now Ahmed Oollah was the leader of the rebels, and a very excellent general he was; and he knew two things, and the exact value to put on them also. First, he was well aware that Sir Colin was in possession of Cawnpore, and that he was all this time not only strengthening the place against that "invincible" Gwalior contingent, but gathering together a great army to attack Lucknow, and, secondly, he knew that if he could completely smash and annihilate General Outram, he, Ahmed Oollah, would be free to sweep down on Cawnpore, cut off Sir Colin's communications, and ravage the country far and near with fire and sword. For those three months then General Outram's position was indeed a perilous one, and the service he was doing his country was a very noble one.

Though separated in person many a letter passed between Willie and Jack.

"What think you, Jack?" said one of Willie's letters. "I've had an interview with Sir Colin himself, and such an interview! It was just after a brush we had with the enemy, in which everybody said I behaved with gallantry, and saved the life of my Colonel. I suppose, Jack, I did save his life, though for the life of me I don't know till this day quite how it occurred. But there was the poor Colonel in an ugly position, and wounded, in a ditch, and three huge, hulking mutineers making straight for him to end the business. Two fell beneath my revolver fire, and one I cut down with my claymore. But more were coming, so I had to run, Jack. Oh, no, I wasn't going to go without the Colonel, so I just caught him up and swung him well over my shoulder, and—ran. Just as I got into shelter a bullet struck me on the buckle of my sporran belt, and down I went. No, not even scratched.

"And, Jack, Sir Colin has made an officer of me. I believe I am a lieutenant, and he says he will get me the Victoria Cross.

"'But, Sir Colin Campbell,' I ventured to say, 'I really don't deserve it.'

"'Why, my lad, why?' he said.

"'Well,' I replied, 'it isn't usual, is it, Sir Colin, to get the Victoria Cross for running away, and that is precisely what I did, General?'

"The dear old man laughed right heartily, and bade me be off like a good boy, and not bother him.

"Oh, Jack, isn't this glorious news! What will mother say? and what will Annie ——. Oh, but I forgot; I must never, never, never think of her!"

* * * * *

I do not mean to describe at any great length the last siege of Lucknow.

But Sir Colin captured the Dilkoosha once more on the 3rd of March, and so smartly did the guns open fire on the rebels beyond the canal that they were soon obliged to retire.

And now it was all one long fight until the 14th of March, when the third line of the enemy's works were turned.

"Then," says Holmes, "the bonds of discipline, already strained by the tumultous joy of an unexpected triumph, were burst by the mad lust for plunder. British soldiers and Sikhs ran hither and thither through the spacious courts within the citadel, firing at the windows; while others, bent upon seizing the treasures that were stored in the rooms, surged around the doors, and dashed their muskets against the panels, or fired at the fastenings.

"By the fountains, and among the orange-groves of the courts, the bodies of dead and dying Sepoys were scattered, while a British soldier, unnoticed by his heedless companions, was leaning against a statue, gasping out his life, and at every gasp deluging the white plaster with his blood.

"The groans of the dying were drowned by the yells of the combatants, the frequent reports of fire-arms, the crash of shivered window-panes, and the roar of a fire that the plunderers had wantonly kindled in the middle of the court. Ever and anon soldiers came streaming out of the rooms through the shattered doorways laden with plunder, and, laughing at the threats and entreaties of their helpless officers, flung all they could not carry away—pictures and furniture and china vases—into the fire."

Majendie tells us that when the last of the rebels were driven from the city, about the 21st of March, the appearance of the city was sadly different from what it had been nine months before.

"The gilded domes, the minarets, and the long façades were battered and riddled with shot; swollen and distorted corpses were floating down the river, and foul birds of prey were hovering over them. The once gorgeous rooms of the palace were strewn with shattered mirrors, battered furniture, broken statues, and putrid corpses; artillery horses were picketed in the gardens; soldiers in their shirt sleeves were smoking and drinking in the corridors. The bazaars were deserted; and in the squalid streets in the meaner portion of the town no living thing was to be seen, save here and there a pariah dog, a decrepit beggar, or a lurking budmash; for the bulk of the peaceable inhabitants had fled in terror; and the Sepoys and rebels had gone to join the implacable talookdars, who still bade defiance to the British power."

Strangely enough Willie and Jack, the former accompanied by brave Sergeant McKinnon, met in the deserted town at the very spot where, in the hour of victory, the gallant Scot Neill had fallen in that terrible rush to the Residency—Havelock's first relief of Lucknow. He had been shot through the head, and fell dead from his horse. Truly a soldier's death!

Under the shadow of an archway then, that spanned the street and hid a portion of it from the blinding glare of the sunlight, the two friends met once again.

Jack was alone, and so bright was the sun's glare, that when he heard footsteps under the bridge he could see no one; so his hand mechanically sought his sword-hilt.

"Jack, my boy, we meet again. And here is my trusty friend the sergeant."

Then hands joined hands.

"I tell you what it is Jack," said Willie, again referring to McKinnon, "my friend here bears a charmed life. He is ever in the thickest of the fighting, but he never receives even a scratch.

"And," added Willie, "it isn't once that my friend here has done a deed that deserves the Victoria Cross, but a dozen times."

Jack extended his hand, which stalwart McKinnon took modestly enough.

"I am truly glad," said Jack, "to shake hands with a brave man."

"Toot, toot, lads!" replied McKinnon, blushing like a schoolboy. "We've all done our duty; but, alas! many and many a man has earned the Cross who will never wear it, because they lie cold in death."

"Ay," said Jack, "that is true. And poor Hodson, of Hodson's Horse, is among the number, and McDonald."

"I saw them both fall, sir," said the sergeant.

"McDonald," he added, "was killed first. I think he had a presentiment that day he was going to die, for before the fight he pulled a rose, and gave it to that bravest of surgeons, Dr. Munro. 'Good-bye, dear friend,' he said, 'keep this for my sake.' Though he was a captain, you know, sir, he was only a boy. He was wounded first by a splinter from a shell, but refused to go to the rear. He led his company bravely through the breach, and was killed inside while waving his sword above his head.* Wood then led the charge, and with us went Hodson as a volunteer, so fond of fighting was he. When we got out of the ditch around the Begum's palace the fight raged for two hours, and poor Hodson fell in a doorway, sabre in hand. He just got out the three words, 'Oh, my wife!' when blood choked his utterance, and down he dropped."

"Ah!" sighed Willie Saunders, "after all, war is a terrible thing. Just look at the gloom and desolation all around us now!"

"It is too terrible to think of. Come, I am going to the tree-shaded Dilkoosha. It will be far more pleasant to talk of home than of war. Come, men, come."

* Forbes-Mitchell.

CHAPTER XIV.

WILLIE'S LETTER TO HIS MOTHER.

THE heather was once more a-bloom on the moors, and high above the Lodge of Balaklava it covered all the hills and braes with purple and crimson. Glorious times for sportsmen, but sad for the grouse, for dogs, ghillies, and guns were skirmishing here, there, and everywhere, and the sharp ring of fowling-pieces singly, doubly, and sometimes even in little volleys, could be heard sounding afar on the crisp, clear mountain air.

The two lairds, Saunders and Morrison, were as usual out together, and about two o'clock they had thrown themselves down beside a turf-wall, to enjoy their luncheon along with their faithful dogs.

While they sat there, laughing and talking together, the sharp excited barking of a collie could be heard. It was Bruce himself—Willie's friend—and behind him came running a bareheaded kilted urchin of a boy.

At first Saunders thought that something must be

wrong at the Raven's Nest, but the glad look on the lad's face—I might almost say on Bruce's too—quickly banished this idea.

"Well, Robbie," said the laird, "what is it, lad?"

"Oh, gin [if] ye please, sir, the mistress says ye maun a' three come hame to the Raven's Nest to dine the nicht."

"What!" cried Laird Saunders, "has your young master returned?"

"Na, na," said Robbie, "nae sic luck. But the mistress has gotten a letter, and oh, sir, it maun be good news, 'cause she was greetin ower 't [crying over it], but smilin' through her tears a' the same. So ye 'll nae forget."

"Not likely, Robbie. But there, sit down and have a bite and share the snack with Bruce."

So down sat Robbie and Bruce, and I don't know which of the two looked the happier.

Yes it was a gladsome letter Mrs. Saunders had received, and it was from Willie.

Was Willie well?

The answer to this question is that he had had the usual luck of a soldier. He had fallen in battle, severely wounded. But in a month's time he was so far recovered that he was able to stand the journey to Calcutta, whence he was to be sent home with many more invalids, not only from his own regiment, but from others.

That was a very happy dinner-party at the Raven's Nest, for, not content with inviting Colonel Lindsay and Laird Morrison from the hills, Mrs. Saunders had sent word to Balaklava Lodge for Mrs. Lindsay and Annie also to drive over. So here they all were in the cosy drawing-room after dinner. A bright fire burned in the grate, for in August the Highland winds are keen, and all sat round it, while Mrs. Saunders read that letter with the Calcutta postmark on it, and the strange and foreign-looking stamps.

I am of opinion that that collie dog Bruce knew his master was coming home, for all the time Mrs. Saunders was reading he sat by her side with his chin resting on her knee, and his bonnie brown eyes fixed lovingly on her face.

"Dearest Mother," the letter began, "I have so much that is strange, and, alas! so much that is sad to tell you, that I hardly know where to begin. You must have been very much frightened when you heard that I was dangerously wounded. Well, there might have been some danger, because Dr. Munro said so, and he is the bravest surgeon ever I knew. He was always in the front, and as often under fire on the field of battle as any of us. They say, mother, that I shall receive the Victoria Cross for conspicuous bravery in the presence of the foe, but I am sure I do not deserve it half as much as Munro. Well, I have one or two regrets, and one is that I was not wounded in a great battle instead of in a mere skirmish. And I regret also that I was wounded at all, because I should have liked to have stuck to my company and seen the very, very last of this terrible rebellion. You must know too that it was honest Fergus MacKinnon who saved my life. He bandaged up my wound on the field of fight, and afterwards helped to carry me to the rear with his own hands and his own crimson sash. Ah! mother, that was a bonnie sash once, but it is now only a dark blood-stained ragged rope.

"I am writing this letter on board the ship that is going to take us all home. I and another invalid officer have got a cabin all to our two selves, and Jack Morrison is sitting by my side as I write. When I finish it he will go on shore and post it.

"Fancy dear old Jack coming home with me, mother. I was lying in bed in hospital thinking how little I should enjoy the long voyage home, having no one to talk to, when I heard a voice just outside the door that I knew at once belonged to no one but just Jack, and next minute the honest, brown-faced fellow was bending over me."

"That's my boy," interrupted Laird Morrison with pardonable pride. "My own lad, God bless him, and send the boys safely home."

"Well, mother, I have been getting better every day since Jack took charge of me.

"But I am not the only one that Jack has in charge, mother, and hereby lies a sad and sorrowful tale. There have been so many terrible things happening every day in India that I do not wish to grieve you by a relation of half what I know, so I must be very brief. Besides, mother, it is Jack's story, and he will, I hope, before many weeks are over, tell it to you by word of mouth at our own fireside.

"Well, you know, Jack had a very happy and comfortable home at Agra. He dearly loved the children, Jessie and Teddie, and his chief Mr. Mayne also; and Mrs. Mayne, he says, was just like a mother to him.

"And during all those dreadful months in Lucknow and at the fort of Alma Bagh he never ceased thinking and praying for their safety. But somehow, he says, he had some forebodings that all was not well.

"The misery began as far back as June 5th, 1857, and not at Jack's home in Agra, but in Jhansi. Some time before this Mr. Mayne had business of very great importance that took him to Gwalior, and curiously enough his wife insisted upon going with him and taking the children too. It was a strange resolve, but resolve it was. Well, they were there when the mutiny broke out at Jhansi. Jack tells me he knew the Ranee personally. She was the Queen, you must know, and a tall, beautiful, and splendid woman she was, but a bitter foe to British rule. Perhaps she had cause to be, for we Britons had annexed Jhansi, and the Ranee, a widow of the late Rajah, was meagrely pensioned off. Moreover the English had insulted her religion by slaughtering cows in the city, and she was burning for revenge. Her time came soon after the first awful outbreak of the mutiny at Meerut, and on the 5th of June the Sepoys seized some forts outside the city.

"On the afternoon of the 6th the mutiny became general, for on that dreadful day the Sepoys rose in force, and murdered all their officers with one exception. Then gaols were broken open, and the convicts, joining the townspeople, marched upon the forts where the Europeans had taken refuge.

"It was a hopeless defence our people made. They had neither ammunition nor supplies to stand a siege, and there was no hope of help coming from anywhere.

So on the morning of the 7th three messengers left the garrison to visit the Ranee and beg for mercy. Her answer was, 'I have nothing to say to these English swine. Away with them to the death they so richly deserve.'

"In a few minutes more those poor fellows were murdered.

"The Ranee after this sent to the garrison to say that all she required was possession of the forts, and that if the Europeans would lay down their arms they, with their wives and little ones, might march forth, and would be safely escorted to another part of the country.

"It was death in either way. But oh, mother, what follows will hardly bear repetition. For instead of keeping her promise the wicked Ranee gave orders for a wholesale massacre, and neither man, woman, nor helpless babe was left alive.

"It was shortly after this that the mutiny at Gwalior broke out.

"And here the Maynes were at the time.

"It is sad to think that but for the utter folly of the Brigadier, many a precious life might have been saved.

"I must not tell you, mother, of this massacre further than it concerned the Maynes. It broke out like many others with the firing of the nine o'clock gun. At that moment, as though it were a death-knell, the Sepoys rushed into their huts and seized their guns and sallied forth.

"A minute or two after the rattling of musketry fell upon the ears of Jack's unhappy friends, accompanied by the yells of the murdering Sepoys, and many a piercing scream and piteous appeal for mercy.

"There was not a moment to lose, but where could the Maynes fly to? Mrs. Mayne, however, caught Jessie in her arms, and her husband took Teddie, and together they rushed forth to hide in the bushes in the garden of the bungalow where they had been living. To have gone farther would have been but to court earlier death, for the darkness was everywhere illumined by the blaze of burning dwellings.

"They lay concealed here for hours, expecting every minute to be discovered and put to death. They saw the bungalow stripped and looted, and then set on fire, while the demon mutineers danced and yelled and fought for the loot but a few yards from them.

"Two hours after this the din of fire-raising and murder sounded farther off, and the darkness had once more settled down around them. Worn out with fear and fatigue, poor little Jessie and Teddie had sunk to sleep, while their wretched parents sat beside them, dumb with a grief too deep for tears. Well they knew that with the daylight discovery would come and then ——. But in the moonlight that followed soon after twelve they saw through the bushes where they lay concealed the flutter of white garments, and immediately after heard the voices of their own two faithful Sepoys who had come from Agra with them, and that also of the ayah.

"Cramped and miserable though he was, Mayne crept out from his concealment, and presented himself before them. He could not be sure even that they would be faithful. But they were, and Jack tells me that this was by no means a solitary instance of native servants remaining faithful and true to their European masters.

"They were taken to a hut not far of, and there concealed, Jessie and Teddie still asleep.

"What a terrible awakening they had, poor little things. For at daybreak they were discovered by some Sepoys, and, oh, mother! Mr. Mayne was killed there before the very eyes of his wife and children.

"Is it any wonder that the poor lady was dead to the world from that hour?

"Jessie's gentle ayah told Jack all the pitiful story when he went at last to Agra. How the two Sepoys and the ayah herself managed, during the darkness of the next night, to take the lady and children out and away into the jungle, and how they then all began their terrible march to Agra, hiding all day in the jungles like wild beasts, and only coming out at night to resume their journey. How they suffered from hunger and from thirst, how their shoes were lost and their feet cut, and how their clothes were torn from their backs with the thorns, and how poor wee Jessie and Teddie cried with fear and dread to hear the wild beasts roar around them, as they hurried on through the darkness towards the distant city of Agra.

"No; Mrs. Mayne never recovered her reason, and it was probably best, mother.

"But they reached the city and fort at last, and then the lady sank and died.

"This is not a tenth part of the terrible story, mother,

but it is all I now can tell you. Jack himself will do the rest.

"And what do you think Jack has done? Why he has constituted himself, or been constituted, guardian of these helpless infants, and they and their faithful ayah are coming home with us in the same ship.

"The children are not poor, mother; but Jack says that if they had not a penny in the world they should live with him, and he should be a father to them."

There was much more in Willie's letter to his mother, with which I need not trouble the reader.

But when she had finished there was a few moments of silence; then Laird Morrison held out his hand to Saunders.

Neither spoke. They simply shook hands.

But that hand-clasp spoke volumes.

And perhaps, as hand met hand, a prayer went up from each—a prayer which breathed thankfulness to God who had given to each a son, for whom he never yet had cause to blush.

CHAPTER XV.

TWO YEARS AFTER THE MUTINY.

THE Royal Lady who has ruled so long over this great country has a soft side towards "puir auld Scotland."

Nor need the English be at all jealous of this, for she dearly loves her people one and all. But it was, it will be remembered, at Balmoral, under the shadow of the grand old hills, that she spent her younger and her happiest days, when her children were bairnies all, and when the Prince Consort himself, like Byron in bygone times,

> "Rov'd a young Highlander o'er the dark heath."

It was the proudest day in Willie Saunders's life then, when, with her own fair fingers, Her Majesty pinned the decoration of the Victoria Cross upon his manly breast. Naturally enough our hero's head was all in a whirl, and he could hardly afterwards remember what it was the Queen had actually said to him; but the words were somewhat as follows:

"It is brave men like you, who make and uphold empires."

For a whole year after this Willie held his commission in his regiment, but there was no prospect of war, and garrison duty became terribly monotonous to him after a time. Besides his father the good laird was not getting very much younger. People don't as a rule. So, everything being taken into consideration, Willie determined to retire from what, under the circumstances, could hardly be called active service.

He had only been once home at the dear old Glen since his return to England, and that only for a week. He had taken good care, too, to choose a time when he knew that Annie Lindsay and her parents were in London. Willie believed he had quite gotten over his passion for Miss Lindsay by this time, and that he could come back to Raven's Nest, and even visit at Balaklava Lodge with perfect impunity.

How little we know our own hearts!

* * * * *

So Willie Saunders doffed his uniform at last, and came back to the Glen, and at once began to settle down to his old life and his old ways. To see him now as he rode down the strath, or up to pay a forenoon or evening visit to his friend Jack Morrison, at the Firs, as Jack's new house was called, anyone would have taken him for a handsome and well-to-do young farmer; but few, indeed, could have guessed that he had come through so much in so short a time—entered the army and risen from the ranks through attention to duty; fought and bled in his country's cause; been gazetted and won the Victoria Cross; all in the space of four brief years.

Many who knew him thought and said that his career had been all too brief, but they prophesied that if ever his service were needed again he would once more draw the sword he now had sheathed, and once again lead his company to battle and to victory.

But there never would be any more war. So preached the young minister from the pulpit on the very first Sunday after Willie's return. "The time was fast approaching," cried this juvenile enthusiast, bringing his white hand down with a convincing bang upon the pulpit cushion, "nay, the time was already here, when peace had spread her white wings on the balmy breeze, and war flown far away.

"The beam that shines from Sion hill
Shall lighten every land,
The King who reigns in Salem's tower
Shall all the world command.

"No strife shall rage, nor hostile feuds
Disturb these peaceful years,
To ploughshares men shall beat their swords,
To pruning-hooks their spears.

"No longer hosts encountering hosts
Shall crowds of slain deplore;
They hang the trumpet in the hall,
And study war no more."

The minister who droned from the pulpit is older and wiser now, and knows that men's hearts and the souls of emperors and kings cannot be changed by one brief war.

But let us follow Willie to The Firs. The Firs is a new house entirely, and prettily do its grey gables look, peeping up through the greenery of the woods on the brae yonder on this beautiful day in early summer.

Jack himself meets Willie at the gate. The same blue-eyed, brown-faced Jack we knew before, only he seems altered just a trifle. He is rounder in the face, and has lost the weary, haggard glare he had in Lucknow.

"Come in, Willie. Come in. We were expecting you. Of course you'll stop to dinner. Yes, we are all at home—my wife, and Teddie, Jessie, and all."

It is soon evident enough that Jessie and Teddie were, for they come in with a rush through the casement window that opens on to the lawn, followed by a pet lamb that has almost grown into a sheep, and a huge deerhound dog.

The children run to welcome "Uncle Willie," as they call our hero, and Teddie insists on scrambling up on his knee.

Bruce, Willie's favourite collie, thinks it rather strange for a sheep to be admitted into the drawing-room, but Oscar, the great deerhound, explains, and Bruce is content.

Then the curtain is drawn back, and Lily Wood herself enters the room.

Ah, but Lily Wood is Mrs. Morrison now, and has been so for some time.

The conversation now becomes general, and is proceeding quietly and easily enough, when two more visitors are announced.

Colonel Lindsay and Miss Lindsay.

It is the first time that Willie has seen Annie since they parted years and years ago, though he has frequently met the Colonel.

How very beautiful Annie is!

Willie can't get up to shake hands with her, because Teddie is on one knee, and Jessie on the other; but as Annie comes quietly and smiling towards him, all the blood in his body seems suddenly to get up into his head and face. It is soon over, however. The dreaded meeting is past, but Willie Saunders has made one discovery—he loves Annie Lindsay still.

I wonder who it was who first proposed that picnic to distant Glen-Orla? I have had the impression all along that Lily, that is, Mrs. Morrison, had something if not everything to do with it, and some day I mean to ask her. Well, everybody who went to it was very happy. It was a very beautiful day, and the sunset was a wonderful one, so was the moonrise.

I do not know how it fell out, but Willie lost his way in taking a cross-cut through a birchen wood, in order to rejoin the party and prepare for the return. Somehow he did not seem to mind it very much, for Annie was by his side. Had he been very grieved about the matter he could have easily referred it all to Bruce the collie, and he would have put them on the right track in a very brief time indeed.

But they found their party at last. The moon was pretty high by this time, and casting a flood of silvery light over hill and dell.

"Jack," whispered Lily to her husband as the truant

pair came slowly back, "Jack, isn't it delightful? they are walking hand in hand."

Yes, that is true, reader, they were hand in hand, Bruce walking close behind, and looking very knowing and very pleased indeed.

And hand in hand for the future they would walk through the vale of life.

* * * * * *

* * * * * *

"Peter," said Willie Saunders one day about seven weeks after the picnic, "we can't be so near to dear old Dover without calling at the Albyn."

"Oh no, sir; we must go and see the sairgent."

So the beautiful yacht on which Willie and Annie were afloat on their bridal tour quietly entered the harbour.

Two hours after this Captain William Saunders and his one-handed valet, Peter McKay, walked right straight into the cosy little parlour of the Albyn Inn.

And in with a rush and run came Ellen herself, and smilingly stood before them, both hands extended, and the bonniest blush on her face that ever you saw.

But hand-shaking over, she ran into the passage once more.

"Oh, Fergus," she cried to her husband, now landlord of the Albyn, "come quickly, the two soldier lads are here."

What a pleasant hour that was the three old friends spent together!

"I'm just as happy as happy can be," said Sergeant McKinnon, "and you've no idea what a dear little woman of a wife Ellen makes me."

"I *have* an idea," said Willie, "because I've just got married myself, and Fergus, dear old friend, before you are a day older you have got to come and see us, and bring Mrs. McKinnon with you."

And so he did.

And so ends my story.

FINIS.